PRAISE FOR *Staying Married is the Hardest Part:*

"Because of her background as a therapist, Comfort brings a unique level of insight... making this memoir both deeply personal and incredibly thoughtful... She captures the reality that marriage isn't just about love; it's about constantly adjusting, making choices, and sometimes facing hard truths... A deeply honest look at what it means to share a life with someone."
— **Readers' Favorite**

"... a profoundly personal memoir ... Read it and you will understand the secret sexual disappointments that so many American women experience."—**Ruth Rosen, author of *The World Split Open: How the Modern Women's Movement Changed America***

"Drawing from her professional experiences as a psychologist and her own complex marriage, Comfort offers a candid look at the challenges couples face... A heartfelt exploration of love, compromise, and resilience ... Perfect for readers seeking inspiration for navigating the rocky terrain of long-term relationships."—**Deb Miller, author of *Forget the Fairy Tale and Find Your Happiness***

"In this captivating memoir of her marriage to a Hollywood screenwriter, psychologist Bonnie Comfort bravely exposes the sexual and power struggles that plagued her relationship, showing how old wounds and coping styles fuel conflict between partners. A startling and beautiful story that will inspire readers."—**Mike Consol, host of the *Novelist Spotlight* podcast, author of *Love American Style***

"*Staying Married is the Hardest Part* is an in-depth analysis of falling in love and staying in love. Bonnie Comfort creates a pervading intimacy with a string of stirring, insightful moments that are both funny and tender and honest."—**Antonia Dauphin, screenwriter, *Children of Yesteryear***

"Admirably honest!"—**David Shields, author of *Reality Hunger***

"Psychologist Comfort shares her compelling and challenging marriage . . . that gives us hope for our own power struggles, sexual incompatibilities, and strains in long-term relationships. This wise and profoundly moving book is an ode to enduring love."—**Jan Baross, author of *Jose Builds a Woman***

"As a psychiatrist, I'm drawn to this fascinating portrayal of love, but this is also a moving account of losing an irreplaceable partner and how to grapple with what comes next. I'd recommend it to anyone navigating love, loss, and the search for meaning in the aftermath."—**Jayne Laszewski, MD**

staying

married

is the

hardest

part

staying married is the hardest part

A MEMOIR OF PASSION, SECRETS, AND SACRIFICE

BONNIE COMFORT

SHE WRITES PRESS

Copyright © 2025 Bonnie Comfort

All rights reserved. No part of this publication may be reproduced, distributed, or transmitted in any form or by any means, including photocopying, recording, digital scanning, or other electronic or mechanical methods, without the prior written permission of the publisher, except in the case of brief quotations embodied in critical reviews and certain other noncommercial uses permitted by copyright law. For permission requests, please address She Writes Press.

Published 2025
Printed in the United States of America
Print ISBN: 978-1-64742-944-7
E-ISBN: 978-1-64742-945-4
Library of Congress Control Number: 2025903939

For information, address:
She Writes Press
1569 Solano Ave #546
Berkeley, CA 94707

Interior Design by Andrea Reider

She Writes Press is a division of SparkPoint Studio, LLC.

Company and/or product names that are trade names, logos, trademarks, and/or registered trademarks of third parties are the property of their respective owners and are used in this book for purposes of identification and information only under the Fair Use Doctrine.

NO AI TRAINING: Without in any way limiting the author's [and publisher's] exclusive rights under copyright, any use of this publication to "train" generative artificial intelligence (AI) technologies to generate text is expressly prohibited. The author reserves all rights to license uses of this work for generative AI training and development of machine learning language models.

Names and identifying characteristics have been changed to protect the privacy of certain individuals.

Contents

Part I

Chapter 1	The One	3
Chapter 2	A Decent Compromise	13
Chapter 3	Yes, I Will	20
Chapter 4	A Jewish Heart	34
Chapter 5	Persephone in the Palisades	51
Chapter 6	Sailboats in Bed	66
Chapter 7	Ashland	76
Chapter 8	Ways of Leaving	95
Chapter 9	A Licensed Psychologist	112
Chapter 10	Killing Each Other	123
Chapter 11	Making a Leap	138

Part II

Chapter 12	A Strange Confluence of Events	153
Chapter 13	Pinky Swear	168
Chapter 14	The Hotel del Capri	187
Chapter 15	Transitions	205
Chapter 16	"Bye, Bon"	214
Chapter 17	Humpty Dumpty	223
Chapter 18	He's in Room 9	234
Chapter 19	Owls	245
Chapter 20	Epiphany	257
Chapter 21	The Great, the Awful	269

Author's Note	281
Acknowledgments	283
Book Club Topics and Questions for Discussion	286
A Note on Sources	289

In memory of Min and Bob

Introduction

Marriage: a hopeful, generous, infinitely kind gamble taken by two people who don't know yet who they are or who the other might be, binding themselves to a future they cannot conceive of and have carefully omitted to investigate.

—Alain de Botton, *The Course of Love*

During the winter rains here in Portland, Oregon, there are times when my office smells of faint cologne, baking chocolate from St. Cupcake downstairs, incessant coffee, wet fleece, and leather. At the end of a psychotherapy workday, my trash can is crowded with tear-soaked Kleenex and used Starbucks paper cups. The room feels full of a palpable desperation from my patients, who want their lives to get better. There are laughs and light-hearted moments, too, but it's the sadness that stays with me, the painful stories of abandonment or conflict.

Married couples stress me the most with their raised voices, anxious sweat, and tired, angry faces because they don't know how to turn their complaints into something constructive that might stop the bickering at home. Couples worry about their children, their finances, and their self-destructive late-night

x   staying married is the hardest part

habits of hidden cookies, another glass of wine, or clandestine watching of porn in the bathroom. Spouses hide and withdraw from each other, and when they start telling the truth in my office, their conversations are full of blame, hurt, and sarcasm.

At the end of such a workday I'm worn out by the human longing to be understood, rescued, forgiven, cherished, loved, soothed, and to feel hopeful.

One evening at home after a marital therapy day like this, I peeled off my clothes in the bedroom, grateful to let go of all the sadness and frustration I'd witnessed that day, glad to push away the constant hum of need piled up in those Starbucks cups and Kleenex. I sat down on the edge of my bed and glanced at a framed photograph of me taken by my husband, Bob. Although I'd walked by it a thousand times and barely noticed it on the wall, this time, the waning light illuminated it at an angle that caught my eye. I picked it up off its hook, sat down on the bed, and studied it. Although we were only a few years into our marriage when this photograph was taken, Bob had already shot thousands of photographs of me using his Canon AE-1 SLR. That camera was his single most important possession, and I was his favorite subject.

I angled the photograph to the light and noted I was wearing a dress that had been a favorite of mine back then, a filmy black chiffon blouson with tiny red flowers scattered over it. I was perched on the kitchen counter in our long-ago Pacific Palisades house, next to a hot air popcorn maker and a beehive glass honey jar. In this photo, one of my knees is up, that foot resting on a chair, my elbow on that knee, my hand propping up my chin. There is a slight spread between my perched leg and the other one, enough that you get a glimpse of black stocking and garter. Wide-open love shows in my eyes as I look at Bob. My face is wistful and vulnerable.

That photo was taken decades ago. I ran my fingers over the framed glass and then stopped, resting on the image. I was young. I was trusting. I was in love with my husband and eager to please him. I didn't know then that my need to please him would lead somewhere darker.

No matter how great a marriage is, there's always a shadow side. I was a psychologist doing marital therapy, but my patients might have been surprised at how deep the shadow side was in my marriage.

Part I

CHAPTER 1

The One

It was inevitable that we fell in love, in spite of the red flags, in spite of his old-man car and the glass pendant on a white string he wore around his neck, in spite of my sensible shoes, and my insistence that I had to live on the Westside rather than in Pasadena, and my being Jewish and him being a refugee from a fundamentalist Christian upbringing. We ran toward each other like people whose every experience led up to that moment of meeting, whose separate needs fit together in a crazy, compelling pattern that propelled us forward into a shared life. Now, I think that's how long-term love is. You fall in love with magic in the beginning. You learn to live with its fraying edges, but—if you're lucky—there's still some magic that remains at the core.

In June 1977, I met Bob at an afternoon party I attended alone. The Los Angeles sun beat down on my yellow Volvo as it climbed up the narrow streets of Laurel Canyon onto Hermits Glen. Up the hill, violin and bass music played under the sound of distant voices. My interior decorator, Barbara Kellard, was giving the party. For a whole year, I'd had fun hunting through stores with her, and now my West LA apartment was filled

4   staying married is the hardest part

with earth-toned colors, custom-made furniture, and affordable antiques. We had shared secrets, become soulmate girlfriends, and I had come to love that wide-open grin of hers, her infectious laugh, and her buoyant spirit.

The fragrance of Asiatic lilies and coffee swept me along into her backyard, where I paused, taking in the carefully tended garden, the scattered tables and chairs, and the guests dressed in silks and chiffons. It was instantly apparent I was underdressed in a plaid, cotton short-sleeved shirt and pink overalls. My mother would never have worn such an outfit. She was always tastefully dressed in classics, beautifully accessorized with white gloves, pearls, and high-heeled shoes. A funky hip look like mine that day was not in her repertoire, even in Winnipeg, Manitoba, on a hot summer afternoon, but she was there in the city where I grew up, and I was here in the city where she grew up, and I could wear whatever the hell I wanted now.

Barbara hugged me and offered me white wine, but had to greet others. I stood like a doofus alone, gulping that wine and looking around at my options. There was one table with two men sitting at it and an empty chair at their table. Not one familiar face in the whole place.

I asked if I could join the two men. "Sure," one said and pulled out a chair for me. "I'm Bob, and this is Phil." I sat down and watched them joking and laughing. I noticed Bob's comfortable body, his easy laugh, and his spot-on quips about guests milling around.

A tall, tanned guy walked across the lawn, his walk like dancing, and Barbara rushed over to him and hugged him. "Who's that?" I asked Bob.

"That's Rick Kellard, my writing partner."

Rick! The husband from whom Barbara was now separated, although she had spoken of him with great fondness. "Oh," was all I said. In fact, I didn't say much of anything else. These guys had their own style of banter, competing for jokes. I sat and listened and laughed.

After a while, I excused myself and discreetly slipped away. Loneliness filled my car as I drove home, my long earrings tinkling in the air conditioning's blast.

Two weeks later, Bob called and asked me out on a date, but I was busy serving dinner to yet another doctor I was seeing. "Yeah, okay," I said, sounding lukewarm. I couldn't quite picture his face and couldn't really have this kind of conversation in front of another man.

"I'll call you later in the week," he said.

He didn't, and I forgot about him while busy planning to leave for Winnipeg—the yearly summer ordeal of visiting my family.

Although I'd left home at twenty-three, my parents continued lobbying for me to move back to Canada and marry a financially successful Jewish man who would look after me and make them proud. For nine years, I'd had a thriving career as a clinical social worker in prestigious LA hospitals, and now, at thirty-two, I was studying in an LA school to become a psychologist. Nevertheless, they still held fiercely to their desires, despite my saying, "I'm never moving back."

I returned from Winnipeg discouraged by the way I had regressed with my family, even after years of psychoanalysis. The ugly sight of brown smog over LA was a relief. The smell of jet fuel and ocean air reassured me. I was home again, safe from my mother's judgments and the constant feeling that I had to prove my choices were good. The first thing I did was

6   staying married is the hardest part

drive to Santa Monica Beach and run on the sand, inhaling the salt, feeling the warm wind on my face, and embracing the utter safety of being here in my chosen home, the place where I could be whomever I wanted.

Back in my apartment, an ache settled under my breast-bone. Throughout my twenties, I'd had four long-term boy-friends, interspersed with intense bouts of dating, but I'd finally realized I needed to rely on myself more, so this previous year, I'd chosen to live alone and focus on work and school. I had no long-term boyfriend, lots of studying, and I didn't even date.

I paced around my apartment, restless like I imagine an alcoholic must be after she's stopped drinking. I straightened my closet, vacuumed, and paid a few bills. Then I thought, *Oh, what the hell,* and phoned Barbara. "Hey, that guy at your party? Bob something? He called me last month, but he never called back. Can you tell me about him?"

"Sure. Bob Comfort. I think you'd like him. He's Canadian. And very funny."

"Where does he live?" I asked, an important piece of infor-mation in LA.

"He's staying with a longtime friend in Pasadena."

"Why doesn't he have a place of his own?"

"He goes back and forth between here and Edmonton."

Hmmm. Odd lifestyle. And Pasadena. Too smoggy and hot. I was already starting my assessment. But okay, fine. If Barbara said I'd like him, I'd at least call.

Our get-to-know-you conversation lasted a whole hour. Something about the way we talked to each other without even being in the same room already seemed intimate. Questions led from one topic to the next, each of us ready to be transpar-ent, each curious. I laughed often.

At one point, he said, "So why did ya call me now?"

"I was lonely."

Later, he told me he loved that I'd been honest with him like that. He was lonely, too.

When I opened my door to him, I discovered Bob was over six feet tall and very cute with big brown eyes, and dark hair spilling over his forehead. Over his worn jeans and a white T-shirt was an open, long-sleeved shirt. "Nice place," he said, looking around my newly decorated living room. My dining table was covered with the pieces of a stained-glass window I was constructing.

Bob's voice was resonant, just the right shade of deep. Something about the energy radiating from him seemed to fill up the whole room. He pulled a flat, oval stone from his shirt pocket. "I brought you a good rock from the beach," he said. The rock had a perfect small hole in it. I took it and felt its smooth surface. I was impressed with how flat it was and the novelty of this gift, which was so different from flowers, chocolate, or wine. I liked standing so close to him in my loose, gauzy dress and flat sandals, but I was self-conscious of my huge plastic-rimmed glasses, the extra five pounds on my belly, and my short, unvarnished fingernails. I knew this much about him: he was a TV comedy writer and producer and was likely to encounter very beautiful women. I thought I was attractive enough compared to people in the hospitals where I worked, but I was definitely not showbiz beautiful, and I could already feel something stirring in me toward him. Maybe it was his fragrance—spicy and sweet—or his height, or his open face.

He was also wearing a very odd thing around his neck: an ordinary white kitchen string holding a teardrop pendant of clear blue glass with a white piece in the center and a dark blue

8   staying married is the hardest part

dot in the middle. The effect was a blue eye on a string. "What is that?" I said.

"It's a *nazar*. I bought it when I was doing stand-up on a Canadian Forces show tour of the Middle East. It's supposed to keep you safe from the evil eye."

Did he believe that?

Although Bob was only thirty-seven, he was driving a Buick sedan big enough for a family of six. It was just after Labor Day, and the soft, warm air was fragrant with frangipani and gardenias in West LA. We drove to a casual bistro on Wilshire Boulevard in Santa Monica.

Once we were seated, our connection grew by the minute. Frosty glasses of gin and tonic for me, Canadian Club and water for him. Me at utter attention, fascinated by his personal stories, the mischievous Canadian small-town boy who left for LA at seventeen, the brash US Marine, the daring showbiz writer not afraid to talk to a studio executive. I learned that he'd had a very successful talk radio show in Edmonton, and a successful entertainment company there, but he'd walked away from both because he and Rick were writing, producing, and acting in a CBS kids' Saturday morning show called *Wacko* and he had to be in LA until the show was finished taping.

Bob's face was incredibly animated, changing from minute to minute. He had expressive mobile eyebrows, a huge toothy smile that rounded his cheeks, and a prominent nose with a flattened spot about an inch and a half up from the tip. When he smiled, tiny crow's feet wrinkled at the edges of his big brown eyes. At different angles, he was cute or handsome but also flawed, with a double chin, a face too round for his head, and eyeteeth that stuck out a bit and overlapped the others slightly. His tall, comfortable body was also very appealing to me, but the quality that hooked me was how self-revealing he was.

"I had a great time doing my talk show in Edmonton. I could drink all evening, sleep in till ten, and then be full of controversial topics for the show. But I want my voice out there in a bigger way, and I want more money, and nothing compares to Hollywood for those things."

As we exchanged stories, I also told him so much about me it was as if I was in a first session with a new analyst. I barely touched my Dover sole and green beans, so intent was I on talking. He bit easily into his burger and fries, and his direct eyes were totally fixed on me as if he was watching a movie of my life. Here we were on a first date, and there was no barrier between us. Magnet to metal.

On the way home from dinner, Bob offered me some "Smarties" in the car—the Canadian version of M&M's. It made me laugh that he called them Smarties, even though it was, in fact, a package of M&M's. I hadn't heard that word in a decade.

Back at my apartment, Bob and I settled on the sofa. There was a level of rightness and familiarity different from anyone I'd been with in a long, long time. His best friend in Edmonton was married to a woman who'd been in my grade-school classes in Winnipeg. We discovered our mothers had the same Coronation silver flatware and English bone china teacups. The British Commonwealth tradition of tea was something I hadn't encountered with any of my American boyfriends, and it was one more thread of connection that began building between us.

I cuddled up to him, and we kissed, and I liked how he felt. When I got up to get him a glass of water, he watched me walk

10 staying married is the hardest part

past, and I felt good until he said, "You kind of dress frumpy. Do you ever wear high heels?"

I thought my sandals were cute. I thought my loose gauze dress was sexy. I took a few extra moments in the kitchen, slowly stacking ice cubes one at a time into a tall glass, standing still, hesitating a few more moments before filling the glass with a thin stream of water. The other men I'd been with seemed to like my wardrobe.

I stepped back into my living room and handed him his water. "I don't wear heels," I said. "They hurt my feet."

"But they look so good! You wear social worker shoes."

"That's not very nice," I said. I sank down into my custom-made sofa and watched him gulp his water, noticing how his double chin made his neck look so fleshy.

He set the glass on the coffee table. "I'm sorry," he said in a much softer tone. "I didn't mean to hurt your feelings." Hurt your feelings. Homey. Simple and to the point. Something we said as kids. "It's just that you've got good legs," he said. "High heels would look terrific on you."

In coming years, I would see how important this moment was, but at the time, what I noticed was how quick he was to apologize, and I liked that. He opened his arms, and I scooted over and cuddled up to him. We kissed. Heat rushed to my face. We kissed more. I was ready to toss off my clothes and get naked with him.

He pulled back and patted his hand on my knee. "Let's not do this tonight. Why don't you get into your pajamas and brush your teeth? And I'll tuck you in and go home."

It was the 1970s, for God's sake. This was LA. Nobody did that anymore.

The women's movement and political protests had been in full swing for years—drugs, casual sex, rock and roll, and social

bonnie comfort   11

upheaval were the norm in LA. Vietnam vets came back emotionally broken and anguished, and some professionals I knew experimented with pot, cocaine, and LSD as they searched for new meaning. In that hotbed of chaotic social change, I came to believe you could tell everything you needed to know about a man by getting in bed with him—how considerate he was, how giving, how creative, how fun, and how observant of someone else's needs.

Most of my girlfriends were having casual sex, too. We were taking birth control pills, so no worries about pregnancy. Syphilis and gonorrhea were plagues of the past. Herpes was a cold sore on the mouth that everyone had now and then. AIDS wasn't around yet, and no one had heard of chlamydia or venereal warts. So, in the search for The Right One, why wait? It was more efficient to hop into bed with an interesting man to figure out quickly if he might be a good fit. For my friends and me, the quality of sex was important.

But now, here was old-fashioned Bob, and suddenly, that felt nice.

I dutifully put on my nightie and got into bed. He tucked the bedspread tightly around my hips and waist. He kissed me on the lips sweetly. "I have a feeling I'm going to be spending a lot of time on that side of the bed," he said, pointing next to me. Cozy, familiar, charming, and comforting. A list of words like that floated through my head.

He made me promise to turn on CBS the next morning at 10:00 a.m. to watch *Wacko*.

Although I'd lived in LA for nine years, Bob was the first person I'd met who was in show business. My world had been hospitals and clinics, and the sum of my Hollywood experience had been standing in line once behind Lucille Ball at the Chalet Gourmet in West Hollywood and chatting with Groucho Marx

12   staying married is the hardest part

in an elevator at UCLA Hospital, him in his hospital gown and slippers, his left hand hanging onto a wheeled IV pole.

The next morning, there was Bob on CBS wearing a bright yellow chicken suit, and in the next sketch, wearing a huge Viking hat. I had never seen on the screen a man who'd been in my bedroom the night before. I was Alice stepping through the looking glass, stunned by the utter weirdness of crossing into a world I'd never known. The skin on my forearms tingled. My cheeks heated up, and I laughed out loud.

When he called a half hour later, and I told him I'd watched, his words tumbled out all at once: "I just want you to know I had a wonderful time last night, and I think I'm going to fall in love with you and don't break my heart."

After all those doctors, lawyers, hospital administrators, and businessmen I'd dated, careful ones who were so cautious about saying how they felt, I listened to those words of Bob's, and tears welled in my eyes. A man who wasn't afraid to say he liked me. A man not afraid to talk about his feelings. I plopped down on the sofa behind me as if someone had just hit the back of my knees. I pressed the phone receiver hard against my ear as I felt the room spin. "I had a great time, too," I said. *And you might be The One.*

CHAPTER 2

A Decent Compromise

We had sex for the first time a few days later. He kept his *Wacko* T-shirt on—a baby blue cotton number with a bouncing kangaroo in the center. The sex was all about intercourse without much foreplay. I was disappointed because although I found intercourse exciting, I never fully reached orgasm that way. What I needed was a man's attentive tongue, which got me off and was preamble to great intercourse.

I understood this was only our first time, though. I'd give it more room. After all, had I ever been with a man who had had sex with me in a silly T-shirt from his own TV show?

A week later, we walked around my neighborhood in the evening, holding hands. "Have you ever done it in the bushes?" he asked.

"No." I didn't tell him about the astonishing number of strange places I had done it, including on the nurse's desk in a dialysis unit where I'd worked, the smell of bleach in my nostrils.

"I like to do it outside sometimes," he said. "And I like to peek—see something I'm not supposed to. In my family, sex was a sin, so as a kid, I'd get excited just seeing the outline of

14   staying married is the hardest part

a girl's breast in her sweater. And by thirteen, I got aroused if I accidentally saw a woman in her underwear, or if her bikini top slipped down. Getting a glimpse of the forbidden, you know?"

This seemed quite ordinary to me. For years, I'd done research on people's private sex lives as a way to figure out my own. I usually asked girlfriends and boyfriends to share their experiences, and I did so in return. I read erotic books of the time—*Lady Chatterley's Lover, Tropic of Cancer, Fear of Flying*—and professional works on sexuality, my favorites being by a UCLA psychiatrist who wrote groundbreaking books about erotic experience and sexual fantasy.

So, as Bob and I were walking around and talking, I didn't make much of his confidences. I already knew that if you scratch the surface of any adult, you'll find sexual secrets that are rarely told to anyone because of shame or fear of being judged.

Years before I'd met Bob, I'd lain on the analytic couch discussing my own sexual fantasies, and I'd been told they were a sign I wasn't fully mature. That turned out to be an erroneous theory. Sexual fantasy is a kind of magic that appears in your head unbidden in late childhood, and the particulars are so unique to your childhood experience that although they may sound strange or perverted to someone else, those fantasies remain what excites you most throughout your life, and they usually contain a little story which pops into your head when you masturbate. What the human mind can invent that sexually excites is wildly variable, and each of us has very specific fantasies.

That evening, when Bob and I got into bed, it was the same as before: he encircled me completely, his breath sweet like a baby's, his body warm and fragrant with a faint smell of Old Spice, his hands roaming over my skin, my breasts and thighs, all of which made me super receptive to the intercourse which was intensely arousing. Still, it didn't matter how fabulous the intercourse was, I still couldn't orgasm without more attention to my specific needs.

Lying next to him afterward, both of us flushed, I felt compelled to address the issue—me of the many past men, me for whom good sex was part of my identity as a "liberated woman." I rolled toward him. "Hey—you were wonderful—but I didn't quite make it."

"Oh. Thought you did." He rolled on his side toward me and stroked my arm. "You sounded like you were really into it."

"I was! But next time, could you start by doing me with your mouth?"

He looked down, and in a soft and sad tone, said, "I—I can't—just—can't do that."

That was a surprise. Most men I'd been with assumed I'd want that and would offer it. "Is it the taste? Or the physical position?"

He rolled on his back and ran his hands over his face and hair as if to push it all away. "No. Being that close—my face down there—it scares me."

"*Scares* you?"

He looked up and away at the ceiling. "I feel skittish about touching or kissing you there. I'm awkward. Afraid I'll get it wrong or hurt you, or it won't work, and I'll feel worse."

I stroked his chest, liking its shape. "But you could get better at it. I could show you."

His cheeks looked hot. He turned toward me again and studied my face with those direct brown eyes. "I've tried. I'm just so uncomfortable with it. I was raised in a crazy religion, and it left its mark. The first time I said *fuck* I was eight, and I was sure God was going to strike me dead on the spot."

16 staying married is the hardest part

"But—you know now those teachings aren't true—"

"I do know, oh boy did I reject it. But I still feel self-conscious. Like embarrassed to be too romantic. I've had some loud complaints."

"What about using your hand?"

"I wish I could say yes—but I've tried quite a few times. I don't have the gift."

I hadn't been the perfect bedmate either. I could still hear the damning comments from an old boyfriend whose opinion mattered the world to me: "You're taking too long," "I didn't have this problem with other girls," "There's something wrong with you, and it's psychological."

When I was twenty, those remarks had seared into me a belief that I was sexually defective, and it had never left me. The result was a self-consciousness in bed that prevented me from giving myself over to sensation if I didn't know a man well, or if I cared too much what he thought of me.

Instead, I defaulted to faking orgasm if I wanted to delight a man and I knew it wasn't going to happen for me. Some women fake it because they want the sex to be over, but that was rarely why I did it. Raised in the 1950s, I had learned the number one rule for women: be pleasing to men. By the late 1960s, that meant being willing to have sex, but I was caught between the old standards and the new feminism, so if I couldn't please a man by having an orgasm with him, I developed this secret and shameful habit of sometimes faking it.

I sat up cross-legged and faced Bob. "I've been afraid of complaints myself. I got hooked on my parents' back massager as a vibrator when I was eight. Addicted to it, but secretive about it."

bonnie comfort   17

When I was eight, I had wandered through my parents' open bedroom door one evening and saw my mother lying next to Daddy, facing away from him in her bra and slip. He was running something across her aching low back—an electric vibrator like the scalp massagers in drugstores. Within days I snuck into their bedroom and tried it on myself. Wow, what a surprise!

That was the first secret I kept from my mother.

Four years later, when our health teacher gave us *Facts of Life and Love for Teenagers*, I read it three times before I realized what I'd been doing with the family vibrator was bringing myself to orgasm. I had never heard that word.

The book also said if a young woman used a vibrator, it might interfere with her ability to have an orgasm "the normal way." Now I was doing something unapproved, secret, and shameful—something that could make me abnormal—and there was no one I dared ask about it, because there was no way I was going to give it up.

I looked down at my lap as I kept talking to Bob. "Over the years I've ah—sometimes used it with a long-term boyfriend, but never with someone new."

At that time, a vibrator was something used in porn movies, not something tucked in every woman's bedside table, so I found it embarrassing and was afraid the man would feel alienated by it or not like that I needed it. Mine wasn't a penis-shaped device. I had no idea where to find something like that, nor did I want to. It was simply a replica of my parents' drugstore scalp massager, which was the only thing readily available in those days.

"I'm embarrassed when I can't fully let go," I said. "Sometimes I've faked it so a man wouldn't know when I didn't

18   staying married is the hardest part

come."

I hung my head in silence. It was a measure of my growing trust in Bob that so soon in our relationship I'd made my shameful confession about faking it.

He put his warm hand on my knee. "So just use your vibrator with me! Then neither of us'll be worried!"

I picked at a hangnail on my thumb. I knew what was best for me—a man who was confident of his own sexuality, who loved giving oral, and with whom I never felt I was imposing. "But I'd rather you pleasure me . . ."

"Hey—I can fuck you all day long. I just can't put my face down there. I know it's crazy irrational, but for me it's the same as dancing. It wasn't allowed. So now I can clown around on camera with fake dancing, but real dancing? I can't do it. Same with this. I'm so uncomfortable with it. That's why I like the idea of you using your vibrator."

"It's not the same. The vibrator works, but it embarrasses me to use it in front of someone, and to have a man give himself to me is way more intimate and sensuous."

His eyes were round and serious and directed at my face. "But can't we use it as a workaround? It's a guaranteed orgasm for you every time."

"Yes," I said. "That's true."

I didn't want to keep pressuring him. Things still felt too new, too fragile. And I was already enchanted with him. Maybe over time he'd change?

We kissed. "Get out your vibrator right now," he said.

Bob held me while I used it, but the old shame resurfaced afterward. I always felt more "normal" if I reached orgasm with a man pleasuring me. Yet, Bob's uneasiness about giving me oral would ruin it for me anyway, feeding as it would into my fear that I was imposing and taking too long. My vibrator was the next best thing. He even said he thought of the vibrator as his "friend."

By the end of that evening of honest sharing, of him welcoming me with my own sexual quirks, and me accepting his limitations, our love deepened. In that sense, Bob did me more good than seven years of analytic work, and my consent to our compromise softened years of him feeling inadequate.

CHAPTER 3

Yes, I Will

Bob was staying with Claire, a platonic friend who was now divorced and raising two kids on her own. Her ex owned The Ice House, a comedy and folk-singing club in Pasadena where Bob had started as a bartender and graduated to doing stand-up. Pretty and funny herself, Claire had made Bob part of her family and her two kids milled around him when he was there, laughing at his jokes, playing cards, and watching TV with him.

A few days after our sex talk, I drove to Pasadena to celebrate Bob's birthday with Claire and friends. "Hi!" she said with a big welcoming hug. She was tall, with long, graceful fingers and striking blue eyes. How warm and open she was, chummy as if we'd already known each other for years. Bob was clearly part of her family. That's where he stayed whenever he was in town.

Bob grinned at me. "Are you happy to see me?" he asked with that endearing mouth that moved around when he was full of feelings.

"So happy." I loved how open he was without being needy or fawning.

bonnie comfort   21

Over the next few weeks, the heaviness I'd felt under my breastbone after returning from Winnipeg was replaced by lightness and joy during lunches, dinners, late-night cuddling, laughing, and talking. There was not one conversation that didn't trigger a genuine belly laugh in me. He had a knack for telling the truth in a unique and hilarious way. Like after a few times when different guys said hello to me in public, Bob said, "We can't go anywhere without bumping into someone you've dated! If we go to the racetrack, the horses are going to run by, waving 'Hi, Bonnie! Ho! Bonnie!'"

I laughed, but he was right. Attracting men had become my superpower.

One evening after we were hot and heavy, Bob kissed my forehead, and said, "You're kind of a bad girl. . . . Y'know what I mean—naughty. I love that about you."

I chuckled with the pleasure of recognition. I *was* naughty—playful about sex, and willing. The side of me that loved to seduce had had a lot of fun. Besides, what a "bad girl" was in 1959 was just normal in LA in 1977. Everyone was hopping into bed.

Bob stroked the side of my face. "I'd love to see you in stockings and garters."

I hadn't worn garters or stockings since I was sixteen, but I was curious about what his reaction would be. "*Welll*—maybe one day I'll buy some stockings."

He actually started getting an erection again just hearing me say that.

Early one evening, Bob kept me waiting an hour before showing up for dinner, and I said, "I'm worried you're not reliable." He replied, "Sure I'm reliable! You can rely on me to be

22   staying married is the hardest part

late, you can rely on me to drink, and you can rely on me to wear jeans."

I chuckled. At least he was honest.

At dinner, he ping-ponged from comedy bits he'd done that day to discussing a future TV show for him and Rick. His clever inventiveness charmed me. In Canada, he'd created "Metric Melodramas" to help citizens make the transition to the metric system—five-minute films like the old serial cliff-hangers they used to show in movie theaters before the feature film. His character was "The Evil but Oddly Attractive Yardley Footlong" who was always tying "Millie Meter" to the railroad tracks.

On a Sunday afternoon over hot corned beef sandwiches at Fromin's Deli, I saw how much Bob delighted in children. There was a toddler at the table next to ours, and Bob waved and made funny faces to hear the boy giggle. Other times in restaurants, he played hide-and-seek with babies. "Y'wanna have a baby?" he asked as he watched the couple at the next table leave.

"Definitely. I've always wanted to have a baby. I just wanted to get married first."

"I'd love to have kids."

Yikes, were we talking about marriage already? "Good to know," I said, and smiled. The idea warmed me, but I wasn't ready to continue the conversation right then. I bit into my sandwich and looked away at the door as a guy walked in. "He looks familiar," I said.

Bob glanced at the entrance. "George Carlin. He used to play The Ice House."

"Geez, I've gone to lots of comedy clubs, but I've never been to The Ice House."

bonnie comfort   23

He sipped his tall, iced tea and shook his head. "I got tired of stand-up. Most guys say the same jokes over and over, but that bores me. I really like Lenny Bruce. Gutsy and political. And Steve Martin used to come into The Ice House, and I think he's very talented."

I tried looking casual when he mentioned household names that he knew personally, but my admiration must have been blatantly obvious.

"Hey—" he said. "I don't want you to get sucked in by show business. These people just eat and fart and die like the rest of us."

Well I didn't want to come across like a teenage groupie. I toned down that "through the looking glass" feeling I still had.

Later that night, after another sweaty love session, Bob put his hand on my forehead and ran his forefinger down the side of my cheek. "Will you marry me?"

I smiled with pleasure. "Are you crazy?" It had only been weeks, and in spite of how enchanted I was with him, my skeptical inner voice kept something in reserve: Is he reliable? Does he drink too much? Will his income be steady? Can I give up the sex life I've always wanted? What would my life with him really be like? "Ask me in three months!" I said.

Another evening, sitting outside at a café waiting for our dinner, we saw a guy in a sweatshirt two tables away. "Marine Corps," Bob said, nodding his head in the guy's direction.

"How do you know?"

"The way he holds his body. His haircut. That small emblem on his sweatshirt. He's probably on leave for the weekend."

We downed our cocktails and ordered a second. "Why did you enlist?" I asked. "I mean, you were Canadian."

24   staying married is the hardest part

"Didn't matter. I was a legal resident. And after high school, I wasn't sure what to do. I figured it'd give me time to think." He leaned back in his chair, watching the guy two tables away. "After a few weeks in boot camp, I fit right in. When I was growing up I learned that if I made my dad laugh, he wouldn't hit me. Same in the Corps: I learned how to flout authority, but just up to the line so I wasn't court-martialed. I made everybody laugh."

"Give me an example."

"Well—when I was working for Bridge Company, we had a captain who could lift amazing amounts of weight, but wasn't getting any mail from the Mensa Society, y'know? And we were going through inspection where you had to put every single thing on your bunk—clothes, rifle, helmet, boots, and if any clothes were missing you had to show laundry chits for them. My bed had a few things on it but everything else was laundry chits. So he came up, and looked at my bunk and said, 'Where's all your stuff?'"

"'Sir,' I said, 'At the dry cleaners in town.'"

"Then he was *at me*. Checked through everything. Then he looked closely at my dog tags and said, 'What's this *NP* bullshit?'"

"'Well, sir,' I said, 'that's *NP* for no preference.'"

"And he started yelling, 'There are no atheists in a foxhole! You must believe *something*!'"

"I waited till he was done, and then I said, 'Sir, I'm part of a small denomination, but the guys made a little fun of it, so I thought it'd be better to have *NP* on there.'"

"Then he chewed me out, and the whole fucking squad, because whoever had been laughing at me was an example of how not to behave: we were here to save the world, and this was part of it. Then, he asked me what the small denomination was that I belonged to.

"I said, 'Well, sir, I don't like to say it loud,' and I got quiet, and said, 'I'm a Comfortist.'"

"Oh my God!" I said, laughing at Bob's sheer nerve. "I can't believe you said that!"

"Yup. And he got real loud and said, 'What the fuck is a fucking Comfortist?'"

I put my hand over my mouth, amazed at his sheer guts.

"I said, 'It's a very small denomination. And people don't mean any harm, but my feelings are a little hurt.'" He took a sip of his whiskey. "And then he lectured us all on religious tolerance in America, while everyone was trying not to laugh."

His smile faded, and he took another whiskey sip. "But I feel bad now for making fun of him. I was such an arrogant asshole. He was totally loyal to the Corps, and what he said was true. The guys believed it, and I believed it."

For Thanksgiving, we rented a condo in North Lake Tahoe near the Nevada border. Everything about him was new—his terror flying over the mountains in a small plane, how ridiculous his long legs were, skinny from knees to feet, heels jutting out in back, how he loved birds and stood on the balcony in his bathrobe, me thinking how ridiculous those legs were, but how much I liked him.

We wandered around the Cal-Neva casino just over the Nevada border. At a roulette table, he handed me a $100 bill and said, "Put it on red or black." Unnerved by such an extravagant idea, I shut my eyes for a moment and *red* came to my mind. "Yay!" I yelled when the dealer tossed me two hundred-dollar chips. It was exciting to be so cavalier with money.

26   staying married is the hardest part

We slept in a queen bed and watched lazy snowflakes fall outside the window. His Canon camera was with him, nestled in its black "leather" bag, and inside were rolls of RGB film for negatives and slides—movie film, he said, with colors deeper and richer than drugstore film. I had my Nikon with a bag full of drugstore film. We took photos of each other, me in his long-sleeved blue T-shirt from Banff, a camel hair overcoat, my big aviator glasses, him in a blue nubby turtleneck and a blue quilted jacket, his hair blowing away from his face, a silver ring on his little finger.

When we returned, he moved into my apartment with me. Sleeping together every evening, I was confronted more with our sexual arrangement. The vibrator was our "friend," but I still longed to feel Bob fully with me.

In hopes of loosening the grip of his old religious training, I said, "Tell me more about what you believed as a kid." It was a Sunday, and I was stirring eggs for an omelet, having already grated cheese and chopped parsley while he sat at the dining table reading the LA Times.

The paper rustled closed, and he started reciting as if from a memorized poem: "If you're good, you'll go to heaven when you die. Everyone else'll suffer untold agonies in hell. It's a sin to touch yourself. It's a sin to have sex before you're married. Lust is a sin. Even the smallest lie is a black mark on your soul. In Sunday school, our teacher held a glass of clear water to demonstrate, and she said, 'Here's a little lie you told,' and she added one drop of ink to the water. 'Here's you sneaking into a movie,' another drop. 'Here's dancing,' drop. 'Here's drinking and smoking,' two more drops. As the sins mounted, each with a drop of ink, the water became darker and darker until it was a murky mess. 'This is your soul,' she said, 'full of sin. But if you

bonnie comfort   27

pray to God for forgiveness, and you promise not to commit these sins anymore, you can be saved,' and to demonstrate this, she added a solution to the water that completely restored it to clear. It was magic. I wanted to be saved, over and over."

I had stopped stirring the eggs, so unsettled I couldn't do anything else but listen.

"If you were a devout follower of the church, you could be saved, and at some point, you could be sanctified, and those who were sanctified were guaranteed to get into Heaven. But the sanctified people were the arrogant, self-satisfied ones who sat at the back of the church and judged everyone else. They were protected from hell. I hated them. Thin-lipped women with no makeup and sour expressions on their faces.

"This is how much I believed: one night I had a bad dream, and I went into my parents' bedroom to tell them. Usually they snored, but this time they were both lying flat and still, not making any noise. I panicked. Thought everyone had died and gone to heaven, and big sinner that I was, I was left alone on earth and was going to hell. I let out a huge wail, and they startled out of a sound sleep and asked me what was wrong."

I served our breakfast. He read me stories from the paper. I loved being with him.

As I tidied up afterward, I glanced around my living room. For ten years, photography had been my dedicated art, and photography books were strewn around my apartment like recipe books of the world. In evening classes, I'd learned about emulsions, composition, unintended meaning that sometimes emerged from a candid shot. I'd taken photos of my lovers, this one's muscles, that one's hair falling in layers that caught the light in separate shades, one whose smile radiated warmth and fun. Coming out of a family of talented painters, I had this one

28 staying married is the hardest part

thing that was mine—photography. I'd slip my hands inside my developing bag, securing the rolls of film in the light-tight container, and pour chemicals into the chamber using my timing schedules to create my own negatives in long unfurling strips I hung over the shower stall to dry. I created 8 x 10s with my enlarger that sat on my long bathroom vanity counter. But now I was dating Bob, whose recreational art was photography, and I stopped doing it. I had already taken a liking to stained glass and was learning how to design and make windows. But in my mind, it was as if we couldn't both be photographers. I didn't want to compete with him.

His music taste was different from mine: ELO, Queen, Billy Joel, Jethro Tull. My jazz records lay idle—Chuck Mangione, Grover Washington, Jr.—and Bob made fun of the blues ("Well I woke up this mornin' and everything I had was *gooone*. . . ." he sang in a fake raspy voice). I loved the blues, but I stopped playing them. He taught me to enjoy Beethoven symphonies, Mahler, Handel, Vivaldi, all beautiful.

It didn't occur to me at that time how I was once again shaping myself to fit the man I was with. I had thrilled him by pulling up my skirt one night to reveal a pretty lace garter belt holding up black stockings, and I'd bought two pairs of high heels. I'd given up photography, and I was no longer listening to my favorite jazz and blues records. It happened so seamlessly, so subtly, that I barely noticed.

After Bob moved in with me, I discovered how different our lives were. He and Rick would meet for a late breakfast at a deli, toss around ideas, laugh the whole time, take notes, then go to their offices and write. Rick came over to the apartment one afternoon and I saw how appealing he was—tall, skinny, handsome and full of restless energy, he actually took a run at the fake rock wall surrounding my gas fireplace and climbed a few feet up the side before jumping off. Then they went to a pitch meeting. They often entertained studio executives, production company staff, and show runners. They went to late-night bars and drank while I stayed home working on my latest stained-glass window. Bob would come home at midnight, face flushed, whiskey on his breath, and we'd stay up talking and laughing.

On weekdays, I'd drag myself out of bed at 7:00 a.m. to head for work.

"You've got the circadian rhythm of a paper boy," he said watching me get ready to leave while he lolled in bed reading the *LA Times* cover to cover to look for stories.

I want his life, I thought. After three years of working in a mental hospital, I'd had enough of severe mental conditions. I wanted to be a psychologist treating people with mild depression, anxiety, and relationship problems, issues in which I could make a difference. And I wanted way more fun and laughs. Bob was just the man to make that a part of my everyday life.

I was at this point dedicated to my third psychoanalysis, the treatment of choice then for the "worried well." Struggling with self-doubt and mild depression throughout my twenties, I had relied on three different analysts in sequence: the first three days a week, the second four days a week, and now the third, Dr. James Grotstein, three days a week. Analysts had become my gurus, who accompanied me on my search for a deeper understanding of myself as a way of growing up.

Now I lay on Grotstein's couch evaluating Bob. "Show business is erratic," I said. "He makes great money now, but what if his

30 staying married is the hardest part

show doesn't get picked up? But, oh my God, he is the funniest person I've ever known! I mean original funny, in the moment, on the fly. Witty, clever, not someone who tells you jokes. And every day it's something new! On the other hand, he's always late. I've stopped expecting him to show up when he says he will."

Each doubt was met with questions from Grotstein: Did I want a child? Had I admitted to myself that I didn't have another decade? As I responded to his queries, I saw more clearly than ever that the search for the perfect man was a recipe for never choosing anyone.

The next session, a day later, I was restless, moving my legs around on Grotstein's black tufted sofa. I gazed at the wall of books across the room. He knew more than I did. "What about the sex?" I said. "We're not a great fit. I mean it's great in some ways but not in others."

"You'll have to decide what matters most to you."

I mulled this over for weeks. Sex was an important issue in my life, perhaps much more so than for other women, and Bob's skittishness about oral sex went straight to the heart of my own sexual struggles: if I had to demand he give me what I wanted, I wouldn't be able to relax into it. His attempts wouldn't work, and we'd both feel we'd failed. I thought sex therapy might help both of us overcome our inhibitions. I couldn't count on that though, even if he agreed to it.

Therefore, I had to make a choice: accept our compromise or stop dating him. I gave myself more time to see how it felt to live with our compromise.

The next month, our first December together, we had a party. The afternoon of, Bob and Rick brought home gallons of booze, and the ugliest sculpture I'd ever seen—a big jumble of seashells glued together. "This'll be our door prize," said Bob.

bonnie comfort   31

"Oh my God it's so awful! Who would want that?" I asked.

Bob laughed that staccato laugh I came to love. "Awful is the point!"

It began a long tradition of "awful" door prizes at our parties. Bob Goodwin, a close friend of Bob's, won it this time. Goodwin had an adorable smile and a great talent for mimicking voices; years later, he became the producer and director of *The X Files*. The other tradition started was a slideshow of very odd photos Bob had taken, with his running dialogue to go with them. At the height of the party, Bob dimmed the lights and began with a photo of two middle-aged European women in mid-calf dresses, stockings rolled down to their knees, and their black purses slung over their forearms while they climbed up a steep embankment. "Ah, here we have the Romanian women's climbing team," Bob said, which triggered a burst of laughter from the crowd. The next slide was a twenty-five-foot-high statue of a Roadrunner. Bob said, "Here's this bird's personal ad— 'Tall, chesty woman looking for someone to share a life of fast starts and stops.'"

I couldn't believe how fast those one-liners rolled off Bob's tongue, no notes, no preparation, just following his wit. I knew he'd had a talk show in Edmonton and done stand-up for military troops, but this was the first time I'd seen him hold a whole room full of people at rapt attention, laughing, and hanging on his every word.

The ability to spin tales, be witty or profound, or dazzle me with verbal brilliance were more enchanting to me than any other quality in a man. I wanted other things in a partner, too, but words were the siren song. Bob was hysterically funny, a talented writer, and a soulful human being who often said something so right that it was like he had scratched an itch I

32   staying married is the hardest part

hadn't known I had. He brought me silly fun, honest directness, and a lesson I didn't know I needed: that laughing was essential to a good life, not just frosting on the cake.

I also felt cherished by him. He hadn't dated a professional before, and he listened carefully when I talked about my work. He said he was proud to be with me—that I was not only pretty, but would be a psychologist, and he could see how much people liked to talk to me.

Often, he brought me unusual gifts—a hand puppet, a rubber chicken, the pale face of a pelican carved in stone, thirty-three perfect sand dollars. I loved polished rocks, so a rock polisher. Perfectly imperfect things.

One day, he came home from a long-lost movie set on a Culver City backlot with something that looked like a white chess pawn and filled up my hand. "It's from a staircase on the old set of *Gone With the Wind*," he said.

My fingers closed around it, and I said. "You're kidding me!"

"No. Stole it. Shouldn't have. But thought you'd like it." Lips curled up in a half smile.

I shuffled back a step. For a moment, I was fifteen again in my family living room, tears streaming as I read the last chapter of Scarlett O'Hara's saga. "This is incredible! I can't believe it!" Stammering now, "But-but you stole it?"

"Oh, it's all abandoned and very run-down." He waved his hand. "No one'll miss it."

Impossible. Me holding this piece of history with small patches of paint worn off. I never told anybody. I still have it. It was one of our secrets.

Bob plucked me out of my work milieu of serious suffering, and swept me into a life of laughs, glamour, and fun.

I ran toward it like a child seeking play after a day in school. Everything good seemed possible with him.

The week before Christmas, I was straddling him on my bed, his face flushed, his hands on my ass. "Will you marry me?" he asked for the second time.

I felt safest with men who were not like my family. Starting at age twenty, I had no long-term Jewish partners in my bed. With those men, it was like sliding down a long tunnel backward into my family, the dangerous place where I didn't know who I was, where I was always comparing myself to my older sisters, and where the intense closeness of our family threatened to obliterate me. Only Bob had the perfect recipe—not Jewish but Canadian, not formally educated but brilliant and self-educated, tall to their short, emotionally open and giving like them, and funny, oh so funny, quick as lightning with those hilarious life observations that came out of his mouth every day.

"Are you thinking about it?" he asked.

My smile covered my whole face. Even my eyebrows smiled. "Yes," I said. "I will marry you. But not till next summer." That would be ten months together. Enough time to be sure. Still enough time to walk away.

CHAPTER 4

A Jewish Heart

In February, we flew to Canada to meet our families. The majestic Rocky Mountains were visible from the plane as we flew over them to Edmonton, which was flat and piled high with snow. Bob's dad, Ben, was a retired English teacher quoting arcane literature. His Mom, Dorothy, was severely disabled by rheumatoid arthritis, and unable to do much with her floppy, deformed hands, so that Ben had to do everything—shop, cook, clean, help her on and off the toilet, and help transfer her to bed or back into her wheelchair. It looked tragic to me, yet she was cheerful, ready to laugh, and intensely interested in others. Her Christian religion sustained her.

One evening when we were all watching TV, there was some oblique reference to fellatio, and Dorothy said with great emphasis, "Oh boy, if a man ever put that thing in my mouth, I'd bite it off!"

I kept my face still to suppress my shock. Why would she say that in front of me? And if her attitudes about sexual activity were that constricted, how could it not have had a profound effect on Bob? I was reminded of his cousin saying to him, "Aren't we dirty little devils?"

bonnie comfort   35

Bob showed me his collection of ancient, striated rocks in the basement. As a boy, he'd lived and played in Drumheller, a small coal mining town in the badlands of eastern Alberta where dinosaurs had roamed. He'd gone to Sunday school for years, but when he tried questioning the version of history in the Bible, the teacher would shut him down. Once, his uncle found an enormous dinosaur thigh bone that sat on their back porch until a museum took it away. "After that," Bob said, "How could I believe the world started only five thousand years ago?"

We slept happily in a double bed in the guest room where he told me in a whisper that once, when he was in high school and going out for the evening, he came up to his mother's bedside to say goodnight and she said, "Don't ever leave me." That request frightened him and drove him away from home at seventeen, even more than his dad's harshness and temper.

Bob also whispered that his older brother, Doug, had seen their father step into the Drumheller "house of ill repute." I don't know if it was true, but Bob believed it, and he told me that story more than once. His father had been in the Canadian Air Force during World War II, and Bob's model of masculinity was to some extent built on his father being in the military and Bob hearing that Ben had sought relief in whorehouses.

This is how your family of origin shapes you: in ways you admire them, you emulate them; in ways you hate them, you try to be different. In ways you don't realize, you live out what they taught you. In Bob's family, men found dirty sex away from home, and "good girls" engaged only in sex the Bible allows. In my family, sex could be varied and creative, but only in marriage. For both of us, our family narratives worked against us: Bob didn't feel sexually comfortable unless he turned me into

36 staying married is the hardest part

a "bad girl," and I didn't feel guilt-free because I'd broken the virgin-till-you-marry rule. Neither of us could entirely divest ourselves from these narratives.

When we left Edmonton, there were lots of hugs and promises to visit again soon. On the plane to Winnipeg, Bob settled into a seat with a shiver. "*Whoo*! I hate that Edmonton cold!"

"Ha. You ain't seen nothin' yet."

By my late teens, I hated Winnipeg, particularly in winter. Outside, it hurt to breathe, and parking places had electrical outlets to charge car batteries, or they'd be dead in an hour. The weather never seemed to bother Daddy, who'd grown up there, but Mom was from LA, and she grumbled as she stamped her feet in the foyer to get the snow off. She shook her head some mornings when she gazed out the kitchen window as the snow blew sideways across the frigid drifts.

As a child, I sensed a thread of regret running through Mom's life—how she described the avocado and fig trees in her family's backyard, the wide, clean streets, and the abundance of flowers year-round. She had left LA to marry my father, but her yearning leaked out in her private habits—the *Vogue* magazines she read with reverence, the letters she wrote to her mother and brothers, the occasional remark she'd let slip, as in "You have to get a professional degree, Bon. It doesn't matter if you're living in a woodpile. It's something you'll always have." And I knew Winnipeg was the woodpile.

I adored my mother when I was young. As a kid, I had coined a nickname for her—Min—and for my whole life, I called her that, and I was the only one who did. It was a special bond between us, even when things were strained. Long after she could pick me up, she hugged me, cut and washed my hair, and rubbed my back or stroked my arms and legs. If I was sick, she took my temperature and brought me toast in bed with tea in a little china cup. She did that for all of us, but since I was the youngest, she had more time for me as my sisters matured. I admired her and wanted her to see me as the unique person I was.

Now, I was nervous. It had been nine years since an awful confrontation between us in my first LA apartment, and although I had dutifully visited once a year, the frost between us hadn't melted. At age twenty-three, when I walked up the jetway to fly to LA, I turned one last time to see my parents holding back tears, but an iron resolve made me keep going. The suffocating, closed box of the life they were pressuring me to choose would kill me. I even ran screaming from Canada itself. In a small, dingy immigration office in LA, I claimed my American citizenship, a privilege I had because I was the daughter of a US citizen, a woman who had never been willing to give up her own American identity.

Five weeks after I arrived in LA, my Grandma Esther died. Min called to say she was coming to the funeral. She stayed in a hotel, and for the event wore a black Chanel classic—straight skirt and choker pearls that fit perfectly atop the collarless boxy jacket. "I'll ride to the cemetery with Uncle Joe and Aunt Bess," Min said after the service. Cold as a Winnipeg winter.

After the shiva at Uncle Joe's house, I asked Min if she'd like to see my apartment. She agreed, but the hard glint of her eyes behind her glasses told me nothing between us was okay.

The only sound on our drive was the V-8 engine of my used Mercury Cougar. It was awkward when I opened the flimsy front door of my West Hollywood apartment. For a moment,

38   staying married is the hardest part

I saw it through Min's eyes: the threadbare carpet, the thin sofa cushions with a cigarette burn in one corner, the cheap prints, the student era bookcase. I might have felt humiliated by her disdain of such a modest place, but no. I felt proud of it. Triumphant. These were my Picasso prints, my board-and-brick bookcase, my British pewter mugs. I was finally making my own choices.

She perched on the edge of the old green sofa as far away from the cigarette burn as possible, and I sat in my used armchair across from her. We chatted about nothing until she abruptly stood and turned around, facing the wall. Her Chanel skirt showed the rounded outline of having sat in it for hours. Her black sheer stockings had a catch at the back of her left calf. I had no idea why she was standing there like that.

She didn't move. I looked at the wall she was facing, then at the other wall, then at the rug. Was she taking it all in? Was she going to finally tell me my new life was okay with her?

I studied the back of her, and the clasp of her pearls—a double moonstone, pale blue, translucent and surrounded by rhinestones. It was the one string of her pearls I'd always loved, and years before, she had promised that one day she'd give them to me. There was something vulnerable about the way her feet splayed out slightly, her shoes with a small protrusion in the leather on both inner sides where her bunions pushed out.

She still didn't move. And there I was, looking at her back for a full minute, completely puzzled. Finally, I said, "Min— *what are you doing?*"

She practically whirled around, and then glared down at me, high color in her cheeks, her voice loud and hard. "That's what you did to me!" she said. "You—turned—your—back— on—me." She spit her words out.

bonnie comfort   39

She turned her head slightly and a shaft of sunlight from my front window caught the lenses of her glasses, and I couldn't see her eyes. I saw only LA light reflected back.

A moment later, when I did see her eyes, they frightened me. They burned with anger. I sat immobile, unable to speak. I was twenty-three and she was fifty-eight, and I didn't understand yet that a person could be all ages at once, that a fifty-eight-year-old could have parts of herself that were very young, with the kind of confusing, powerful emotions a twenty-three-year-old has.

"Min," I said, pleading quietly. "I'm just choosing my life. I'm—sorry. I—had to leave."

We drove to her hotel in silence. It was two miles from my apartment, but the longest drive of my life. Later that week, in spite of our differences, she bought me dishes and glassware and cutlery. My rich cousin treated us to an expensive dinner at Perino's where pink and peach tablecloths and warm little yellow lights made everyone look young. I loved the place.

This was my city now, with my fancy restaurants.

Min downed flute after flute of Dom Perignon, looking away from me, soothing her anger with too much alcohol until we stood to leave. I'd stolen the life she'd intended to have here. There was nowhere else on earth I could have moved that would have been more painful for her than LA.

On this visit to Winnipeg, I felt protected by Bob's presence. When we walked into my parents' house, Min greeted me with open arms to hug me close. Always tastefully dressed, on this day she wore a finely woven long-sleeved sweater, her single strand of choker pearls, and a knee-length straight wool skirt. "Bon!" she said as always, truly overjoyed to see me.

40   staying married is the hardest part

"Min!" I said, smiling with a rush of blood to my face as I remembered how much we loved each other, particularly when I was young and believed she was perfect. I inhaled her familiar scents—Jergen's hand lotion and Shalimar. Dad wore his usual three-piece suit, white shirt, suspenders, ever the lawyer, ever the formal Victorian gentleman, but I felt deep love between us, too.

"This is Bob," I said, stepping aside so he could greet them directly.

"Glad ta meetcha!" he said, shaking each of their hands. He was a good half foot taller than they were, but open and unguarded as always, which seemed to put them at ease. After we settled at the mahogany dining table, I felt proud of the smart way Bob talked to them, asking my dad about his law practice, and eager to see Min's paintings. For thirty years she'd been painting at home amid the smells of linseed oil, turpentine, and oils, and after we chatted a while, she took us on a tour of her latest—huge canvases mounted on every wall, bright colors, flowers, tropical scenes. I oohed and aahed over her work, mentioning the bold red here, the clever shadows of leaves there. She needed that, and I could give it.

Min was only five foot two and 118 pounds, but she always seemed bigger. On this afternoon, she brought out her best china and silver for afternoon tea, her sugar cookies, and little white bread sandwiches with the crusts cut off. Her china plates with the gold leaf pattern shone, and I nibbled on one of those little sandwiches, remembering how much I'd always admired Min's talent as a cook and baker and hostess.

"Cream or sugar?" Min asked Bob, bending to serve him as if he were royalty.

bonnie comfort   41

"Both!" he said. "And another cookie! How did you get them so perfect?"

She smiled, showing her dimples. "Butter is the secret to everything."

How differently she was behaving now compared to years ago when she did whatever she could to control which young men I chose. Min had been the force to contend with at home, the one whose temper could flare. With her, no meant no. Daddy was kind—rarely a mean word from him—but he lacked the vitality and edginess I found so appealing in Min. She had always been in charge of raising us girls. He worked every day of the week.

Until I was ten, Min and I adored each other. Then I began fighting her over piano lessons, Yiddish lessons, Hebrew school, the right clothes for the High Holidays, and my having to get good grades and only socialize with Jews. Her fiercest fights with me were over boys. Min believed her girls needed a strong protector, and that protector would either have to be her or a husband. Yes, she wanted us to do well in school, learn life skills, and earn a respectable profession, but she believed the real trick in life for a girl was finding the right man to marry, and believe it fiercely she did.

In high school, I hung out with Wayne, a gentile boy who wore tight polyester pants and told off-color jokes. We didn't have much in common, but it was exciting to skip out of school with him to buy Butterfingers and Snickers and walk around the neighborhood, our fingers smeared with chocolate, and Wayne pressing himself against me in a back alley.

When the school year ended, Min whisked me off to LA where we lived for the summer with her mother, my Grandma

42   staying married is the hardest part

Esther. I had fallen in love with LA at age five, when my family had spent the summer. Now I reveled in days at Santa Monica Beach—the warm salt air, the cries of seagulls, the smell of hot dogs from the concession stand, and the thrilling crash of waves. When we drove up the San Gabriel mountains, I gazed lovingly at the LA basin where we saw palm trees waving below and heard the chatter of mockingbirds. It was magic for a girl from the Canadian prairies, and I drank it in like an alcoholic sucking up Scotch.

I also watched for letters from Wayne until I received one that had an extra letter behind it, one on my dad's legal letterhead saying if Wayne didn't cease all contact with me he'd be prosecuted. My hands shook as I read this. Bullying my boyfriend like that! And for what? Didn't they know I would never marry so young? I walked a whole square block, ready to hurl rocks and break windows. They would never trust my judgment! And to go behind my back like *this?*

When I returned to Grandma's house, Min sat at the dining table having tea. I flung that letter down in front of her, and the letter's edge landed in her teacup, slowly wilting. My voice rose to stadium-level yelling. "This is so horrible! *How could you do this?*"

She picked up the soaking letter and crumpled it into a ball. "Seems like that's what we had to do to stop you two."

Rage surged up in me like bile. I didn't speak to her for days, but a mantra formed in my head that stayed with me for decades: *After I leave home, they'll never be able to control me. I'm going to live in LA come hell or high water.*

As a child you live under the scrutiny of a giant who looks after you and controls you, but you're not a lump of clay to be shaped. You come with a personality and life force of your own, and how you navigate the love and wishes of your giant determines only partly who you become.

The rest is your authentic self.

Min sipped her tea and asked Bob a veiled question about how his career was going. He said, "Well—show business proves the Golden Rule, y'know? He who has the gold rules."

Min gave a wry smile. "That's a truth in so many businesses . . ."

Bob shrugged. "I just keep pitching my ideas and having faith in them. We're going to do the Alan King special next month."

Min clasped her hands together. "I love Alan King!"

Of course she did. She loved laughing, she was funny herself, and every Sunday evening in my teens, we watched the *Ed Sullivan Show*, and the stand-up comics were her favorites, and yes, they were almost all Jewish—Lenny Bruce, George Burns, Henny Youngman, Mort Sahl, Alan King, Don Rickles, Jack Carter, and David Steinberg (who was from Winnipeg).

"Next year we'll be doing a two-hour Kenny Rogers special," Bob added, which made Min's eyebrows go up. He chose exactly the right things to share, being modest, but emphasizing his future potential.

Min flushed cheeks betrayed her excitement. She leaned over, placed her hand on Bob's arm, and in a more hushed tone said, "Bob? I think you're going to grab the brass ring."

He flashed one of those wide grins of his. "Maybe! But right now, I'm thinking of a different ring. And I think y'wanna know if I'm good husband material for Bonnie, right?"

44 staying married is the hardest part

Min gave him a smile that I recognized when she was impressed with a truth she'd heard, a small smile accompanied by a slow nod. Bob said, "So I came all the way here for you to eyeball me and see that I really love her, and I'll give her my best."

"That calls for a sip of sherry, don't you think?" she replied.

We drank it from her sparkling crystal wine glasses. A warm relaxation spread through my limbs. I had brought home the prize; I saw it in both of my parents' faces. Min's warmth and humor matched Bob's. He was The One in her mind, too, and after all the fighting and worrying she sighed, relieved that I'd done well for myself.

Before we left, she looped her arm through Bob's, pulled him aside, and I overheard her say, "Bob, I know you're not Jewish, but you've got a Jewish heart."

We flew back to LA in a cloud of relief and joy. Bob returned to his show business, and I resumed my professional life at the VA psychiatric hospital. For years at UCLA and Olive View hospitals, I'd provided emotional support to people with cancer or end-stage kidney disease. Hospital gowns, pain, the smells of deteriorating bodies and chemical rescue, the sounds of moaning, machines beeping—this had been my milieu, and I served as handmaiden to doctors, empathetic ear to people facing death, and support to grieving spouses. I learned an astonishing amount about medical illnesses and their treatment, and the pecking order and administrative subterfuge that is part of any medical facility. It was an important job, but it was not doing psychotherapy, the work I hoped one day to do full time.

Now, as a psychiatric social worker in an inpatient unit, I was one step closer to my ultimate goal, but these patients were psychotic or actively suicidal or manic and not really candidates for the kind of insight-oriented psychotherapy I loved. Vietnam veterans filled our wards, wounded, heartsick, and psychotic. Some of them had done unspeakable things in Vietnam. Our ward smelled of strange medicines, disinfectant, and bad sweat. Down the hallway from my office, I sometimes heard howling or yelling. One night, a patient put a fist through the frosted glass window of my office, and I had to step over shards of glass in the morning. Another of my patients hung himself on a weekend pass. The week before, he'd given me a thank-you gift of a brass candy dish, the underside engraved in his own handwriting, "To Bonnie, love always."

So unlike Bob's life, mine was very serious when I met him. I was grappling with big questions: How do you help someone find a reason to live after he has committed unforgivable acts? How do you accept your limits as a therapist when someone kills himself on your watch? Meanwhile, Bob and Rick laughed and strolled down the Santa Monica pier to think up comedy bits.

The week after Bob and I returned from Canada, I was walking along the VA sidewalk toward my building when a patient dressed in a full tuxedo and black top hat walked toward me until he was about a foot away. I wasn't scared anymore by craziness, so when he stopped and looked at me intently, I didn't flinch. "You know what lust is?" he asked loudly.

"What?"

He leaned in so close to me I thought his hat might tumble onto my head. "Lust is that which puffeth up!"

46   staying married is the hardest part

Abruptly, he pulled away and walked on, and I was a bit relieved as I shook my head and went on. Later that evening while Bob and I were getting undressed, I told him about the incident and he said, "That's a misquote from the Bible. It's from 1 Corinthians 8:1."

"*Whaaat?*"

He unbuttoned his shirt and looked me straight in the face. "You're lookin' at a star Bible student. In grade school, I got so many prizes I lost interest. The prize was always another Bible. The accurate quote is, 'Knowledge puffeth up, but charity edifieth.'"

I play-slapped him on the arm. "Listen to you! I can't quote anything from the Bible except somebody begat somebody who then begat someone else . . ."

He hugged me, and I thought of how all that Bible study had shaped his sexual tastes and fantasies. He loved putting naughty nuns in his comedy sketches—nuns who wore stockings and garters beneath their habits, nuns with push-up bras. Later, while we lay in bed, I asked, "So how did you wind up loving stockings and garters?"

"I used to look through the Sears catalog at pictures of women in underwear. That was pretty exciting and racy for a nine-year-old. Then my buddy stole his dad's *Playboy* magazine one time, and we looked at that for days—lacy underwear, stockings, and shiny high heels.

"In the Marine Corps at Camp Pendleton, we went into Oceanside when we had time off. That's when I discovered hookers in stockings and garters and low-cut tops. I loved how blatant they were because they gave me permission."

bonnie comfort   47

There was a constant sexual energy between us. We were so often body-to-body in each other's arms, inhaling the other's breath, hair, skin, and heat. Although I was disappointed with the lack of foreplay, when he was inside me, I heated up as if someone had plugged me into a wall socket. I bathed in his desire for me, choosing me above some of the women constantly around him—actresses with legs to there, faces for the screen, women who found his humor sexy and hung on his every word. For them, he was the writer, the producer, the executive producer, but he made it clear he wanted no one but me, and I ran toward that with everything I had.

For the first time, I stepped inside a dedicated lingerie store and looked for more to entice him. It wasn't so easy to find such items anymore, but this was LA, where you can find any costume you want. And that was how I thought of it: a costume. He wanted me to dress like the bombshells of the 1950s: Betty Page, Marilyn Monroe, Jayne Mansfield, and Betty Hutton. What? I'd worked so hard to be a playful, sexy woman who men loved in a pair of shorts and a T-shirt!

Still, I was my mother's daughter, wanting to please my man. After fourteen years of liberated women's clothing choices, I began wearing tight jeans, filmy dresses, high heels, form-fitting low-cut blouses, and yes, on many occasions, lacy garter belts, and stockings. When I went to the hospital, I still wore my professional slacks and flats, but away from there I was Bob's girl.

He told me I was beautiful. I loved standing in front of him in my new lingerie and watching his erection rise. He was used to long-legged, big-breasted, scantily dressed women whose faces and bodies were camera worthy. I couldn't lengthen my

48   staying married is the hardest part

legs or grow my breasts, but I could buy shiny high heels and wear black lacy bras and stockings.

As I continued in my third analysis, the history of my early insecurities and how they connected to sex was a frequent topic. By 1964, in my last undergraduate year of college, I was afraid to speak up in class, self-conscious of my body, and anxious about getting good enough grades to be admitted to graduate school. I had a longtime boyfriend, the first one with whom I had sex, but books and movies had taught me I should reach orgasm during intercourse, so I started faking it when I thought we'd been doing it long enough that I should have come. I worried my boyfriend wouldn't feel good about himself if he wasn't "successful" with me.

After I broke up with him, I dated like crazy and had sex with a few. In cars or crummy apartments with carpets smelling of dog hair and Pine-Sol, I mastered the art of the faked orgasm, pretending to be a confident woman who got off easily, while reinforcing men's ignorance about women's bodies.

I kept this hidden from my mother. She and my sisters had adhered to the old tradition— virgins till you marry—but by the time I hit nineteen, I was caught up in the new feminism, folk music, rock and roll, flower power, and free love. Sex was my secret way of carving out an identity separate from my family. I didn't admit to myself then that there might have been some truth in their values. Instead, I chose to entice and seduce, and I believed that an orgasm from me was soul-satisfying and affirming to a man, so if I couldn't get there for real, I faked it. Getting the guy to love me mattered that much. Did I know it was a replacement for family? No. It just seemed like a move into adulthood.

Pleasing men wasn't just about sex, either. In each man's presence I tried being who he wanted me to be. If I disagreed with his ideas, I didn't tell him. I emphasized our common interests or tried liking his. I was barely conscious of my underlying strategy: whatever you like, that's what I'll be, because I'm afraid to risk you not liking me. It happened so seamlessly, so naturally, so unconsciously, that until I looked at all these men and how different they were from each other, I didn't know it myself.

I'm a personality prostitute, I realized. Whatever you want, baby, that's who I'll be.

There is, in psychoanalytic theory, the concept of the false self and the true self, the false self being a layer of the personality that develops out of the need to comply with the wishes and expectations of one's parents. Needing to please others overrides one's authentic inner experience, and this can carry into adulthood.

You may be numb to your own inner experience. You may need the approval of others enough that you slip into a people-pleasing mode without fully realizing it. This is what I did.

Once I established myself in LA, I turned to an endless parade of men. Relying on them, I did things I was told never to do: got on the backs of motorcycles, as if my arms wrapped tightly around their waists could keep me from falling off and breaking my bones; went up in a glider plane in Napa, marveling at the green, rolling hills, and the only sound the wind. I fell in love with a Black man and drove with him in his gold Mercedes up the California coast while people in restaurants

50   staying married is the hardest part

looked at us oddly. There was downhill skiing, hiking in the Sierras, riding in open convertibles with no seatbelts. I ate sushi, lobster, and burritos, foods I'd never seen in Winnipeg. I was intoxicated with everything "California," particularly the LA comedy clubs where I went often. I never did much in the way of drugs, but I took birth control pills religiously, never missing one.

By age thirty, I'd had five long-term relationships, but in between those loves, I had leafed through men like you might page through a Macy's catalog, imagining a life with this one or that, taking him for a test drive, and often quickly deciding no. My list of desires in a partner was long. Who could check every box? One was too boring, one too controlling, one wasn't going to make enough money, one was too religious, one smoked, one was a terrible lover, one was cheap, one was too full of himself, one didn't care what I thought. The list of flaws was founded on my belief that someone out there was exactly right. I may have been in LA, I may have too often engaged in casual sex, but I was at my core Min's daughter, searching for The One.

When I met Bob, my incessant search for exactly the right man stopped. He was almost everything I wanted except for the sex issue, and my thinking about that was heavily influenced by my own sexual problem. In spite of all that analysis, I couldn't heal the split between my brazen performing self and the shy, internal me who was somewhat inhibited.

In carving myself away from my family during the sexual revolution and the women's movement, I had set in motion an unresolvable conflict in me which laid the template for my final choice of a husband. I was most drawn to men I saw as brilliant, charismatic, and powerful, the precise men least likely to offer the patience and kindness I needed in bed.

CHAPTER 5

Persephone in the Palisades

When we joined Bob's friends, I learned how comedy writers, producers, and actors blew off tension and anger at show business. I heard the frustrations, the insider stories. One evening, there were five of them, including Bob—writers with whom he'd written TV variety shows—and these guys vied for airtime, the noise level and laughs escalating. I held my stomach from laughing so hard. We were at Du-pars, a coffee shop on Sunset. One of the guys ordered Jell-O, and a worn bowl of red Jell-O was plunked down on the table. We all looked at it warily.

"This must be the Rosetta Jell-O," Bob said. The laughter was mixed with admiring nods.

The next evening, Bob and I argued about where to live after my apartment. We sat next to each other at Casa Escobar, an old-fashioned Mexican restaurant in Santa Monica, eating refried beans, chicken tostadas, and enchiladas. I said Pacific Palisades. He said Pasadena, near his friends and the studios. I said ocean, my Westwood school, the air quality, and summer

52 staying married is the hardest part

temperature. We both had good reasons, but he said okay, Pacific Palisades.

I planned every aspect of our wedding, including teaching myself calligraphy to address the invitations. Min called her wealthy niece, who offered her beautiful Beverly Hills home for the event. Two months before the wedding, Bob and I went to pick out a wedding dress.

Does every woman remember with such clarity the day she was fitted for her wedding dress? Unlike the guipure lace Parisian gown both of my sisters wore, I chose a $200 pale beige Victorian gauze dress with a cotton underskirt. Bob and I met at the shop in Encino, and while I stood on a riser, the woman carefully pinning my dress, Bob looked into a locked glass cabinet. When she finished pinning, Bob asked her, "How much is that little owl in the cabinet?" She unlocked the glass door and placed the item on Bob's palm.

"Eighty dollars," she said.

Bob said, "I'll take it."

I said, "Really? $80?"

He held up his palm to me. "Look!"

It was a one-inch-high Great Horned Owl standing on a green book.

"It's from Hungary," the woman said. "Hand-painted metal."

"Very fine craftsmanship," Bob said. "It's my present to you."

The generosity of the man, the charm, the quirkiness, the casual spending of too much money for something non-practical—it was all there. I smiled and let go of concern about the money. "Okay!" I said. "It's tiny, but it's beautiful!"

Driving away from that dress shop in my five-year-old Volvo, I was flooded with happiness, and this thought made me laugh out loud: *the cure for depression is getting what you want!* My decades-long fog of sadness and confusion had cleared. All those years in analysis, hoping a deeper understanding of myself would fix me, had helped me feel stronger and more confident, but only finding the right man to share my life with—one I could take home to my parents to show I'd made the right decision—could lift that fog.

In May, I notified the VA I'd be leaving in mid-June. By that time, nobody at work was surprised. My mind was obviously elsewhere as I talked about my classes and my upcoming wedding. I sat in team meetings practicing calligraphy. I wanted to fully embrace my new life and leave the misery of a psych ward behind.

The two-story rental house we found on Monument Street was perfect, with a huge, rectangular swimming pool protected by a high, long hedge, and the Palisades village two blocks away, where there was one of everything—a small movie theater, a local drugstore, a car wash, a Chinese restaurant, a deli.

At the beginning of June, we began packing to move. Bob went through his things, mostly music and mementos, and he pulled out a photo to show me. "Remember I told you I went up to Alert, near the North Pole, to do a show for the troops? This is me there."

A black-and-white photo showed him dressed in a heavy, long jacket and big rubber boots, and he was vamping for the camera, pretending to hold up the round nose of the turbo-prop cargo plane that had flown them there. It was so like him to make a silly pose like that!

54   staying married is the hardest part

"You're adorable," I said. "Save that for me. I'll have it framed."

Returning to packing clothes and kitchenware, I became anxious under the weight of the moment. What if this gamble of marrying Bob turned out to have too high a cost? What if he didn't get another TV job? What if, what if, *what if*?

I chided myself. *You've made your decision, and it's a good one.*

But what about the sex?

After taping up another box, I said, "Maybe we should go to sex therapy?"

He knew what I was talking about. He laid down the newspaper he was using to wrap my stemware and put his arms around me. "I'll try to do better. If it's not better in a year, I'll go with you to therapy."

"Really?"

"I promise."

In the pool at our new rental house, Bob taught me how to swim in deep water by saying, "Why don't you wear a snorkel mask?" which cured my distaste for putting my head underwater. After that, I swam every day, the repetitive motion a meditation and release from all thought. "Fifteen laps today," I'd report to Bob. "Twenty." I'd emerge from that aqua therapy like Persephone, goddess of spring, reborn into my new life, breathing the cool ocean air, walking the clean Palisades streets. Bob gave me this, even though he often had to commute an hour to Studio City to pay for it.

Our wedding took place on July 30, 1978, in the backyard of my cousin's home. For the first time in ten years, Min came to LA, along with my sisters, their husbands, and one niece, none of whom had visited me there before. My dad was already far enough into dementia that he couldn't come, but it did put to rest an issue I might otherwise have had to address—I wanted to walk down the aisle alone. I didn't like the old tradition of a father who owned me giving me to a husband who would own me.

A few days before the wedding, Min and I went for lunch at my cousin's house to look over the backyard and make last-minute decisions. My cousin loved Min, who was her old charming self in my presence, and later, when I dropped her off at her hotel, I felt the threads of connection between us begin to knit together again. "Do you want to borrow my pearls?" she asked, referring to my favorite of hers—the single strand with the moonstone clasp she'd worn to Grandma's funeral.

"Oh, thank you! You know I love those! But my dress has a high collar, so that won't work." We hugged, and the familiar feel of her arms around me felt better than it had in years. However, I was very busy for the next few days and didn't see her again until the wedding.

My family welcomed invited guests as drinks were served before the ceremony. The scent of roasting potatoes mingled with the fragrance of gardenias as I stood in an upstairs bedroom alone, all dressed and ready, hearing the steady murmur of voices, dishes banging, people laughing. I drank champagne to calm myself. I was nervous about being the center of attention at such an emotional moment, everyone looking at me as I walked down the aisle toward my lifelong dream.

I heard Bob and Rick laughing outside, Bob with his staccato laugh, Rick's lower and quieter. They were wearing custom-made suits by a costume designer from CBS, and I

56   staying married is the hardest part

chuckled, remembering Bob once saying, "If there was a fire in Rick's home, he'd throw himself on his shirts." Now he, too, was wearing something fine, even though fashion was never his thing. I peeked out and saw them both handsome, tanned, and drunk on the patio below.

As I walked up the aisle by myself to Pachelbel's famous Canon, I saw Bob and our dearest ones waiting at the front for me, and it took every bit of energy not to burst into tears and ruin my makeup. I held tight to my bouquet of white gardenias and pink roses, with a white ribbon trailing to my knees. Walking back down that aisle we clutched each other's hands as if we had just won the biggest prize of our lives.

After cocktails, there was a buffet with cold poached salmon covered in translucent rounds of cucumber, roasted vegetables arranged in patterns of green, orange, and red, and sautéed rice with baby peas. I laughed and talked with everybody, loving the aroma of Bob on me—that mix of Old Spice deodorant and pheromones and whiskey on his breath.

When the DJ announced our first dance, Bob was nervous. The song was Billy Joel's "Just the Way You Are," and although that later became elevator music, at the time, it was new, and the lyrics had meaning for us. When we finished the dance, Bob held my face in his hands and kissed me so tenderly and sweetly that everybody clapped.

After that, I danced to the fast tunes with my friends and had a joyful time. My sisters danced to the DJ tunes, and I saw Min actually laughing and dancing with my brother-in-law, Nate. Then, the three-tiered chocolate cake with ganache frosting, shiny and dark, topped with small pink flowers, was spoon-fed to me by Bob—in the photo of that moment, it looks like he's feeding a baby bird, me with my mouth open wide.

bonnie comfort   57

I finally had the man of my choosing, in the city of my choosing, with my family as witnesses. Their presence and participation felt to me like the recognition from them I had wanted for so long: respect for my choices, maybe even some admiration, and acknowledgment that I was permanently living in LA, asking for no financial help from them, and in love with a tall, adorable, funny non-Jew whom I was proud to call my new husband.

In the wee hours, Bob and I enjoyed our fancy L'Hermitage suite, doing it next to the mirrored wall, the image of us mysterious in the dim light, a flash of white from my garters, our two heads touching, him over me, one white stockinged foot of mine moving up and down, the smell of vacuumed carpet and my hairspray mingled with the sound of our breath, hot and loud.

The morning after our wedding, we were so worn out that we canceled our planned trip to San Francisco and escaped alone to our new home. Such joy it was to swim naked in our own pool, the cool water slipping over our skin, the aqua blue reflecting a hundred flashes of sunlight. Bob was there with his camera, taking photos of me naked, semi-naked, stockings, garter belt, and smiles.

After that, a new freedom lightened my body. There was something so novel about Bob, an unpredictability that was fresh and exciting and different from all the steady guys in the past with whom I could see my days stretched out in front of me like an endless row of house, work, babies, housekeepers, nannies, tasteful furniture, sex on Saturday nights, kids' birthday parties, college entrance exams, cancer at eighty, death.

58 staying married is the hardest part

We talked more about having a baby, but for me, it was "not yet." I knew if I didn't get my PhD first, I might never finish it. In the meantime, we decided to get a basset hound because they're one of the funniest dogs on the planet. At the breeder's ranch, the cutest puppy was a male with one brown eye and one perfectly good blue eye, and when I brought him home, Bob said, "Let's name him Frank for 'Old Blue Eyes.'"

We laughed at how Frank's ears grazed the ground when he walked, how he'd point his muzzle to the sky and bay when an ambulance went by, and how his balls hung down to his back elbows and tossed from side to side as he trotted.

While I was swimming and studying that first year, Bob was busy with TV variety specials. At the height of these, he and Rick went to Texas with Kenny Rogers to do a biographic special. In a rare moment, Bob smoked pot with the crew, then picked up a microphone at the Houston Astrodome and belted out a few lines of "Ebb Time" to the empty stadium.

Relationships shifted. Rick, now divorced, found the woman he would marry, a sloe-eyed beauty named Jane who loved adventure, family, and show business just as he did.

The guys came home in alligator cowboy boots and big cowboy hats with a new friend, Cort Casady, who was so perfect for my friend Barbara that I insisted they meet. He was handsome, musically talented, a writer, a Harvard graduate, and as good-looking, blond, and California-bred as she was. Later, Cort said when Barbara showed up for their first dinner, she said, "I didn't know what to bring you, so I brought my curiosity." He loved that. And she loved all of him, including his humor, his excellent housekeeping, and the sense that he was utterly reliable.

bonnie comfort   59

She introduced me to my husband, and I introduced her to hers.

In that first year, though, I sometimes told Bob I felt I was disappearing in his presence. I zoned out when he talked about politics, just the way I had with my family. When we were with his hilarious friends, I laughed a lot but didn't feel I could join in much. These reactions were my responsibility, but at the time, those old insecurities caused me to fall silent.

One afternoon, after we'd had a swim and sat next to each other on our lounge chairs, we started discussing local politics, and no matter what I said, Bob had a counterargument. There was a small table with a bowl of popcorn on it, and I began eating those popped kernels continuously, automatically, hand-to-mouth. Finally, I said, "Why don't you ever say, 'Yes, you're right,' when I say what I think? You just morph the subject into something else!"

"Yeah," he said. "Because you're an 'Oh-I-see' person and I'm a 'Yeah-but...' person."

"But I want you to give me the recognition of having made a good point!"

"You'll have to fight for that," he said.

I didn't know how to fight for it with someone I respected so much. With my family, when they debated politics or national issues, I never felt brave enough to join in. Friday night dinners in my late teens were an ongoing ordeal. My sisters, with their husbands and children, descended on the place like loud locusts, and we took our places at the dinner table. Immediately, the discussions began, lively and loud. My sister Carol's husband was a judge and had little patience for debate. The few times I tried expressing an opinion, he shot it down immediately with his own pronouncements. My takeaway: whatever I knew or thought was of little consequence. I said nothing back to him. I shoveled food into my mouth.

My other brother-in-law, Nate, was smart and funny, but in a caustic and hurtful way that made me avoid being in his firing line. He was beautifully mannered in his eating style, cutting his food carefully in a way that would suit royalty, but he would dismiss me sometimes by pointing his knife at me and saying, "How old are you?"

I sat through those dinners, silent and afraid, certain that whatever I had to say wouldn't be good enough and that if I was challenged, I'd embarrass myself by not knowing how to defend what I'd said. My head was full of literature and psychology. I knew very little about history and politics. Besides, Nate could cut an argument to shreds in two sentences.

Year after year, at that table, I shrank into myself. The only way I knew I existed at those times was by putting food in my mouth—chew, swallow, chew, swallow—which kept me in touch with my body. The rest of me was numb, invisible, and inaccessible.

I envied Nate's confidence in his mind—brilliant, authoritative, funny, the center of his own world. I wanted to be like that. I believed I could never be so bold. That lack of faith in myself fueled my attraction to brilliant, articulate men like him who were not afraid to risk an argument by speaking their thoughts. I knew how to be an admiring partner to someone like that, hiding behind the orator. So, instead of honing my debate skills, I worked on being pretty, sweet, and nice enough to get men like that to love me.

However, even Bob didn't like arguing about our relationship issues. If we had words with each other, we'd both shut down and withdraw, me tumbling into a heavy pressure in my chest, and a sudden fierce energetic bout of housecleaning, him sinking into a TV boxing match, and a long evening on the sofa, TV remote in hand. In those first few years, it was always him who would rescue us when he was ready. "How long do you think you'll be mad at me?" he'd ask. And I'd be forced to say, "I don't know," to which he might reply, "Maybe another hour? Or till tomorrow?" And then I'd stand, dishrag in hand, with our bathroom towels fragrant with Tide and neatly back in the closet, and feel that pain in my chest dissipate. Whatever we were fighting about didn't matter as much as how he fixed it. He'd say, "I see why you're mad," and he was usually spot-on, saying for me what I couldn't say, telling me his side too, and offering a resolution until neither of us was mad anymore.

One day, after a bad fight over something stupid, he went to work, and I was miserable all day until he called, sounding cheerful, telling me something hilarious he and Rick were writing. That evening, when he came home, he hugged me, smelling of car leather and whiskey, and I said, "How is it that when we fight, I'm miserable all day, and you go away, and you're fine?"

"I get over it. You should, too. It's just anger. You don't have to be so afraid of it."

In one sentence, he cured me of the fear I'd developed growing up—that anger between people who love each other is frightening and dangerous. He wasn't afraid of my anger, and I didn't need to be afraid of his. After years of Min's hard silences, this was like a helium balloon I'd been holding tightly in my tense hand forever, only to discover I could just open my hand and let it float away. Now, being in school full time,

62 staying married is the hardest part

the pace of moving toward my degree accelerated, and I found myself speaking up in groups the way I never had before.

I'd learned something about marriage. Far below the fussing about a wedding, the rings and flowers and logistics, is a new bedrock for each of you: someone has loved you enough to choose you, publicly and legally, and you have done the same. Each of you, with all your unpretty parts, has claimed the other. It's a public affirmation that lasts your whole life, even if you get divorced. Somebody loved me enough to choose me and let the world know.

One hot August morning, the sky a hazy oven, Bob and I cruised down the highway toward San Diego, and he regaled me with stories, including one of his favorite amusements: people who die in silly ways. "Two this week!" he said. "A wannabe bank robber who spray-painted his face as a disguise and then died from the fumes. Poor asshole."

Chuckling, I shook my head.

"And then a man who died of a self-inflicted stab wound after testing the ability of his new stab-proof jacket." My laughing made my skirt flutter in the A/C vent.

We checked into the Hotel del Coronado, a national landmark, a grand old Victorian with a red shingle roof and turrets. The original buildings were an utter firetrap, and there were prominently displayed fire extinguishers, but the hotel was saturated with history. Kings and queens had stayed here. Our room was lovely—a huge bed and an old-fashioned tiled bathroom.

We dropped our suitcases on the floor, rifled through them for our bathing suits, and then headed down to the huge back patio of the hotel to meet Cort and Barbara in front of the sea. The smell of salt air gave me that ocean high I love. The surf was strong enough that we could hear it, a soft soundtrack of music under everything, and the water was gorgeous: frothy and balmy.

Barb and Cort were already drinking. We ordered our favorites and joked and shared stories. I marveled at how beautiful Barbara and Cort were and how perfectly they fit together. After they left to visit family, Bob and I headed for the pool. While I dangled my legs in the cool water, Bob swam a few laps at a leisurely pace, just enough to burn up some of that Canadian Club. We sat next to each other in lounge chairs. The warmth of the sun relaxed every muscle. Languid and tipsy, we headed for our room.

We lay together on the bed. His hands felt so warm against my cool breasts. He squeezed them like he was testing an avocado for ripeness. We kissed, we caressed, and I became very aroused, and yet he didn't take the time to attend to me. My hand was on his chest, fingers in the fine, sparse hair in the center where his heart thudded away quickly. When it was over, my own heart was still thudding. I was aching with need, and my vibrator was not there.

I wanted to ask him for what I needed, but what was the point? He had clearly given himself permission to say no to me, and I had accepted it. Why he felt he had that right was kind of shocking in that day and age, but so was my lack of willingness to confront him about it. Was I going to blow up at him now? After we'd made our deal? And married?

A momentary rage heated up my face, but I said nothing. The worst part for me was that if he weren't freely committed to doing it as long as I needed, pressuring him to do it would

64   staying married is the hardest part

never work for me anyway. He had his problems with oral sex, and I had mine.

I lay there as Bob turned on the TV and started watching the news. The reality of my choice was sinking in. After so much sexual experience, knowing what I liked and the exact recipe I needed, the one person I finally chose to marry couldn't freely and spontaneously give it to me. I had weighed the pros and cons and decided that what Bob offered me was unique and precious enough to make it worth accepting our sexual compromise. I just hadn't anticipated there might be times when I'd feel so frustrated and hurt.

I escaped to the bathroom and quietly locked the door. The flooring was small hexagonal white tiles, exactly like the ones we had in my childhood home. How odd, I thought, as I pulled a towel off the rack and laid it on the floor. There was no place else I could do this, just like in my long-ago home. I turned on the faucet and left it running before lying down on the towel, those little tiles just inches from my face. The sounds of the handsome TV newscaster leaked through the bottom of the door. I took care of myself quickly, muffling my tears in the towel. Looking back, I realize I could have told Bob, and he would have held me while I took care of myself, so why didn't I at least do that?

It came down to this: I was still a bit shy about masturbating in front of him, and for some reason, the vibrator seemed easier, or its power overrode my inhibition. I promised myself I'd never leave it behind again when I traveled with him.

My face burned, and a quick shower cooled everything down before I came back into the bedroom as if everything was fine. Later, we had dinner at the Prince of Wales restaurant in the basement of the hotel. The ceilings were low, and the room had no windows. Bob ordered a flambéed steak, and when the waiter brought the rolling cooking cart to our table, he poured a big cup of brandy into the sizzling pan. A huge flame shot up toward the ceiling. Bob and I looked at each other, and he said, "Get ready to run." I laughed so hard I had to blow my nose. In this firetrap, I looked for the exits, but the waiter seemed quite unconcerned. Within a minute, the flames died down to the height of the pan, and we were safe. Later, we laughed about that over and over. Bob said, "The headline would read 'Couple Dies in Tragic Restaurant Fire. Waiter Escapes with Only Singed Eyebrows.'"

Back in our hotel room, the bathroom moment pushed away, I curled myself around Bob, knowing I was utterly at home wherever we were as long as I was cuddled up to him. I fell into a deep and sweet sleep.

The next morning, we headed to Hotel Laguna—a white clapboard exterior and dark carpeted bar, a haven for the wealthy in the 1930s. In the afternoon, on the bed in that hotel, Bob took beautiful photographs of me in my lingerie and high heels. Out of dozens of photos, he picked out one to enlarge and frame. I loved it. It looked like a dreamy, soft-focused photo from the 1920s, me on the floral bedspread, leaning on one elbow, my bra half off, one leg bent so my high-heeled foot is on the bedspread, a gap of bare skin showing at the top of my stocking.

CHAPTER 6

Sailboats in Bed

A year and a half into our house rental, we discovered the pool was leaking. We were spending hundreds of dollars a month to heat water that was draining away. The owner refused to fix the pool but was willing to sell us the house. "I think we should buy the house and pay to fix the pool ourselves," I said. By that time, Bob and I had formed his business corporation. He was President, I was Vice President, and I was in charge of all the accounting. "We have the money to put down," I said. "And we can afford the mortgage payments."

Bob shook his head, his voice hard. "Fuck him! I'm not gonna give him the satisfaction of buying his house!" His face had a stubborn darkness that was new to me.

My body felt heavy, from my shoulders to my knees. The house was a perfect starter for us. "Okay," I said. "I'll call the rental agency."

It was a moment when I felt powerless. Like many men raised in the 1940s, Bob felt entitled to have more of a say in big decisions because he was the one supporting the family. My parents were more progressive than that, and if they'd been party to that conversation, they would have told me to fight him about it. Yet they had also trained me to be nice, compliant,

bonnie comfort   67

and not to openly argue. I should have. I didn't.

When I had chosen to give up my job, I hadn't calculated into our equation the differences in our ideas about money. I was a saver. Bob was more likely to make imprudent decisions based on strong feelings of the moment, and now I was financially dependent on him. There was something in me even deeper: I felt dazzled by him. There was a young self at my core saying, "Me? He picked me? How did I get so fortunate?" I never said that to him. I never said it to anyone. But how can you vie for equal power when that's what you're thinking?

My being dazzled by Bob stretched back to my early days when I was impressed and intimidated by my mother and brother-in-law Nate, who each made funny, caustic comments about people, sometimes right to their faces. I admired that ability, but I was much more like my dad—sweet and timid. I saw how humor and wit wielded a certain kind of power, a power I didn't have, and coming out of my family, I was always therefore drawn to witty people, even though they were sometimes funny at other people's expense. Bob's insights and humor dazzled me, and on rare occasions when he went with me to Winnipeg, I felt safe from the sharp comments of Min or Nate.

Then there was the show business thing, a dazzling world unto itself and a world I never expected to access. Often, Bob came home with stories of famous people he'd had lunch with or met in studio meetings. In our first few years together, I couldn't quite believe I was married to someone in that world, me, who'd only encountered those beautiful people in magazines or on the screen. It was that Alice-in-the-looking-glass feeling until, gradually, it felt less alien.

68   staying married is the hardest part

We packed up and moved to another rental house: Glenhaven Drive, in the Palisades, up a steep hill with a view of the ocean. I was disappointed about not buying, but I loved this new rental. The images of Glenhaven exist in my memory as fixtures: the pale blue fleur-de-lis wallpaper in the bedroom, the mirrored master bathroom, the pieces of my custom black sofa now separated and in different rooms, Bob and I watching the corner TV in the family room where we saw the first MTV videos. And this: I was sitting in the middle of our king-size bed, the filmy curtains open over our seven-foot windows facing the sea. The morning was bright and clear, a perfect spring day before the heat and haze of summer. I was reading the *LA Times*, but I stopped to look out. In the far distance, tiny white sailboats bobbed on the ocean, the horizon a hard strip of blue against the pale sky. I was living my dream, sitting in my bed and seeing this. A feeling of deep contentment spread through my chest. *I've made it. LA is my home for life. I could die right now.*

One afternoon, Bob and I parked on San Vicente to go into a favorite restaurant. A woman parked ahead of us opened her car door to exit. Shapely legs in high heels emerged first, but then the woman had a sour, crimped face. "Good pins, bad mask," Bob said, and I laughed. I was so in love with him and his quirky way of saying things, his lack of deference to celebrities, and his folksy desire for a sloppy burger instead of a spare, fancy plate of arranged leaves.

In that first year on Glenhaven, Bob and Rick wrote a one-hour comedy-drama pilot called *One Night Band* for MTM Productions. The pilot was about a talented country band that traveled from town to town, hoping for success. Cort Casady and his musician friend, Michael Cannon, wrote and produced the music, and we were sure the pilot would get "picked up,"

bonnie comfort   69

but after all the hard work on it, the show was dead because some executive made a different choice. We were all shocked that *One Night Band* wasn't chosen to become a TV series. It was that good.

In response, Bob got depressed. He lay on the sofa, clicking listlessly through the junk on network TV. How could some of that drivel be on the air when his best work was ignored? It was more of a mystery to me than to him since he'd seen way more of what went on behind the scenes. He coped with his depression by staying out drinking with Rick and watching late-night TV. Weeks went by without us having sex.

I knew depression often suppressed libido. Women could have sex even if they didn't feel like doing it, but a man had to have and keep an erection, and if he was really down, that sometimes resulted in temporary impotence. Some men are "automatic performers," men who can get it up and keep it up regardless of the circumstance, but most men I know are not like that, and certainly Bob, as emotionally sensitive as he was, couldn't get interested if he was depressed. I did my best to be patient and understanding.

Bob tried to cheer himself up by trading in his fancy BMW for a Chevy Blazer, a distinctly non-LA vehicle. He knew Michael Andretti, Mario Andretti's son, who had worked on One Night Band, and Michael installed an interior roll bar and off-road tires for Bob's new Blazer. That big SUV helped quell Bob's anxiety because he could see more all around, and he had a metal cage protecting him. He had nothing to haul—not golf bags, skis, or tools. He just liked the idea of being a dude with a truck.

He and Rick started producing the next pilot and pitching more ideas. Their contract with MTM was coming to an

70 staying married is the hardest part

end. They were free again, which meant an income gap but more potential. Their agent arranged meetings with various production companies, directors, and TV executives. When he had to get ready for meetings, Bob would put on what he called his "body armor" —deodorant, antifungal ointment, athlete's foot spray on his toes. Clearly, he was sweating his way through those meetings—doing his "dancing bear" routine, as he called it—where he and Rick made everyone at the table laugh, gave them fascinating ideas for TV shows or movies, and then waited afterward to hear from their agent. Did they get an offer? Had they done well enough?

His show business stresses continued to eat away at his energy and his sexual desire. After having had almost daily sex in our first two years together, our frequency now went down to about once a month. I told him I missed it and wanted to have sex at least once a week, but each time I asked him, he'd say, "I just don't have the energy for it." I'd accept that for a while, and then nag him some more.

Bob made it clear that his diminished sexual interest wasn't directed at me. It was an expression of how stressed he was every time he pitched an idea that wasn't approved or any time he wrote a TV pilot that he loved, which was then tossed on the piles of network rejects. He just sexually shut down, awash in disappointment, frustration, and anger.

In the meantime, we decided it was time for us to get pregnant. I'd just turned thirty-five, and we thought it was unwise to wait any longer. I tossed away my birth control pills, excited to be riding bareback now, and I began taking my temperature and swallowing prenatal vitamins. I let Bob know when I was ovulating, and he made sure we did it at least twice during that week of the month, but the rest of the time, his attention was elsewhere. Knowing how shut down he felt, I was grateful that he made the effort to get me pregnant, but every month, I cried in the shower, painfully disappointed when I got my period.

In September 1980, we had a big fortieth birthday bash for Bob at our house. I catered the party from Mort's Deli, a Pacific Palisades institution at the time. There was an enormous supply of liquor, beer, and wine, and dance music in the living room. At some point, Bob gave a new slide show of odd photos along with hilarious titles for the photos.

At our first party, Goodwin had won the ugly shell sculpture. Goodwin presented Bob with his birthday present at this party—the shell sculpture. I don't know where that thing is now—either in some landfill or on some comedy writer's shelf, but it sure gave us laughs.

Some of us danced in the living room. Bob cut the giant birthday cake. He opened the rest of his presents, and wow, there were some weird ones, including a live mallard, a live baby iguana, and a blow-up ring-toss clown with an enormous penis onto which you toss the rings. We inflated the four-foot clown during the party and took turns tossing the rings.

In spite of his frustrations with TV work and my frustration over the dramatically diminished amount of sex, there was an underlying current of joy in me most of the time. I was having more fun now than the previous ten years combined. One afternoon, we went into a "write your own headline" newspaper store, and Bob had a newspaper made to send to his dad for his birthday. The headline in huge black letters read, "BEN COMFORT REFUSES TO DISCO! HUNDREDS MOURN!"

More than anything else, life with Bob was fun. I was like a kid again, playing. I didn't know I'd forgotten how to be silly with laughs and games, but I remembered now, and I didn't

72 staying married is the hardest part

ever want to lose this attitude correction again. Yet my ability to nurture the love of fun lay much more with Bob than me. I adored him for this gift.

And yet, the sex became a more and more complicated issue.

The floor plan of the Glenhaven house was different from our previous house. There were sliding glass doors to the back patio, one in the living room and the other in the master bedroom. One evening, Bob said, as he often did, "I want to take some photos of you. Get dressed up. Surprise me." Since he always got aroused taking photos of me, I figured this was his way of trying to overcome his sexual shutdown, and yes, I wanted that.

I chose a sheer blouse, a full black skirt, spiked heels, stockings and garters, and fairly transparent white panties. Then, I walked into the living room to have my picture taken.

Bob's face flushed in that special way. "Beautiful. Sit on this chair."

I warmed to his gaze.

"Undo your top button. Lean forward. That's it." He clicked away.

Then, "Lean back, put one leg up on the seat, spread your legs a bit." Ugh. I didn't want to be this kind of model, but I did it, thinking that would be all.

Then he said, "I'm gonna step outside. I wanna watch you through the window."

"Watch me?"

"Play with yourself."

A queasy feeling dried my throat. "I don't want to do that."

"C'mon. Just a little bit. It'll turn me on."

I wanted to turn him on, but my stomach curdled. This wasn't what I wanted. It felt creepy. I knew sex combined with

bonnie comfort 73

emotional intimacy was a tall order, and those of us frightened of being that vulnerable avoid it, but I wanted to try for it, and this wasn't the way.

Nevertheless, I closed my eyes. I pretended I was alone just the way he wanted, but inside me, a small voice, the voice not only of my profession but of my truth, said, *Don't.*

Why didn't I rise up indignant and loud, refusing to endure this painful sham?

I knew one answer to that question: he took beautiful photos of me in my outfits, and I loved those photos. They captured me at my best, figure flaws concealed, a certain something radiating from the image. I wasn't Hollywood beautiful, but the photos made me look that way.

When I was a girl I went to see romantic comedies with my parents. In those darkened theaters, I watched Doris Day tease and refuse a man, which only made him want her more. I watched Marilyn Monroe seduce with innocence, Jean Simmons play hard to get, and the exquisite Elizabeth Taylor have men fall at her feet. Later in the evenings, I'd stand in front of my bathroom mirror, a flimsy scarf around my head, lipstick on my childhood face, repeating the movie dialogue while trying to look coy and imagining men so in love with me.

Now, this sex play with my husband fed my childhood longing for the power of beauty, except by now, I knew my posing and smiling was playacting for love, an act of cowardice on my part, and I had to bury my shame. Although that small voice inside me said, *Don't,* a louder voice in me said, *Humor him. Playact for a while. Then we'll get in bed, and it'll be fun! And the photos will be pretty and sexy.*

After ten minutes, Bob slid open the door and joined me. We had our usual good time in bed, but the prelude to it had

74   staying married is the hardest part

disturbed me, and I ruminated about it afterward. Bob was fighting depression these days, and later, he said he was afraid he "couldn't get it up," confirming my assumption that his asking to watch me was a way of overcoming his sexual shutdown.

Yes, I loved sex with him, but I'd never before felt alienated from myself the way I had on this evening. It was different from wearing stockings and garters for him. It was acting out a sexual fantasy of his that didn't excite me but instead made me feel like I was volunteering to be in a porn movie. I didn't like it. Yet I loved him so much, felt his anxiety, and was grateful that he wanted to overcome his sexual shutdown for me as much as for him.

Still, this moment changed things between us. He had used me to feel better and be able to perform sexually, and although I complied, I resented his being willing to cajole me into doing it after I told him I didn't want to.

It damaged our connection. I withdrew inside myself. I knew it was wrong for me, and I didn't want to do it again. And yet, it was only a brief incident. The rest of the time with him was so good.

As his show business life wore on, Bob tried distracting himself more and more from the roller coaster of "Yes, we love it!" to "No, sorry, we can't do it." I worried about how down he got each time his agent or a producer called and said, "They passed." I hated to see him so deflated, staying up till 2:00 a.m. watching stupid TV, but when he reached for his camera for a few hours, he was buoyed again by seeing me in lingerie and filmy clothes. It excited him and made him forget his frustration and sadness, and I wanted to give him that relief. There were many more times when I dressed up, and he took photos of me at home when I pulled my skirt up or undid my blouse, and those times served me too, how he came back from his pain and made me feel beautiful. I turned a blind eye to my misgivings about my performing self. At the time, it seemed worth it.

You know something, but you don't want to know it. You ignore, suppress, and distract yourself. You tell yourself it will get better. You live around it, not in it. You don't shake yourself by the shoulders like someone who cares deeply about you. You love your shared life, that endearing smile of his, and how much he loves you, too.

CHAPTER 7

Ashland

At school, I continued studying personality tests, criteria for various psychiatric diagnoses, and new medications like Prozac. An unexpected possibility developed for me—I was good at administering psychological tests. I could describe the results clearly, give a diagnosis, verify a problem, and write a good report. I worked to become very proficient at it. It gave me practical, salable skills by which to earn some of my professional income.

Meanwhile, Bob and Rick became more sought after, churning out pilots and movie scripts for Fox Studios, Warner Bros., and independent production companies. In the evenings, we went to parties with actors, comedy writers, and musicians, living a life I had never imagined and could hardly believe was mine. I didn't see I was the exotic one—the therapist among them who had the insight they were looking for. Even though I didn't have my PhD yet, they called me Dr. Bonnie, they with their beautiful faces, enhanced breasts, desperate insecurities, and glossy exteriors.

In the quiet of bathrooms and kitchens, they told me secrets. One evening at a restaurant, an actress pulled me into a bathroom stall so I could feel how realistic her new breasts

bonnie comfort   77

were. I could hear the truth behind their masks and remain a pool of calm and steadiness for them, but I could only share my truth with my analyst and my closest friends. I love him so much, and yet there's this one miserable thing.

Over and over, Bob would get his energy up for writing, make good money for it, and then have his hopes for getting his work produced dashed. We always slept in the same bed, although he'd often stay up till the wee hours watching *The Tonight Show* and weird TV. Sometimes when he woke me getting into bed, I'd roll over and start playing with him, hoping that would cheer him, but he'd say, "Sorry, too bummed. Maybe in a while."

One evening, when we were alone in the house, he again asked me to parade around in the bedroom while he stayed outside watching. "Change your underwear," he said. "Try on different outfits." Violating the promise I'd made to myself, I complied. There are photos of me from that night that I still have, wearing a white lacy bra, garter belt and stockings, and a burgundy sweater first on, then off. There was no digital photography in those days. He used 35 mm movie film he took to a lab in Hollywood where they made 35 mm slides of his photos. Did the men who developed those slides look at them? See me naked or in garters, my hand on my crotch, my smile sleepy, and my eyes serious? Maybe.

I was an actress in a private play, *but this is my husband,* I thought. *The man who is supposed to love me and want to make love to me, and I am here in this charade playing the innocent woman who thinks she's alone in her bedroom while some creep outside is watching her change.* It offended me. Most of all, it hit me in my self-esteem because I was violating my own values and desires.

78   staying married is the hardest part

It did not occur to me then that Bob might be just as embarrassed by his own need and his inability to be present with me as I was dismayed by it. I only thought at the time that this was what he wanted and that he was pressuring me to bend to his will. I liked being his private dancer and being desired by him, but it didn't spark my desire. It flipped me into performance mode.

If what he liked had turned me on, there would not have been an issue, but in this way, we were incompatible, and I couldn't hold my ground.

I try now not to judge myself too harshly for often complying back then with his wishes. I'd grown up when wives were supposed to please their husbands, be pretty and sexy, and look after home and children. Nor can I view Bob's sexual requests through the lens of 2023 without making cruel and unwarranted judgments of him. He grew up in the 1940s, when the husband was the boss, and the wife was supposed to defer to him. There was a power differential between us, not just because of how we were raised, but because, in my mind, I had put him on a pedestal, thinking of myself as less talented and smart, even though I was way more educated than he was and plenty smart enough.

In the third year of our marriage, our sex focus was mostly on trying to get pregnant. Diagnostic tests turned up no reason to explain why I wasn't getting pregnant, so we started doing artificial insemination with Bob's sperm. Bob was a good sport about it, saying, "Where's my date?" when it was time to donate his sperm to a bottle. When I was ovulating, I'd take the bottle to the fertility specialist in Beverly Hills, and he'd spin it in a centrifuge, bathe the sperm in an egg wash, and then insert the liquid into my uterus. Every month, it didn't work. We talked and talked about it, the possibility of adoption, the roll of the dice with IVF, which was very expensive back then, and the chance of a high-risk pregnancy and multiples at birth. Bob was willing to go down either path. I told myself that having a child was about raising a child, not going through pregnancy and delivery, but I couldn't talk myself into adoption, and I didn't want the risks of IVF. We left it up to hope and fate.

Other than when I was ovulating, we stopped having sex. Even my posing and dressing up for Bob didn't help the rest of the time. I understood how discouraged he was about the business. His disappointment was a heavy weight on both of us, but I hadn't anticipated it would shut him down so long in this particular way.

One morning, I pulled on my sexy workout tights and leotard and paraded past Bob. I saw zero light in his eyes. I sat beside him while he read the paper in bed. He put the paper aside, and I leaned down and kissed him, but he kissed me only lightly on the lips, his own closed, and I leaned back. He looked past me to the doorway as if he wished I'd already left. "Sorry, Bonster. I just haven't got the energy for it right now."

I lowered my head and sighed.

"I think you should go out and get it with someone else, and don't tell me about it."

"What!?"

"You're horny, I get it. And I don't know when I'm going to be up for it again. Just get it somewhere else and don't tell me about it, and don't do it with any of my friends."

I was stunned. "How can you suggest that? I'm horny *for you*, nobody else!"

80   staying married is the hardest part

He patted my arm like I was a child, unhappy about not getting an ice cream cone. "I just don't want you to be unhappy. And I can't fix it right now."

"But you'll be able to fix it eventually, don't you think?"

"Yes. I just need more time."

"I'll wait."

I focused instead on my psychology training. I had to take comprehensive exams at school to complete my academics before I could turn my attention to a doctoral dissertation. I learned statistics, research techniques, learning theory, and neurobiology. I memorized the brain's structures and marveled at the complexity of the human body and how a damaged brain could compensate for an injury or a deficit. I also noticed myself speaking up in class, asking questions, and in our mandatory group therapy sessions, saying out loud how I felt. One day after group, a pretty classmate said to me, "I'm so impressed with your opinions."

I don't think anyone had ever said such a thing to me.

As the months wore on, I still pressured Bob sometimes about the sex. I didn't want that special connection between us to fade away. "Look," he said. "I'm doing the best I can."

"Maybe we should go to sex therapy?"

"I don't want to do that. Let's get you dressed up tonight, and we'll fool around."

Did it always have to start with that? "Okay," I said, but I was tired of my wardrobe being foreplay.

We had a good time that night, but the reality of his lack of sexual interest got me down. I never expected his work disappointments would have this effect on him. He was commuting to Burbank and Studio City, and something new developed: panic attacks on the freeway. The only thing that helped his anxiety was a fuzzy blue blanket he took with him into the writing offices, where, from time to time, he'd wrap himself in it and nap on the sofa.

I kid you not. The man was treating himself with a blue blanket.

Often, he and Rick wrote late into the night, ending up in a bar with many laughs to ease the pain. Some people drink, and the ugly comes out. "In vino veritas," he used to say. And his "veritas" was love and humor and classical music. He'd crawl into bed at midnight, put his arms around me, and tell me how much he loved me. On one of his late whiskey work nights, I stumbled out of bed at 2:00 a.m. and found him in the dark living room, only the tiny green lights from the stereo showing his silhouette as he air-conducted a Beethoven symphony. Tears fell down his cheeks.

I was still in my final analysis with Dr. Grotstein, and I asked him for a referral for Bob—someone who was an expert at treating anxiety. He gave me a name. Bob went and learned biofeedback, self-soothing techniques, and progressive relaxation. There was no attempt to explore the underlying causes of the anxiety and certainly no attempt to address his sexual shutdown or his sexual tastes, but at least he was getting some treatment.

At school, my favorite class was object relations theory, the latest psychoanalytic ideas on how the human infant becomes aware of itself, how the self develops, and how experience shapes us. Our professor had handpicked the essential object relations essays by different theorists; each one was a world of its own. I inhaled this stuff. It shaped my thinking about personal problems, gave me ideas about how therapy works, and fed right into my own analysis. It was the knowledge I'd always wanted.

82   staying married is the hardest part

One balmy afternoon, Bob and I decided to walk along the Santa Monica bluff. It was four o'clock, and I loved the warm ocean breeze and watching the coastline from Malibu to Palos Verdes, white sails stretching out to the horizon. We stopped at a picnic table and Bob sat with his back to the tabletop. I stepped between his legs and threaded my arms around his neck. Out of the blue, he pushed me away a little bit and, with a very serious look on his face, said, "I gotta tell you something—I've been thinking about it a lot."

This didn't sound funny at all. I studied his face.

"I don't want to live in LA anymore."

I pulled sharply away. "What!?" That he was even thinking such a thought shocked me.

Downcast, he shook his head. "Too much traffic, too much crime, and the earthquakes scare me. I'm sick of being freaked out. Wouldn't you enjoy living in a little town?"

Horror made my feet stumble backward. Oh LA! Salty ocean air, blue-tinged mountains, temperate sun, beautiful people, gourmet melting pot, entertainment mecca, freedom to be whatever you wanted with whomever you wanted. My Shangri-LA. . . .

My arms flapped against my sides, my voice shrill. "I love it here! I never want to leave!"

As if he hadn't heard me or seen my distress, he said, "There's a beautiful spot in Idaho right on a lake. Sandpoint is the town."

"Idaho? No! Absolutely not!" The devastation of leaving would be enough, never mind considering a landlocked northern state.

"How about Ashland? A sweet little town in Oregon on I-5 just above the California border. Last time I stopped there, the local newspaper headline said, 'Bicycle Found in Hedge.' Any town with that as its main headline is a town for me."

"Why didn't you tell me this before?" My hands flailed again at my sides because I wanted to smack him. "I won't do it! I don't ever want to leave here! And how can *you* leave here? Your business is here!" This was by far the worst thing he had ever said to me. I felt he was threatening to take away the very ground beneath my feet.

He gazed right past me to the ocean horizon I loved. "Writers move out of town all the time. Kind of a status thing. They live somewhere else and come into town for pitch meetings."

"But TV production is here!"

"Only for the weeks the show's being filmed. Then you can go away again. Anyway, I'm starting to hate TV. I want to write movies. You can do that from anywhere."

"But I'm in school here! Our friends are here! LA is who I am!"

"Just come with me to see it."

His persistence made the skin on my arms go numb. "I'll see it, but I'm not leaving!"

We'd been together for three years and married for two when this fissure in our marriage took hold. I was financially dependent on him at the moment. And I had married him, assuming he wanted to build a life here in LA with me. Not once had he suggested otherwise. He was asking me to walk away from the very foundation on which I had built my life.

Mid-December 1980, a few months after our Santa Monica bluff conversation, we drove up to Ashland so I could see "how wonderful a town" it was. We drove because Bob was panicky about flying and loved the control of being in his own vehicle.

84   staying married is the hardest part

I much preferred flying, but the last thing we needed was him enduring more panic.

Around Kettleman City, the thick smell of cow shit filled the car, an odor so strong we practically choked on it. Long before we saw the holding fields, we smelled them. And then there they were, thousands of cows, crammed together, miserable, knee-deep in mud and their own shit. I admit it. I love steak, but at least I want to eat free-range cattle who have not had the short, miserable lives of these guys.

We stayed in Dunnigan, a truck stop town north of Sacramento. Here, Bob treated me to food I hate: wilted lettuce from a bag, beef stew probably from a bag, bad apple pie, and strong iced tea. These are the places Bob loved and felt comfortable, but although it might seem I was having a terrible time, I was not. He entertained me with his constant observations about life, we played music and sang, made up limericks and jokes, and in Bill and Kathy's Diner, we watched people in other booths, and the servers and busboys, and Bob made up stories about who they were. "See that one?" he said, pointing to a tired, bleached-blonde waitress with a potbelly and a missing side tooth. "She married at seventeen, her husband cheated on her and stole the money she was saving to buy a car, and he left her with three little kids and a mortgage. She had to go live with her parents again in their trailer behind the house. She dreams of one day having her own place again. Her feet hurt, she drinks too much at the end of her shift, and she's kind of in love with the fry cook."

I watched this woman with the story in mind. Her fingernails were red and acrylic; the lines around her eyes and mouth shouted sun exposure, cigarettes, and exhaustion. She called me "honey," and she lingered a little too long at the order

bonnie comfort   85

window talking to the fry cook. Soon, she'd be a character in one of Bob's sketches or scripts, a woman who, at first, you kind of disdain until she breaks your heart with her hurt.

In the morning, the landscape became greener and lusher as we got closer to Oregon. Over the Siskiyou Pass we drove, and then surveyed the spectacular valley below, and the picturesque town of Ashland, surrounded on east and west by two different mountain ranges which run north to south.

We drove slowly through the little town. The population sign read 16,000 and change. At that time, LA was a teeming eight million, the melting pot of various ethnic and racial groups, where the energy level was high, competition stiff, and excitement in the air. Now came sleepy little Ashland, with a few pleasant restaurants, one tiny movie theater, and a lovely park in the center of town. Yes, Ashland was home to the Shakespeare Festival, and it had a number of theaters to serve that, but it was five hundred miles from San Francisco or Sacramento, and at that time, there were no direct flights to LA. More than anything, Ashland was a small town, and you have to love a small town to want to live in one. I didn't.

We checked into the only "high-rise" hotel of six floors, the Marc Anthony, in the downtown center. A realtor arranged to show us some houses, and I was already more than miserable: living in this place would suffocate me. No great restaurants, no glitzy excitement, and no ocean for two hundred miles. We rode around to see the different houses, some of which had wonderful views. At the top of a very steep street was a house for sale built into the hill and looking out over the whole valley and mountain range to the east. The view was breathtaking.

I commented on the view, but Bob said, "Let's see the other houses."

86   staying married is the hardest part

The realtor was a man in his forties wearing a plaid shirt, a down vest, and an ingratiating smile. We pulled into a long driveway set far back from the street. An ordinary wooden house was nestled in the trees with an attached garage and two outside decks. I stood at the end of that driveway on Wrights Creek Drive, shivering in my LA clothes. We looked inside: big kitchen, roomy living room, dining room, and another living room downstairs with three small bedrooms. The carpet was a shit shade of brown, the kitchen floor linoleum. A walk-in pantry in the kitchen was nice, and the sink had a greenhouse window, which I liked.

We were now back at the Marc Anthony, drinking vodka (me) and Canadian Club (Bob), and Bob said, "I like the one set back from the road."

"But the view from the other one is so great!"

"Yes, but I like the idea of a house being protected, nestled in among trees, not exposed like the one with the view. This one has a view of trees and grass. That's nice, isn't it?"

"I'm reminding you, as far as I'm concerned, this is a vacation place, not a place to live full-time. But at least if I had a house with that view, it would be easier."

After another sip of whiskey, he said, "Let's get the one I want. I'll probably be in it more than you anyway."

Although that was true, it still felt like a throwback to our parents' era when the man had the final say. It pissed me off, yet he *was* the one making all the money, and that ate into my sense of equality. There was another reason I didn't argue too much: I saw how upsetting LA was for him because his career frustration was embedded in that city. I understood his desire to escape from the reminders, but I also believed that, eventually, his work would win the day for us, and he'd have enough show business success that being in LA would be easier for him.

Maybe Bob was embarrassed later at his selfish statement. From then on, every major financial decision was a joint decision, and he never questioned anything I spent money on.

Unfortunately, neither of us had ever bought a house before, so we didn't think to negotiate. We agreed to the full asking price and signed all the papers. Bob was happy. I was angry and miserable. My sexual dissatisfaction was minor compared to this.

Back in LA, I let my outrage fade. We had a vacation house. So what! Let Bob go there as a refuge from show business. I didn't have to go there any more often than I chose.

Meanwhile, we kept throwing parties and trying to get pregnant. Bob made sure he was in town when I was ovulating, and I was grateful to him for that, but I couldn't listen to my girlfriends' stories about their pregnancies or their babies without feeling a grinding ache in my chest that sickened me. Maybe it would happen for us, maybe not. I tried to focus on the fun we had and how fortunate we were in general.

People loved to come to our house. Bob thrived on an audience and would get everybody in a circle to play "dictionary" or "limerick." Dictionary was a game in which one person holding the dictionary chose an obscure word, and each of us wrote down what we thought was either the true meaning or a made-up definition. In a room full of comedy writers, the fake definitions were hilarious. Limerick was our made-up game: using the traditional format of a limerick, the first player invented one line, then the next person to the left made up the

88   staying married is the hardest part

next line, and so on. We never knew what was going to come out of somebody's mouth. We provided loads of food and liquor, and people laughed till they couldn't catch their breath, stayed until 1:00 a.m., and left with their door prizes and packets of leftovers. After our parties, Bob and I would cuddle under soft blankets, sleep in, eat cinnamon toast for breakfast, and laugh again about last night's highlights.

Frank, our basset hound, was also a constant source of amusement. One morning, Bob and I were sitting in bed reading the paper when we heard the doggy door open and close. We looked up to see Frank walking briskly past the window, intent on something and focused, his ears swinging from side to side. Bob said, "Frank's out on official business this morning."

I could picture the dog in a small suit and tie, his briefcase by his side, and I laughed out loud. What I remember most, though, is smiling at how Bob said Frank took the "filet of bed."

Bob often sang to Frank, "He's a good friend, he's a nice pal, he's a brown guy . . ."

With all the entertaining and story-pitching he was doing, Bob's voice started getting hoarse. We went together to see Dr. Leeds, an Ear, Nose, and Throat (ENT) specialist, who said there was something on Bob's vocal cords that needed to be biopsied. This was horribly frightening to both of us. I couldn't imagine any fate worse for him than losing a vocal cord—like a brilliant painter losing his sight or a world-class skier being paralyzed from the waist down. The only thing that soothed his panic was me playing Chinese checkers with him, and I played what seemed like endless games with him, even bringing the board to the hospital to play it the night before his biopsy. The results were benign, which was such a relief for both of us that we threw a big "Bob Doesn't Have Cancer" party. That was a happy night, but this cancer scare was a wake-up call for both of us—him with his fear that his scripts would never be produced, me with my fear I'd never have a baby—yet we were each doing everything we could to realize our dreams.

Bob began making regular trips to Ashland to relax and get to know people in town. He developed a circle of interesting friends, got a regular poker game going, and began writing in the living room at the big desk we had set up instead of a sofa. In LA, I spent time with friends. I read and played racquetball and continued my studies to complete my PhD.

I missed the sexy fun of our first few years, and I kept raising the issue. This time, it was a morning when he was all dressed to leave. Our bedroom was still humid from his long shower, where he used the pelting water to allow himself to think. I was standing there still in my panties and nighttime T-shirt, and I asked, "Want a quickie?"

He had his "meeting jacket" slung over his arm. His face sunk into a morose downturn of mouth and eyes. "Look," he said. "I think you should get it elsewhere, and don't tell me."

"You're saying this to me again!?" My voice came out loud as I stood a few feet away from him. And then I crumpled into hurt, stepping backward till I hit the mattress and sat down. "Why would you say that?" I continued in a sad tone.

He gave me a tired eye roll. "You've been asking me about this for months, that's why. And I've told you I haven't got it in me right now." He laid his jacket down on the end of the bed and held his arms wide. "I'm not cheating on you. I'm not flirting with other women. I still think you're the best person I'll ever find in my life. But sex is the last thing on my mind.

90   staying married is the hardest part

It happens to me sometimes. Hopefully, I'll rally soon and be able to perform."

"But—but it's not about you performing. If you can't get it up, it's okay. Just let's play and rub each other and give each other pleasure."

He stepped over to me and pulled me up. My hair had curled from the humidity in the room, and he sunk his fingers into it and kissed me. "I'll try to get home early tonight," he said.

Like many other nights lately, he came home that night long after I was asleep.

When Bob suggested I get sex from someone else, it went against everything I believed in—monogamy, loyalty, and working out your differences with therapy and courage. I was currently studying couples' therapy, and we'd covered what came up when people wanted to try "open marriage." The consensus was this: it was no solution to marital frost.

So, I persisted. This time, we were lying by the pool on a weekend day. The air was soft, our roses a brilliant red in the sun, and I asked, "Wanna get naked and swim together?"

"Nah. Gotta a phone conference in ten minutes."

"I really think we should try sex therapy. I know someone good."

"I know I promised I would before we got married, but I'm not up for it right now."

"Then how can we fix this?"

"I don't know. Time. Less aggravation. Right now, I'm givin' ya all I can, and I know it's not enough. I told you—I think you should have a roll in the hay with someone else."

This attitude infuriated me. "But looking for sex with someone else is no solution! I love you. I want *you*. And don't you *care* if I'm with someone else?"

He took off his ballcap, scratched his head, and put the cap back on. "Look. You're a very sexual person, and sometimes I have dry spells. I'd rather you get what you need than have you leave me over it."

The phone rang, and he went inside for his call while I lay on my lounge chair, suddenly cold. I pulled a towel over me and turned to watch the sailboats on the horizon. This reminded me of how he'd asked Rick to take over the first dance at our wedding. Same solution: he didn't feel he could meet my need of the moment, so it was better that someone else did.

In a weird way, it was an act of generosity, but it made me feel he really didn't understand me after all. It was as if he thought I was a car that needed servicing and I could just pull into any dealership for a tune-up, unconnected to my emotional life, just a tune-up to keep me running smoothly. Yet if he was really thinking about me, and us, it made no sense. Sexually, I didn't function that way. I needed emotional safety and devotion for actual sexual satisfaction. And if some random guy was completely willing to give me exactly what I needed sexually, would it work for me? I was deeply in love with Bob, and it was him I wanted. Why would I feel emotionally safe with someone else? A guy who was single and looking? Or a guy who was married and looking?

If Bob really was afraid I'd leave him over his sexual shutdown, it was also insulting. Did he think I was a woman who had to have sex so much it didn't matter who it was? There were so many ways this didn't fit with my history, and he knew my history.

92 staying married is the hardest part

Although I was educated on how to fix someone else's marriage, I grew angry and distant and stopped talking to Bob about the sex issue. Despair crept into my bones. After everything had seemed so right, now everything seemed wrong. Disappointment with sex was one thing, a thing that in some ways I'd signed up for, but I never thought my husband would suggest I go out and find sex with someone else, nor had I ever imagined he'd want me to leave LA.

LA meant everything to me; it had become part of my identity and the opposite of what I'd fled from in Winnipeg. Living in LA represented my promise to myself not to repeat my mother's misery. She had missed LA her whole life. I dreaded the thought of being dragged away from here and always being homesick.

It felt as if my husband had taken off a mask he was wearing and shown me his true self, a betrayal of what I thought his promise had been to me. One morning, I drove down Temescal Canyon to the beach and went for a long, miserable walk along the shoreline. The roar of the surf was the music of my life. The thought of leaving it made that old ache settle in my core again. I removed my running shoes and dug my toes into the wet sand near the surf. As that warm, foamy water washed over them, an alien thought occurred—that if I kept feeling this awful, I could leave Bob. It was painful even to say those words in my head. Leaving Bob. My beloved. But I knew if I could practice as a psychologist, I could at least make a decent living on my own.

Determination eased that core ache: I'd become a licensed psychologist, so I'd always have the option to leave him. Back at the edge of the warm, dry sand, I laced up my shoes with an energy and resolve I hadn't had in a long time.

bonnie comfort 93

When we fall in love, we trust our partner will be the person we knew in the beginning, that lovely, irresistible other who is everything we admire and love. We attribute qualities and delights to that person's character when we put aside everyday life to devote ourselves wholeheartedly to each other. That is our job when we're mating, like bald eagles who mate for life, and court by flying high in the air, joining a talon to the other's, and then cartwheeling downward while connected in a glorious show of togetherness.

It's a love trance. It can't last.

Gradually and inevitably, we grow less patient and willing to sacrifice what matters to us for the sake of the other. We withdraw some adoration and instead assert more of our individuality. Old habits return, and we want the other to accept them. We lose patience and start saying things to each other we never imagined, like "You're always late!" or "Why don't you pick up after yourself?" or "You never have time for me!" or "How much did that massage cost?" We gradually realize we've committed to spending our lives with a stranger.

Psychology theory tells us that our brains create an internal representation of the Other: our story about who that person is. We then relate to that real person *as if* he or she is the person we have in our head. When the real and uncontrollable Other does not behave like the partner we imagine in our heads, we are painfully disappointed.

Even when we notice things we don't like in the beginning, we don't focus on them. The lack of emphasis we place on these things later comes back to haunt us. I knew Bob always drove to Canada and back, and I saw how afraid he was in small planes, but somehow, it never occurred to me in those first three years that he'd *never* go to Europe or Asia or Scandinavia

94   staying married is the hardest part

with me. And he told me he was self-conscious about danc-ing, but it never occurred to me that he'd *never* dance with me. I told him I'd had a lot of sexual experience, but it might not have occurred to him that would make it more difficult for me to do without. And maybe he had no idea how fiercely I loved LA and what it would mean to me to leave it. I hadn't talked about that in our first three years. It never occurred to me that it might come up as an issue. Gradually, we began to learn the ways we were willing to accommodate the other and the ways we weren't.

And there was this: although Bob had told me in the first few weeks of dating that he liked to "peek—see something I'm not supposed to see," that comment had whistled in and out of my head with lightning speed. I never gave it another thought because he repeatedly asked me to wear his favorite lingerie. It wasn't until three years into our marriage that he asked me to pretend I was alone in that lingerie while he watched me from outside. Now it was something I had to deal with after we'd been together, married, and fully committed to each other.

Bob was compelling enough that I was willing to be burned some of the time to stay close to that flame, even though I was beginning to learn what it might cost me.

CHAPTER 8

Ways of Leaving

Bob started leaving me in his own way—more trips to Ashland, more depression and irritability, more frustration with the business, and sex that was occurring less and less frequently. I was in my dream house now but without him. I cried to my friends until they were tired of hearing it, and they told me to either leave him or make peace with my marriage.

When I thought of leaving him, memories of our good times played in my head. I saw us sitting at Don Cuco's in Studio City, a collection of comedy writers, actors, musicians, and friends drinking icy margaritas, mowing through many baskets of hot tortilla chips, stuffing tacos and burritos in our faces, and all the time laughing so hard I thought someone was going to need the Heimlich maneuver. I saw us sitting at Thanksgiving dinners with Chris Cluess, another comedy writer, and his brilliant wife Joyce and their daughters, laughing so hard that someone sprayed ginger ale on the turkey. I had to blow my nose I laughed so hard. I had to hold my stomach till I caught my breath. Laughter made us high.

Even on a bad day when I was pissed at Bob for some reason, he could say something that made me laugh enough that

96   staying married is the hardest part

I'd let go of my anger. An orgasm may last twenty seconds if you're lucky, but a funny line can entertain you, give you the truth, keep you company, and make you laugh a dozen times in the same day.

In the year after my wedding, my dad suffered a new series of small strokes. Min had already looked after him at home for years with his increasing dementia, but she was too stressed and exhausted by it now to keep it up. She told my sister, Brenlee, "I can't do this anymore."

They found him a good nursing home near the house, and there he languished, demented and giving political speeches to an imaginary crowd. She went to be with him every day, brought him his favorite chicken soup, and slogged through the snow she hated to make sure he still knew he was loved.

The following January, Min visited me in LA, although I had to find a month-long rental for her near me because we didn't have a proper guest bedroom. It had been one-and-a-half years since our wedding, and the visit went better than I expected. She was with her family most of the time, but we took walks together and went out for lunch. There was a tentative quality to our conversations, perhaps both of us not wanting it to go badly, but while there, she bonded with a woman named Connie, who was a friend of my Uncle Joe's, and so much did she and Connie have in common that she promised to return next year and stay with Connie, who was a widow and very much welcomed Min's company.

Min's animated account of her dinners with Joe, his wife, and Connie told me how much she missed California. We laughed together as we chatted and I was reminded of how funny Min was, not so much when she told jokes she'd heard, but her offhand comments that were usually spot-on because they held truth, like "Her hair is so thin you could read a newspaper through it," or, "He stands in front of the open refrigerator until frost forms in his nostrils." I brought her to the taping of Bob's TV show, where she met Bill Bixby, a handsome TV actor whom she'd always liked, and that was a rare treat for her.

I had Min over for dinner a few times, proud to show her my LA home and proud of my husband and his showbiz life. I felt the visit had gone well for the first time, but I was still relieved to take her to the airport.

Over the next few months, Bob sank into a more troubled depression. He believed he was wasting his talent in TV. He hated the commercialism, the hypocrisy, and the fact that scared executives who bowed to the network brass refused to put up money for his original stories. So then he ran away to Ashland every chance he got to soothe himself. While there he started writing his own screenplay, and I was glad he could do that without some person from the business criticizing it, but now I was often in my beloved Palisades house without him.

Some things seemed unsolvable: my desperate desire to stay in LA, his desperate desire to escape to a small town, my wanting my psychology career, his wanting to write what he believed in, our sexual conflicts over lack of frequency, and my distaste for him now asking me to indulge his desire to peek. Yet we were still deeply in love and didn't want to part.

One evening, when Bob was in Ashland, I went to a party at a Century City hotel. The guy sitting next to me at the dinner was cute, with an impish smile, and he was single, Jewish, and loved racehorses. I also loved racehorses, their sleek, perfect bodies and hot energy. I had watched the big races on TV. I'd taken riding lessons in the Palisades on warm afternoons while Bob was at the studio. Racehorses are magnificent creatures, and I'd never known someone who actually owned one like this guy did. After a few glasses of wine, we danced, his huge dark eyes focused on me. As people left, we did, too, and walked the hotel's dark corridors, holding hands. I leaned back against the wall and kissed him. Was I really going to cheat on my husband? For a while now, Bob had been suggesting that I try this. How guilty did I need to feel? And I had told this guy I was married. If he chose to be with me, it was his choice.

The fragrance of someone's room service meat wafted over us as we leaned against the corridor wall. During the evening, this guy told me he had a patchy relationship history and that he wasn't good at talking about his feelings. But what did it matter if I wouldn't choose him if I were single? I wasn't. I was just looking for supplemental vitamins. Still, I stopped him from going any further that night. He walked me to my car, and we kissed again. Before he left, he gave me his business card and told me he hoped I'd call.

Over the next few days, I argued with myself: *you already know from your work that affairs damage a marriage. They can be the beginning of the end! Do you want that? No. So, you already know it's a bad solution. But still, Bob thinks it might help me cope with his lack of interest. Is he right? Can I do that trick of splitting myself in two? Would he care?*

The temptation was too great. I was alone in bed every night that week. And Bob, having suggested multiple times that I try a "roll in the hay" with someone else, had eaten into my moral reserve. I found the guy's business card in my purse and called him. Racehorse guy owned a very successful carpet business and asked me to visit him at his showroom in West Hollywood. We spent a fun afternoon together, lunch, kissing in the parking lot, and the heat building between us. At his suggestion, I met him the next day in the lobby of the famous Ambassador Hotel where Bobby Kennedy was shot. Old chandeliers, red velvet upholstered chairs. A vast suite with a living room. He didn't seem to mind spending money on me.

It was so strange to taste someone else after four years of Bob. Champagne in an ice bucket, room service filet mignon, a man who devoted himself to my body. It felt pretty good, as long as I didn't care how little he talked. It was a makeshift solution to a temporary situation. Would I do this again? I didn't know, but I gave myself over to that afternoon with one exception: I didn't reach orgasm with him no matter what he did. It was as if I were single again, in my early twenties, the chameleon who presented the aspects of me I thought a man would like, including, sadly, faking an orgasm.

We had a few things in common: both Jewish, both loving gourmet food, and both captivated by thoroughbreds. I wanted to go to Santa Anita with him. I wanted to learn more about racing. I decided to subscribe to *The Thoroughbred Record* to learn more about the racing and breeding business. I fantasized that maybe I'd buy a piece of a racing mare someday. When Bob returned home from Ashland a week later, I told him I wanted to get a box at the Santa Anita racetrack, the classiest track in town. He never wondered out loud why I'd suddenly developed a passion for racing. He loved to gamble. We got a great four-person box over the finish line for the Oak Tree meet, and I was thrilled.

100   staying married is the hardest part

I began a genuine affair with Racehorse Man. We talked on the phone every day. He took me to the kind of high-end restaurants Bob rarely liked—La Scala in Beverly Hills, Bernard's in the Biltmore, and L'Orangerie. He lived with his sister, so we went to hotels. One afternoon, when I came back from being with him, I found Bob at home much earlier than usual, and the sight of me in a flirty skirt aroused him that time, and we tumbled into bed, me worrying that I might seem too wet although he didn't seem to notice. I felt terribly guilty that day, but my guilt faded as, once again, Bob shut down sexually for another month.

Instead, Bob and I focused on having fun, and now fun also included going to the track. We took our friends with us, and once in a while, we'd make money when we bet on fast-sounding horses' names. At the track, though, I felt split in two, aware that my lover might walk by if he was there to look at a horse. I somehow managed this emotional juggling act of having fun with Bob while I was glancing around for that familiar face.

I still loved to be with Bob more than anyone.

I saw more hotel ceilings that year than the previous fifteen years combined, but for me, it was only about a man being hot for me. The true, shy sexual me needed safety and love for release. Instead, I playacted at being the sexiest of women. Racehorse Man snorted cocaine right before sex. A few times, I tried cocaine, thinking it might get me over the edge, but drugs and alcohol were never my thing. All it took was two separate times of feeling exhausted the next day for me to say no to another white line.

After a while, that guy whispered in darkened hotel rooms that he loved me, and I began feeling bad. I was keeping him from finding someone for himself. "Do you date?" I asked. "A little," he said. A wave of possessiveness and jealousy overcame me, although I had no right. And he wanted more of us, but I could not.

We agreed to quit seeing each other. Right after that, I went to Ashland for a few days and missed that guy with a sick yearning. I realized the yearning really belonged in my marriage. It was Bob I wanted. Always Bob. He had told me, "I give you everything I got," and I knew it was true. So I dressed up for him, and him being at his most relaxed in Ashland, loved it. He tapped into his old self then, hot for that performer Bonnie, and we had a spate of frequent sex, but the private me who wanted to be truly met felt lonely.

It was an unresolvable difference between us.

One day, while we were both back in LA, Bob said, "Come live with me in Ashland." We sat in Fromin's Deli on Wilshire Boulevard, drinking flowery iced tea and eating warm, salty corned beef sandwiches on rye with new dill pickles—food we couldn't get in Ashland, land of white bread and ham. *Don't push me*, played in my head. *I won't leave this ocean, my friends, the palm trees, the excitement.* I looked at him and kept chewing. Then I said, "I can't live there full time."

He fell silent, and our usually fun deli lunch was ruined.

I focused on my studies, determined to get my degree and psychology license. You could say I was calculating about it—making sure I could support myself if I left Bob—but I didn't want a divorce. I wanted the sexual and geographic conflicts in our marriage to get better.

After that, Bob went to Ashland every chance he could. When he was in town, which was three-quarters of the time, we usually went out for dinner, then settled in at home to watch the news. No matter where he was, Bob called me multiple times a day and always opened with, "*Hi!* How ya feelin'?" He really wanted to know. I loved that about him, and we'd share whatever was uppermost in our minds. Our talks gave me a constant sense of togetherness. And there wasn't a single conversation in which I didn't laugh. No matter what he had to tell me, there was something funny in it, even if it was just him describing how he'd seen three network executives walking side by side that breezy day, all with a hand on the head to secure their toupees in the wind.

I was happy to be in Ashland for a few weeks now and then. After all, it was with Bob. Often, we ate breakfast at the Ashland Bakery and strolled through the beautiful Lithia Park, which had duck ponds and footbridges over a stream. The town was charming, but no way did I want to leave LA.

A classmate named Rachelle became my best friend—a petite woman with a face as beautiful as a Renaissance painting—a little turned-up nose, perfectly shaped and full lips, and smooth olive skin. We confided in each other; we loved the same psychoanalytic classes, and she educated me about Jungian theory. As we got close to completing the academic portion of our degree, we began studying together to take the doctoral exam. Many days, while Bob was at a studio working with Rick, Rachelle sat with me at my dining table in the Palisades house, one of my stained-glass windows hanging in the window behind her, and we grilled each other about theory, statistics, and therapy techniques.

I was a nervous wreck the night before the final exam, but Rachelle and I both passed. Next for me was a one-year postdoctoral fellowship in the psychiatry department at

Cedars-Sinai Medical Center, but now the pressure was on to finish my dissertation so I could graduate in time.

In January 1982, a year after Min's first visit, she arrived for a full six weeks of staying with Connie. Min loved the hot winter sun and the easy walking out of the house without heavy coats and boots. It was an echo of her younger years. There was a skip to her walk, a relaxed smile on her face. What a loss it must have been to leave this big, wide paradise.

A few days after Min's arrival, Bob went to Ashland for a few weeks, angry with studio executives who had paid for but refused to make a clever Western movie Rick and he had submitted. Bob did his best to recover by sitting at his desk in Ashland, gazing at our oak trees, and continuing to write his first solo screenplay, *Green Sky*. When Bob came back to LA, his agent began shopping it around. It was a lovely script, a "small movie," and eventually Paramount bought it but never produced it. To this day, it languishes on some dusty shelf because Paramount is not willing to release the rights without a million-dollar fee.

While Bob was gone, things were easier and more comfortable between Min and me. In my younger years when I listened to Min talk about family or friends, I learned there was much more to understand about a person than what you could see on the surface. She would comment on vanity or arrogance or the way someone tried to hide something that was obvious to anyone else. Listening to her, I had learned to look deeper.

Now, I took her as my date to a Beverly Hills party for a friend—a dance floor laid down outside for the occasion, fancy food stations around the dance floor. While Min was at

104   staying married is the hardest part

the dessert table, I bumped into a real estate developer, a man I'd known and been attracted to in my midtwenties, but he was already married. He was comfortable, familiar, lean, and fit, with a great, sexy walk. We stood at that party talking, standing close, the air between us electric.

I trusted him. The next day, he called and said, "So why did you give me your number?"

"I'm attracted," I said.

"Me too," he said.

We made plans to have lunch later in the week. Guilt and uneasiness crept in.

That afternoon, I took Min shopping at the Westside Pavilion. At Sisley, one of my favorite Italian restaurants, we ordered pasta e fagioli soup and white wine, and in the turmoil of guilt and longing, I leaned forward and said, "Min, I don't know what to do . . ."

Min was smart and often right, like when she told me the exact thing I never wanted to hear about an old boyfriend— that he hadn't treated me well. She was also right about other things: wear classic designs in clothes, they'll never go out of style; use the best ingredients in your cooking, it really makes a difference; and be generous with people.

Now, for the first time since that horrible rift between us thirteen years ago, I asked for her advice. The light in Sisley was dim, and I was already on my second glass of wine. "I love Bob," I said, "but we don't have sex for weeks." I shook my head and added, "And I don't want to leave him."

Min took a sip of wine and held the glass up, her pinky finger high. She leaned closer and in a conspiratorial tone said, "Honey, if I were you, I'd get a little on the side."

I laughed out loud. "Really? Well, I am doing that. In fact, he told me to do that and just not tell him! But I don't like it. I feel guilty."

Min shook her head. "That's what you have to do sometimes. Don't tell anyone, cover your tracks well, and whatever you do, don't tell Bob." Her cheeks were flushed now from the wine, and she seemed different to me—more like a trusted girlfriend than the larger-than-life controlling mother.

She said, "Was it that good-looking fella I saw you talking to last night?"

She didn't miss a thing.

Min's permission felt like a great gift to me, and the next day, I had lunch with the married real estate developer. And the day after that. I didn't tell her the details. I didn't think she really was a girlfriend, but by the time I dropped her off at LAX, he was my lover.

I knew Bob hadn't intended for me to develop a close, emotional connection with someone else, but this lover was not like the last: he was the kind of man I could have seen myself marrying. So, mixed in with my "well-Bob-told-me-to-do-it" anger was more guilt.

Bob came back to LA, but a deep friendship grew between this man and me as we spent many days looking at his properties, walking, talking, and having sex in his model homes. Bob was usually out the door early every morning and often not home till late evening, so it was easy to cover my whereabouts. I worried more about this guy's wife finding out, but she worked an hour away in Santa Clarita, and he seemed unconcerned.

I loved this man, I have to say. Not the way I loved Bob, but this guy was part of my social life prior to Bob; we shared some

106   staying married is the hardest part

friends. He felt like family. We discussed our marriages, the music we liked, and the people we knew. Sometimes, we had sex in his private office—on his cushy wool carpet, in his tall cream leather chair, on his huge single-slab Parota wood desk. I couldn't come, even though he was patient and understanding, but with him, I didn't fake it, and this time, I felt bad more for myself than him.

After being with him, I started hurrying home to brush my teeth, shower, and reorient myself to Bob, but Bob was so aggravated and preoccupied with work that he didn't notice me being distracted. I tucked the images of another man's naked body into a locked compartment in my head. Bob was my one true love, and even then, I knew my sexual inhibition with that guy was a form of being faithful to Bob. Go figure.

Five months after we began meeting, my real estate guy called with big news: "My wife is pregnant. I—I never expected this, but it's happened."

I sank down on my living room sofa, a hollowed-out feeling in my chest.

"I'm sad to say I have to stop seeing you. Truly sad. I'll miss you. But I can't do this to her. And I want this baby."

I imagined his mountain-top house full of diapers, teddy bears, and musical mobiles. I respected his priorities and appreciated how kind he was in breaking it off with me, but for weeks, I walked along the ocean, missing our days together and our comfortable conversations. The sadness was made worse by knowing my friend would have a baby and I wouldn't.

In February 1983, Bob's mother died while sitting in her recliner in their Edmonton home. We'd been told she was fighting some kind of cancer, but her death still came as a shock. We went up for the funeral, standing next to each other at the back of the church, holding hands, and me feeling what a loss this was for Bob.

When we returned, I focused on my dissertation. Bob and Rick agreed to a new TV contract with Lorimar Productions, housed on the Columbia Pictures lot in Culver City. It was a lucrative contract that would secure our financial future for a few years, and in response, I pressured Bob to buy a house in the Palisades. Reluctantly, he agreed to buy, only for me. This made me happier: it was a firm anchor in LA, and it would be ours.

In June 1983, I was awarded my psychology degree, but oddly, after all that time and hard work, it seemed like a non-event to me. I put my bound doctoral dissertation on a shelf and carted it, unread, to every house. I had worked hard to write that dissertation, but only because it was required of me. It reminded me that I'd always been good at doing what others wanted, just not so good at being me. I still had to do three thousand hours of postgraduate training before qualifying for my licensing exam, the biggest hurdle of all.

Cedars-Sinai Medical Center in Beverly Hills is a prestigious private hospital. I was assigned to the outpatient psychiatric clinic, and I could now introduce myself as Dr. Comfort, a thirty-nine-year-old newbie. Although the patient population was very different from the VA, back in a hospital setting I was home.

The clinic was fronted by a guy named Cecil. Behind him on his corkboard was a black-and-white photo of Lucille Ball in her Lucy outfit. I imagined his home was a shrine to her silliness, which made me feel at home with him.

108　staying married is the hardest part

The therapists' offices took up two long corridors—nine small offices per corridor with sound-insulating doors. Cecil showed me to the office assigned to me—a good location halfway down the inner corridor. I met a mild-mannered psychiatric resident from Australia on one side of me and a tall, thin one on the other side.

I immediately dove into the whole program, doing therapy, charting, reports, watching art therapy, and attending meetings. I did case presentations and was supervised to improve my therapy skills and professional judgment. It was exactly the training I needed.

My first patient was a stunning twenty-four-year-old actress with shoulder-length blonde hair and impeccable skin who wore all her clothes inside out. She couldn't bear to be apart from her boyfriend for five minutes, but she was angry, depressed, and tired of him at the same time. I couldn't help wishing I looked like her for just one day, minus the clothing arrangement. I also recognized an exaggerated version of the youngest part of me, dependent and angry and presenting my physical-self first, but it was an old part of me. I'd outgrown my kittenish side.

Another of my new patients was a guy who was obsessively bonded with his horse. Because of my racehorse days, I felt a kinship with him, but gradually, I learned he slept in the stall with the horse, jacked off about thirteen times a day, and jacked off the horse, too. I kept a straight face when he told me this, and I made notes. The next day, in a clinical conference, I presented the case, and it was pointed out that his hypersexuality was typical of bipolar disorder, and I had missed the diagnosis because he didn't come across as manic. He was a high-functioning bipolar, and his horse was very relaxed.

bonnie comfort   109

At home, Bob was gone during the day to Lorimar, where he and Rick were writing and producing their new series, hoping for a big on-air score. In the mornings when Rick was often late arriving, Bob worked on a new screenplay of his own called *Dogfight*. Although we still slept in the same bed, our lives stayed very separate. It was lonely in that sexual way, our incompatibility a nagging sadness. The deepest sadness, though, was over my not getting pregnant. I noticed pregnant women and babies in strollers everywhere.

On a Wednesday morning in early December, I was getting ready for work and thought it might rain later. I put on my suit and a pair of shiny black boots that clung to my calves like a sleeve. Bob stopped on his way back from the shower and put his hands on my breasts. He loved seeing me dressed up for work, and this time he wanted me to stop and play with him because he was so turned on by my office outfit. The time crunch made taking care of my needs out of the question, and I thought he knew that, if only unconsciously.

On that morning, if I'd been ovulating, I would have pulled up my skirt instantly, but it wasn't that time of the month, and doing it would make me late. I said, "I should leave," and he said, "Just a quickie," and in spite of my wanting to go, I did my best to rush through the sex as fast as possible. I was doing it solely because—well, because I still wanted to have sex with him even if it wasn't how I liked it. I still loved to inhale his scent and feel him inside me.

This is how a marriage goes forward: You get enough of what you want to forgive your partner for the ways he doesn't serve you, and you also forgive because you understand why he makes the choices he does; his particular brain map of relationships has been laid down long before you, and it's not his

110   staying married is the hardest part

fault. You can ask for change, and maybe, maybe, like water eroding rock, it eventually changes the stream's course. If you can live that long.

At the hospital, I kept bumping into a cute psychiatrist who walked with a loping gait like he was half running. Turned out he was an obsessive runner. He was so pink-cheeked and handsome that I said I wanted him to help me develop a running program for myself. We started meeting on Ocean Avenue to run down to the pier and back. Three times, I went with him to his apartment, faking the orgasm but feeling real about this: I could still attract and seduce a good-looking doctor with a big future. Pretty soon, we stopped seeing each other.

Once that year, I had sex on the floor of my little office at Cedars. It was a guy I met at the Palisades car wash. We were standing next to each other, and he looked down at my feet, nodded, and said with a grin, "Red shoes. Love the red shoes."

I said, "I'm married."

He said, "I don't care."

The next day, he was in the clinic waiting room, and I took him back to my office as if he were my patient, locked us in my little room, and lay down on the floor. It was one more affirmation: I was being told I was pretty, sexy, and desirable. I never saw him again. I look back on it now and realize how horribly risky that was for multiple reasons, and yet, at the time, it didn't seem so. In 1984 LA, casual sex with someone you barely knew was so common it came up often in conversations as the latest fun adventure. It was just before AIDS burst into consciousness in California, and everything changed.

I justified my infidelities by telling myself Bob had instructed me to do it. Now I wonder why he chose to do that. And why I didn't question him about that choice. He could have tried therapy to free himself sexually or lessen his reaction to career disappointments. I could have humored him more often with his sexual requests. I could have given him an ultimatum. I could have challenged his definition of show business failure and how that depressed him. It's only in hindsight that these other alternatives come to mind sometimes.

One of my colleagues that year confessed privately to me that he sucked his thumb at his desk in between patient sessions. One resident confided to me that she'd made an almost lethal suicide attempt the year before. And there was me, engaging in brief, unsatisfying sex with a stranger on the floor of my office.

Sometimes, I thought, the only thing that separated us from the patients was the desk.

CHAPTER 9

A Licensed Psychologist

In the spring of 1984, Bob and his buddies wandered through Bandon, a tiny town on the southern Oregon coast, where they went crabbing. A few days later, I flew up to join Bob in Ashland, and he talked me into going with him to see Bandon.

Bandon is an hour-and-a-half drive northwest of Ashland. Its beach is broad and fine sanded, and in the first hundred yards of water are giant sea stacks—tall rock formations—that give the beach a stunning beauty and perspective. It's one of the most spectacular beaches I've ever seen, but it's often cold and overcast and the wind is strong during parts of every day.

In town, we wandered past a realty agency listing properties on its windows, and while eating fudge from the Bandon Fudge Factory, one property caught our eyes. I agreed to see it.

Even though this beach was much colder than I preferred, the raw beauty of it, the lack of people, and the feeling of eternity were all there. The house was magic. Constructed of river rock and rough-hewn timber, it sat on a low bluff that faced the sea—you could walk down to the sand over a gentle, short slope. And the picture windows faced this astonishing

bonnie comfort   113

vista—the massive sea stacks and the constant roiling water up and down the empty coastline. I loved all of it instantly.

The entrance to the property was a long driveway from Highway 1 almost to the ocean. The next morning, we sat at the highway entrance and talked. The property entrance was marked by a run-down wooden drift boat, with gold metal letters hammered into place: 4000 Beach Loop Road. The peeling paint on the boat was baby blue, the gold letters shiny and large.

I looked at Bob's face, grizzled from a one-day beard, and a few silver hairs caught the light. His smile was soft, and those big brown eyes a bit moist. This time, he didn't make the decision. He patted my thigh and said, "I'd like to buy this for you. If you want it." The car windows were rolled down, so the fresh salt air filled our noses. I heard the crashing of the surf, and I loved this man for bringing me here and finding this and wanting to give it to me because that's what it meant—he was still the one earning money, and he wanted us to come here often and search for shells and play in the tide pools and watch whales during the day and stars at night. I looked at that run-down boat and laughed with sheer pleasure.

"Yes!" I said, "Yes, yes, yes!"

A month later in May 1984, we took possession of the house, and I flew up to help Bob move some of our Ashland possessions over there. Sleeping in that place to the sound of the crashing waves was hypnotic. We walked and walked along the empty beach, and in the evenings listened to music and did a huge jigsaw puzzle.

That Bandon house was, for me, the best compensation for being in Oregon at all. The cost of buying that kind of property

114   staying married is the hardest part

in California would have been prohibitive. The view was unfettered, and the beach was always empty except for a few people and dogs and the hordes of sandpipers and gulls with their haunting, lonely calls. I adored that place, how deeply I slept while there, and how restorative it was to watch the waves and look for whales through our binoculars. In the mornings, before the tide came in, the breeze was gentle, and you could examine the tide pools, search for shells, and love the place completely. The afternoons were always windy, but at night, the beach was calm again, the stars astonishing—plentiful and bright—and way more visible than you could see looking at the sky from the LA basin.

Back in LA, while I was weighing in on conferences at Cedars, Bob was doing a mock *On the Road* documentary for HBO. They had an on-air deal for eight episodes, and Bob loved the comedy sketches—Rick and Bob visiting a man on death row and having the audacity to eat his last meal while they interviewed him; Rick and Bob investigating a man who believed he had developed a serum that could make you invisible, and to demonstrate he injected himself and walked around naked, believing no one could see him; Bob interviewing a Reverend from the Holy Church of Amplification—a man who believed that God wasn't dead, just hard of hearing, so he broadcasted his prayers through a giant satellite dish. The Reverend had a very sexy brunette for vespers. Underneath her demure clothing was a pair of jean shorts and a red top with a lot of cleavage. Bob managed to put Frank, our basset hound, in that sketch, and at the end of it, he drove away in his vehicle with Frank and the sexy girl.

Sadly, a few weeks after that, Frank stopped eating and seemed particularly lethargic, even for a basset hound. The vet told us Frank had lymphoma, and there was nothing he could do to save him. Bob did me the kindness of taking Frank to them for his last day. I couldn't bear the thought of watching him die. When Bob brought back the collar and ID tag, I attached it to a small wooden heart and hung it on our bulletin board, where it stayed for years. In red ink, I wrote: "Frank: July 1978–April 1985. We loved him."

Our lives continued to be very separate. When my fellowship ended in September 1984, Rachelle and I opened a private office in Westwood. She was licensed as a Marriage and Family Counselor, and I was licensed as a Clinical Social Worker, so we could do therapy, but I still had another fifteen hundred hours of supervised work to do before I could qualify for the daunting national psychology exam.

I took a handful of long-term psychotherapy patients with me from Cedars and also worked three days a week in a neurologist's office, doing neuropsychological testing under supervision. My skills evolved, and I was glad to become proficient at this kind of testing because it would be a lucrative way to make a living once I was a psychologist.

Our office was in a charming two-story brick building in Westwood. The suite had an oak parquet floor waiting room, and I furnished my inner office with a peach sofa, a gray laminate desk, a cream barrel chair, and a tall, potted palm in a white woven basket. Most importantly, I paid Min gallery-level prices for three of her huge oil paintings, which I framed to go with the decor. By paying her well, I wanted to show respect

116   staying married is the hardest part

for her talent and hard work. Those particular oils of hers were California patios and interiors, a perfect fit for my office. I saw in them how she must have missed LA to have created those scenes with that soft southern light.

When I brought Bob to see my new office, he said, "Beautiful!" and we immediately had sex on my new sofa. Odd venues and me in my professional clothes were his jam.

For months after that I loved to sit at my desk and hear the A/C vent sigh in this peaceful space that now was all mine. The palm fronds cast finger shadows on the wall. I could dim the overhead lights to just the right soothing level. Rachelle and I did couples therapy together in my inner office.

In January, Min arrived again for her yearly visit to stay with Connie. A new phase in my relationship with Min began. I was now the one who looked after her, took her places, and treated her to restaurants and upscale stores. I loved showing her around LA, eating sand dabs in lemon sauce at the Bistro Garden, or smoked tuna salad and gnocchi at I Cugini on Ocean Avenue. After one glass of white wine, her cheeks would turn bright pink, and she'd slide into her imitations of our relatives in hilarious, perfect form.

The biggest thrill for her during that trip was to arrive at my office and discover on the walls her paintings in expensive frames that showed them at their best. Her eyes shone with tears of gratitude, but there was still a danger between us, topics we couldn't discuss. It was as if my life had begun when I married Bob, and all those years didn't exist from the day I left for LA until the day I married. It seemed those years were a painful dark hole she never wanted to discuss. The energy between us was very tense and weird if I ever made a casual reference to that time. It was a no-fly zone.

She did now ask about my marriage and my encounters with other men. I downplayed these issues and said I no longer had a lover. Some squishy tingle in the center of my stomach said those topics were better left alone, that they would be gossip to take back home to my sisters. The quiet way she nodded and studied my face told me she realized I'd drawn together the curtains again. Superman, with the X-ray eyes, had nothing on her.

After she left, I began studying intensely for the national psychology exam. In April, I passed the written test. I sailed through the state oral exam right after that. Finally, at age forty, I was fully hatched as a clinical psychologist in California. It was a big milestone.

To celebrate, we drove to our Bandon house to walk on the beach. I lay in our bed next to the open window that night and felt the great relief of finally having overcome the last hurdle to my decades-long goal. I snuggled up to Bob's back and wrapped my arm around his waist. Regardless of our differences, if I left him, it would not be because I was no longer in love with him. It would be because the shattering of so many of my assumptions about our lives together was more than I could bear.

A few days later, after we'd packed up the car and driven to the end of the driveway, Bob stopped and reached over to pat my knee. "I'm really proud of you. You've accomplished a lot." I warmed to his hand, which he rubbed up and down my thigh through my jeans. "But y'know what I think?" he asked.

Curious, I angled myself toward him.

"I think now you should write a novel." This said with that confident face he always had when he was encouraging his friends to take daring career risks. He loved challenging people

118   staying married is the hardest part

to get outside their comfort zone and do something great they might not think they could do.

"What!?" I said. "Now? Why do you think I should do that now?!"

I'd written poems and journals during my adolescence and twenties, and yes, I loved to read. But me? Write a novel? The idea never crossed my mind. And other than a poem or greeting card here and there, Bob had never read anything I'd written. Why on earth would he suggest this? Now, of all times, when I'd just reached this professional milestone?

Bob shrugged, "I think you'd enjoy it."

The possibility was intriguing, an idea I'd never had about myself, and coming from Bob, whose opinion I valued so highly, it felt like a great compliment. He thought I could write a novel! It was a sudden turn in my vision—that I could have a writer's life like he had. No more studying dictated by a school or the state. I had fulfilled all those requirements and secured my permanent option to work as a psychologist. Now, I could read whatever I wanted, set my own pace, practice psychology or not, write or not, exercise and take photographs, or go back to designing stained-glass windows. What would I write? Did I have a good story in my head?

My brain was spinning. I looked at the peeling paint on the wooden rowboat at the entrance to our driveway. It was one of those snapshot moments you never forget, like exactly where you were when you watched TV coverage of the 9/11 attacks. "Really?" I said. "You think I can write a novel?"

"Yes!" he said. "You'd have fun doing it!"

"*Hmm*," I said. "Well, if you think I can, maybe I will," as if he were suggesting I order pizza for dinner, but I was not going to walk away from my new psychology practice. That was a given, written in years of study and sweating over the exams, and deeper than that, written in my love for understanding how the human psyche works. Still, the pressure on me was over. I could work part-time and do whatever else I wanted. He would continue to support us.

He studied my face, eyes truthful and open. "You realize this is part of my grand scheme to get you out of LA."

Some of the loft inside me deflated, and an angry heat flushed my face. "Well, my grand scheme is to stay in LA, so even if I try writing, I'll still develop my psychology practice."

"Of course."

Back in LA, I certainly didn't toss aside my hard-won career and start writing. Instead, I began doing psychological evaluations for personal injury, Workers' Compensation, and insurance companies. LA was saturated with therapists all vying for well-heeled clients. What I had to offer was rarer. I trained myself in forensic psychology. I testified at depositions, and occasionally in court. My first love was psychotherapy, but diagnostics paid my office bills.

Meanwhile, Bob and Rick continued working under their contract with Lorimar. In between writing half-hour TV scripts, Bob pounded away on his electric typewriter to finish his second solo screenplay, *Dogfight*, which was loosely based on his Marine Corps experiences.

His TV work kept paying the bills, and Bob loved their mockumentary for HBO, but HBO didn't order another season when the series ran out. Bitterly disappointed, Bob and Rick moved on to a show not created by them, one Bob thought was stupid but kept our lives afloat.

It seemed both of us had lost so much of what we'd hoped for. He was unhappy most of the time, cranky and frustrated

120   staying married is the hardest part

at work, writing his own movie on the side, and increasingly disgruntled with show business. I was sad over the loss of my dreams—baby, happy sex, a life committed to LA. Although we slept together each night in the same bed, we were more distant from each other than we'd ever been.

I talked about my marriage with Rachelle. Of course I did. Frequently. It was one of the great blessings of our friendship that we analyzed our struggles together, hoping that by sharing insights, we'd find a new way of looking at whatever was troubling us.

I was clear that I didn't ever want to leave LA. I would resist in every way possible.

The other issue was more confusing: how Bob's unhappiness shut him down sexually. I usually didn't mind the lingerie display, and I often liked it, but pretending I was alone in the house while he watched from outside added a layer I didn't like. The raw fact of it was embarrassing, that he wanted it, that I often playacted to arouse him, and that his desire for me without the lingerie and the playacting had disappeared. I'd long ago given up the desire for oral sex from him and made my peace with using my vibrator with him, but taking care of myself alone felt excruciatingly lonely and seriously made me wonder whether I should stay in the marriage. After all, I was only forty years old, and I'd already proved to myself that I could still attract other men. Walking away from Bob would be hard, but it also held the hope of a better partnership with someone else.

There seemed to be no solution for my conundrum because there was no one else like Bob for me. I knew every relationship had its shortcomings, and I could trade in Bob for another man who was a great bed partner, but there would, of course, be something else I didn't like. Rachelle suggested I have a consultation about the sex with her analyst—a woman analyst for a change. She had a lot of respect for Dr. Hilda, and I had a lot of respect for Rachelle.

As I walked up the path to Dr. Hilda's private consulting room, I was hopeful that maybe she could help me figure out how to fix the sexual issues in my marriage. Her office was in a modest residential area of Santa Monica, in a converted garage behind her house. It was quiet, carpeted inside, and homey with giant ferns and soft lamp light.

I settled on a ladder-back chair beside Dr. Hilda's desk, and she sat in her rolling desk chair, obviously not the analytic chair next to the sofa nearby. I only had this one hour reserved with her for a consultation.

I poured it out quickly: how much I loved Bob, how he stubbornly continued to ask for lingerie and peeking at me and sexual distance, and how I didn't like that. I told her I had agreed to give up oral sex from him, but it was another disappointment. I, too, had a sexual problem of inhibition sometimes, and with all my years of analysis, I had not been able to overcome it.

"I want a more normal, loving sex life," I said. "Do you think treatment might help us?"

Dr. Hilda's hair was a soft, wavy gray, short to her head, her blue eyes were faded but clear. She fixed me with those eyes and said, "Your husband has fetishes, and the research I've read and clinical experience I've had indicate fetishes are extremely hard to change. I don't think sex therapy or couples therapy will help you in that regard. This is something you either live with or leave." She paused. Then, "Regarding treatment addressing your inhibitions, you've already seen how variable that can be.

122   staying married is the hardest part

I'm not sure more analysis would help. If Bob was willing to go through a course of sex therapy with you, both of you might overcome your inhibitions with the practical techniques they use."

I looked around her peaceful consulting room and wanted to smash every last carefully chosen object in it. Bob didn't want to go to sex therapy. What was the point of my going alone?

My anger and frustration settled into a resigned disappointment. At the end of our session, I said, "Okay. Thanks for your time."

I walked out of her property over the same path I'd been an hour earlier, only this time with little hope. Okay, fetishes wouldn't change. And my wearing lingerie for Bob was pretty okay for me. It was his pressure for me to role-play that was worse. I didn't like indulging his desire for peeking. Sometimes, it was brief, and the sex afterward was good, so I was willing to put up with it. Other times, I hated it. I decided I'd refuse when I wasn't up for it.

CHAPTER 10

Killing Each Other

In my new psychology practice, I saw some psychotherapy patients, but most of my freelance work was doing diagnostics and reports for lawyers, and some I met in person. My playful, seductive side resurfaced. *Why am I doing this?* I asked myself. *I wouldn't tell a patient to have affairs to fix a marital problem! I'd tell her it's no solution at all!* But I kept doing it—out of anger, out of wanting affirmation, out of hopelessness that Bob could change. I can look back on that now and compare it to the many patients I've seen who compulsively make self-destructive choices because they can't give up the temporary soothing, the next drink, the next bag of potato chips, the next shopping spree. I get it, me with all the training, compulsively indulging in infidelity rather than actively changing.

The first lawyer was very guarded. Originally from a Middle Eastern country, the way he ran his manicured brown fingers through his short, straight hair was very sexy. The few times I went to his office, he took me to the Bistro Garden, a high-class restaurant where they knew him. One time, after gin and tonics, playful conversation, and an invite to come back to his office, I came home with rug burns on my knees that Bob

124   staying married is the hardest part

never noticed. What he did notice was the peach straight skirt I was wearing with a low-cut ruffled blouse. Within minutes of me being home I was on all fours again, on our bed, enjoying my husband.

The second lawyer was a bad boy who drove a car with darkened windows so he could toke up on the freeway. He felt dangerous—a guy with a professional cover over wildness—but he had burning, translucent blue eyes and an insatiable appetite for sex. His fragrance engulfed me, a mix of baby powder and sweet hair gel that I had to soap away before Bob got home.

Our marriage had become a house of cards. I saw other men, and we had bought three houses, all held up by Bob's big TV income, but Bob hated TV more than ever. He burned to transition to writing and producing movies.

One day, Bob came home early. In a bitter fight with the network that was airing the show he hated, he had quit his job—told a network executive to go fuck himself—and then walked off the studio lot and said he was done. Rick was forced to finish that series alone. At the time, I wasn't worried about the money. Bob was done with TV, but he was so talented that I was sure he'd create something better. The fact that he couldn't contain his temper and be diplomatic was more concerning to me. He and Rick split up their partnership, too.

We suddenly had almost no income.

I began scrambling. Bob was the creative one, but I was the practical one with the business sense. In five weeks, I sold our Palisades house, and we made a small profit on it. I found a large, airy Brentwood apartment on Gretna Green Avenue, and we pared down and moved. Then Bob pitched movie ideas almost every day while I marketed myself more as a forensic expert. Movies were what he'd always wanted to do. Now, he had his chance.

The second script he completed on his own was *Dogfight*, which wove together an unusual love story with the account of four guys who were a tight group during their first year as Marines in the early Vietnam era. The characters were based on young Bob and his Marine Corps buddies. The female lead was partially based on a young version of me. One of my favorite moments is when the male and female lead are in her darkened bedroom kissing, and a buzzing fly aggravates them. He offers to kill it. She turns on the light in her closet, and when the insect flies in, she quickly shuts the closet door. He says, "That was neat, Rose. I'da just killed the sonofabitch." She says, "That's the difference between us. You're trained to kill; I'm trained to lock stuff up in the closet."

In January 1986, Bob's *Dogfight* script made the rounds in Hollywood and people loved it. At that time, no company bought the script, but its quality resulted in new offers for Bob to write. One was a proposed movie for Johnny Rivers, a popular singer of that time, and the setting was a small town where the last drive-in movie theater was going to be torn down. It was a perfect premise for Bob and he was thankfully hired to write it.

While I was trying to make enough to keep up with our bills, Bob worked on his script and met with Johnny Rivers and Gary Hendler, the TriStar producer who had hired him. The movie embodied Bob's unique voice, and I was hopeful it would be made, but for one reason or another, the movie was never made. Gary Hendler died. Johnny Rivers continued to perform and write music, but the script still lies dormant and, according to Bob's agent, is now owned by Berry Gordy. Bob's

126   staying married is the hardest part

script will probably go into yet another estate of a deceased executive.

In May 1986, my dad died of a final stroke, and I flew to Winnipeg for the funeral. I stood in the side chapel of the synagogue with Min and my sisters as the rabbi pinned to each of our lapels a black ribbon with a cut in it to signify that our hearts were broken. I wore my dad's cuff links with his initials scrolled in them, and I kept my arm around Min, who was thin and sad. His long, lingering illness had worn her out, and I knew his death was both a relief and the final loss. We clung to her and each other, and I took home with me a few precious things of his that Min gave me: his royal blue velvet case holding his two white satin yarmulkes, a photo of him in his handsome young days as an attorney, and some large format records of speeches he'd made when he was a city alderman. I had the recordings transferred to CDs and gave them to Min and my sisters. I still wear his cuff links and remember with gratitude his kindness and his teachings about birds and plants. Occasionally, in the Portland spring, I hear the distinctive honking of a migrating flock of Canada Geese overhead, and I whisper to the sky, "Hi, Dad."

On a bright blue LA afternoon that June, Bob came home early from his pitch meetings. His white T-shirt had a spaghetti sauce stain, and his open plaid shirt looked tired. In the bedroom, we hugged. I had just gotten home from work myself and was still in my business clothes. Sun played on the beige walls as I stood facing him in my red pencil skirt and high-heeled shoes. He sat on the bottom edge of our bed, his jeaned legs open in that sexy way I loved. And for some reason, he looked up and said, "So, have you ever fooled around?"

My mouth went dry. I didn't know where to look.

"C'mere," he said.

Heart thumping like a race car engine, I stepped between his legs, and he slid his hand up my skirt. "C'mon," he said. "Tell me."

The faint smell of Old Spice deodorant was pleasantly familiar, but my mouth was now so dry I could hardly open it. A strand of my hair caught in my mouth, and I pushed it away. Yes, he had told me to do it, but I had a lot to hide. I pulled away and walked to the window as if there was something important I needed to see outside.

"I promise I won't be mad," he said.

"I don't believe you," I said, still looking out the window.

"So you have, then."

I stood by the window, watching the eucalyptus leaves sway above the mottled bark, the strips of it hanging off the trunk in long curls.

"Honest, I won't be mad."

I stepped toward him to study his face. His eyes were steadfast and clear.

"I promise I won't be mad," he said. "After all, I told you to do it." He stretched out on the bed, arms behind his head. "Bon, I promise. Really. Tell me."

My breathing sounded loud and labored. I stood at the foot of the bed and stared at the carpet. "Yes, I fooled around."

Bob patted the spot next to him on the bed. "C'mere. Tell me every detail."

His face was eager, eyes bright, and no sign of anger, but five years in my sexual world was a long time. I tossed off my

128   staying married is the hardest part

heels and crawled up beside him. I didn't say I'd thought of leaving him; I didn't say I was fed up with being sexually distanced and I wanted a full marriage. I was so guilt-ridden and scared that it didn't occur to me to ask why he had raised the issue now.

Instead, I began regaling him with my sexual adventures.

As I lay next to Bob, telling him the details, he stroked my arm, his face flushed. "Bonnie, Bonnie, Bonnie," he said. There was a smile on his face, an affectionate tone, a headshake that told me he was enjoying all of it, truly not mad, admiring me even. I was shocked by this generous-hearted, smiling reaction. "I knew you were a bad girl," he said. "But I had no idea!" His pink cheeks scrunched high in a smile as he chuckled.

I chuckled, too, but it was not with the same pleasure. If he'd been looking, he might have noticed my absence. If he'd cuddled up to me more often, he might have smelled the lingering scent of another man. If he'd listened to the countless times I'd told him I wanted sex with him and done his best to meet me halfway, I wouldn't have done any of this, but his attention had been on his career and having laughs to keep from wanting to kill network and studio executives who fought him or didn't buy his achingly lovely and heartfelt scripts.

As we lay side by side, Bob wanted every detail and couldn't get enough. It turned him on, he said, and we had sex that afternoon, and for the first time, he said to me, "Okay, I want you to stop that now. I want to be your lover. I'll do what you like."

We had a hot time that afternoon. It was everything I had missed from him, but sadly, it didn't last.

At first, I was relieved to tell Bob the truth. I was tired of leading a double life, and I'd never really relaxed sexually with any of those men. My private experience had been hollow and sad. The deep internal split between my shy sexual self and the brash, brazen seductress was acted out over and over. I told Bob this, but truly, it was the brazen aspect of me he wanted; he was turned on by the fantasy me, not the real shy me.

Nagging and pressuring began in earnest from Bob now in a way it never had before. Whereas he'd been content to take photos of me or watch me undress, now he became obsessed with witnessing other men seeing me, or us having a threesome, or me displaying myself in public to other men in his presence. There was a crassness to his language that hadn't been there before, a harder edge to his requests. "Let me watch you. Bend over and show him your tits. Let's do it in the window so the gardener can see." Something about another man seeing "what was his" made him proud and triumphant. He wanted it desperately, and I didn't want to do it at all.

I had put new gears in motion by telling him about my affairs, and I had no idea that the telling would result in his developing a massive obsession to witness me with other men. If we needed to pull into a gas station, he now chose the "full service" option so the attendant would wash the windshield and Bob could get me to spread my legs so the guy could see up my skirt. It wasn't that big a thing to do, so I did it to please him. His requests escalated.

Every time we were on a road trip, Bob made sure to drive in the middle lane of the freeway so a trucker in the right lane could come up parallel to us. Then he'd say, "C'mon, show him your panties. Undo your top so he can see." Sometimes, I complied because I'd see the ruddiness blooming on his cheeks and the

130   staying married is the hardest part

bulge in his pants, and I felt that old Elizabeth Taylor moment of sexual power. Other times, I said no, sullen and quiet, and we'd drive in silence for a while, both of us resentful. That's when my mantra played in my head: *you've got your license, now work harder*, because that made the option of leaving him viable.

I could have fought him and consistently refused his demands, but I feared that would bring alienation, anger, frustration, and distance. As the saying goes, I had done him wrong, and that compromised my position. I was guilty. I had also degraded myself in the process of taking his suggestion and having affairs because I wasn't in love with those other men or getting the sexual satisfaction I was supposedly seeking. It felt like we each had a terrible personality flaw, me in my way just as fucked up as he was in his.

To complicate things even more, the fact was that when we weren't fighting over his sexual demands, I was happy in his presence. I always loved Bob's company. He was still the most interesting person I'd ever known.

Here's what you get in a marriage: a whole package, some of which is great and some of which is terrible, and if the great outweighs the terrible, you stay.

The following April, we stopped for the night at Morro Bay, a little ocean-side town in mid-California. Morro Bay's outstanding visual is a huge sea stack near the shoreline with a commercial fishing wharf. The sky partially cleared as we parked and sauntered down to the dock to watch the boats unloading their day's take. Seagulls flew around the fishing nets, yelling the news. Fishermen unloaded their catches, tourists watched the process, and workers washed down the boats and the dock.

One fisherman was interesting in his knee-high rubber boots, tanned face and hands, and hair trained straight up from his head. Fish blood streaked his yellow slicker. We joined other onlookers watching him work. Bob dipped his head down to my ear and whispered, "Undo your top two buttons and go ask him a question."

I clenched my teeth, instantly pissed off. I was sick of this activity and how it embarrassed me. My tennis shoe toe dug into a gap in the floorboards, and I shook my head no.

"*C'mon!*" he whispered in my ear.

My whole face felt like it was shutting tight. I shook my head again.

"Go ahead. He'll like it! It's a reward for all the work he did today!"

Not only did I shake my head again, but I backed away from the group and stood about six feet behind everyone else. In a minute, Bob turned around, looked at me, and walked right past me as he said, "Let's go."

We drove through town. Neither of us spoke. He pulled into the entryway of a pale blue motel, and I went in to arrange for a room. In silence, we drove around to the back and brought in our things. It was a typical motel Bob liked and I tolerated: a thin, paper-wrapped bar of soap in the bathroom; small, rough towels that smelled of disinfectant, a flowered bedspread under a seascape print bolted to the wall. Outside, dusk was descending.

Bob stretched out on the bed, turned on the TV, and completely ignored me.

I couldn't stand the whole thing—the anger, the silent treatment, the earlier scene of pressuring me yet again. "I'm going for a walk," I said.

132   staying married is the hardest part

He didn't even look at me before I left.

I had no money, just the motel key. I wasn't hungry even though we'd skipped dinner.

I started walking around the huge block that surrounded the motel. It got dark, and because it wasn't a familiar town, I kept walking around the same block over and over. Tears dripped down my face. *I have to leave him. I can support myself now. He's never going to give up this crap.* I kept walking, walking, walking. *How can a psychologist who knows so much about fixing relationships stay in one like this?*

The ocean air blew fog inland, and I started shivering in my thin rain jacket, but I walked till I was numb with cold. Walking, walking. It was long after dark now, and my hands were stiff. Defeated to have to return, I headed back to the motel room and entered quietly. The only light was the TV flickering on Bob's face, his face unsmiling, closed in a way it rarely was.

He's not going to change. What's wrong with me?

I took off my clothes and got into bed. He opened his arms, and I scooted up to him. We didn't talk. The relief of being close to him again warmed me. I turned on my side, facing away from him, and he shut off the TV and curled himself around me. All night, we cuddled up like that, turning over now and then and always spooning.

That summer, 1987, Bob was invited to the Sundance Institute, where his *Dogfight* screenplay was workshopped. It was a thrill for him to meet big-name actors and producers—Karl Malden, Sidney Pollack, Robert Redford—and watch scenes from *Dogfight* being acted out. He called, sounding so happy. The experience solidified his reputation as a new and exciting screenwriter. Afterward, fresh from the conference and newly bonded with Peter Newman—a warm and funny New York producer—they met at Warner Brothers with executives who bought the script and committed to making the film.

We were entering a new era in our lives. It was a huge leap forward for Bob to get a movie deal with a big commercial studio. Most writers work in obscurity and never have that happen. This was life-changing. No matter what happened after that, he'd be known as the writer of a motion picture produced by a major studio. It was his advance advertisement, his verified credibility in one of the most competitive businesses in the world.

Meanwhile, Bob had to keep slogging through TV jobs to pay our bills, because my income was still minimal. The worst blow was losing our Bandon house because we couldn't keep up the payments. After it was gone, we felt particularly sad whenever we talked about it.

I focused on Bob's suggestion that I write a novel. An idea had planted itself in my head and taken hold like a volunteer flower. I began to noodle around with writing, using my professional knowledge as a base. At first, I only had the kernel of a story—how an LA psychologist takes into treatment an attractive, obnoxious lawyer who develops a persistent sexual desire for her. The process of research alone made me fall in love with writing. I experienced firsthand what I'd only observed with Bob—studying something for the purpose of incorporating it into a character's life made the research very vivid and alive.

The following spring, 1988, I was in the bedroom of our Brentwood apartment, sitting at my big white desk, happily working on my manuscript, when the front door slammed,

134   staying married is the hardest part

and Bob walked into the bedroom holding his typical equipment—a yellow legal pad, a black roller ball pen, and some handwritten notes. He took off his baseball cap—a black corduroy with the Sundance logo—and laid it and his writing stuff on the bathroom counter. When he bent to kiss me, Old Spice mixed with faint pitch-meeting sweat hit me—a smell of him I loved.

"Come lie down with me," he said.

Mockingbirds shouted their songs outside the open screened window. A gentle breeze infused the air with the fragrance of eucalyptus from the tree outside. At that moment, a leaf blower started, the deafening sound of West LA on any weekday afternoon. I shut the window, then settled alongside Bob, my head resting on his chest, his left arm around me. My head fit perfectly in that spot because he was six foot one, and I was only five foot five.

"I gave them three movie ideas," he said. "*The Red Car, The Idiot Factor,* and *The Vivaldi Machine.*" These were his own "small" movies, requiring low budgets—no car chases or special effects, just complex characters coping with interesting events.

"Who did you meet with?"

"Michael London, Jerry Weintraub, and Amy Pascal at Columbia. I liked Amy. Smart."

These were names I would see for years, people who rose to prominence inside the business. Sony bought Columbia Pictures a year later, and Amy eventually became Chairman.

"So? What did they think?"

"Too farfetched . . . not enough conflict . . . tough casting."

I was not surprised. Bob's creative ideas were more like those of Mark Twain than Steven Spielberg. Bob's bookshelves were full of Twain, John Steinbeck, Kurt Vonnegut, J. P.

Wodehouse, and books about mythology, history, and physics. He struggled with an unresolvable contradiction: he wanted the money and power that came with big films, yet he wrote small, touching movies that rarely drew big profits. Exciting action, special effects, fear, and sex all sell, and selling is what the movie industry is about.

Still, the fact that Warner Brothers now had *Dogfight* in production was a huge triumph for him, a benchmark moment when a big studio had bought his touching small movie. This fact gave him a known name in Hollywood, and why these prominent executives had "taken meetings" with him to see what else he might pitch to them.

His voice was slightly hoarse. He'd been joking and pitching for hours.

"Did you have lunch?"

"Pink's," he said, one of his favorite LA haunts—the iconic hot dog stand with the red-striped awning on La Cienega Boulevard. He told me the moments in his meetings when he felt the wind go out of his sails: "Amy loved *The Red Car*, but she said she didn't know how to sell it. Michael London said he was excited about *The Idiot Factor* but said he didn't feel hopeful." Bob took his arm away from my shoulder and shifted toward me. "So, on the way home, I'm sitting outside at Pink's, and two guys at the next table are clinking cups because they've just sold a superhero movie, and I'm thinking, what the fuck am I doing here?"

The pattern of fine lines at the outer edges of his eyes attested to the thousands of hours he'd laughed, but he wasn't smiling right then. "I gotta talk to you," he said, and something about the way he said that gave me a queasy and tight feeling in the center of my chest.

136   staying married is the hardest part

I moved to sit cross-legged, facing him. Outside, the whine of the leaf blower ceased, and the room vibrated with silence. His big brown eyes looked directly into my face. "I have to leave LA," he said. "I mean, really leave. I love you. I want you to move to Ashland with me. But if you won't come, I have to leave anyway. If I stay here, it'll kill me."

I'd been in LA for twenty years now. I'd found my neighborhood, doctors, favorite haunts, and best friends. I belonged here. LA was who I was. And now I was looking into the face of my one and only, and he was asking me to walk away from what I'd so carefully and passionately created. And he meant it out of desperation, not out of lack of love for me.

My stomach felt as if I'd swallowed a ball of ice. I unfurled my legs and flopped back down, my eyes gazing at the stupid popcorn ceiling in this big, airy, beautiful LA apartment.

Our sexual fights paled in comparison to this.

He said staying in LA would kill him.

I felt leaving LA would kill me.

Married couples fight over multiple issues, but there's usually one thing that rankles more than others, something complex and not easily resolved. It might be a chronic fight over parenting or a sexual incompatibility. It might be a substance use issue or a long-standing feeling of being ignored or unheard. Whatever it is, both partners are entrenched in wanting what they want, and they fight for it either directly or indirectly with blame, criticism, or distancing. This is the "power struggle" in marriage, and things can get mean and ugly. Sometimes, couples come to see a marital therapist to get beyond their stalemate. Sometimes, the disappointment is too much, and they divorce.

In our case, our most thorny issue was where to live. As with other tough issues, this one carried the weight of childhood. Bob's fondest memories were of his boyhood years in Drumheller, a tiny town in the badlands of Alberta. He had romanticized his years there when he and his older brother roamed the area as mischievous boys having tremendous freedom and fun. I, on the other hand, hated small towns, and even Winnipeg, a city of 500,000, seemed painfully backward and small to me compared to LA and New York. We locked horns about other things, most importantly sex, but where to live was our most unresolvable issue.

A power struggle is normal in marriage. Working it out requires stepping outside your own view and trying hard to see the other's. Listening and hearing your partner's rationale can help you find a way through. That's not an easy task when there's a lot at stake. Some people spend a lifetime of marriage in the power struggle, bickering, dissatisfied but stuck.

I resisted. I struggled. I thought many times about leaving.

People often come to see me with a request for "tools" to cope with difficult emotions and conflicts. Well, "tools" for fixing oneself or one's marriage are complex and take a lot of practice. You each want what you want. You can't control each other. Only genuine acceptance and the willingness to compromise can get you beyond the power struggle. It helps to know that your version of reality is always a view through your own particular set of glasses. Empathy requires you to see through the other's lens. It's that which enables each of you to understand what the other needs and work to find compromises you can both live with.

Bob and I engaged in a power struggle that lasted years.

CHAPTER 11

Making a Leap

You think your life is about one thing, and then it's about something else. You're remodeling your kitchen when you discover your spouse is having an affair. You're training for a marathon when you find a lump in your breast. You're cutting coupons and living on canned beans when your invention sells, and you're suddenly rich. Life is like surfing: you can't anticipate every wave. Learning to keep your balance and stay on your board is a better strategy, but it's a tall order when what happens to you is nothing you'd order up for yourself. I loved Bob, and he loved me. And our dreams for the future were mutually exclusive.

Bob traded in his Chevy Blazer for a new Toyota Land Cruiser, a solid, masculine rig that perfectly suited him. He packed up most of his things and moved them to our Ashland house.

I wasn't willing to leave LA. Instead, I had some things shipped to Ashland and then found a one-bedroom apartment off Barrington in Brentwood. We agreed to try a hybrid life: me one week of the month in Ashland, him one week in LA, and us two weeks apart. Although we loved dogs, we'd been without one for two years and couldn't get another one, with neither of us living full-time in one place.

As Bob and I began living this peripatetic life, I was often crying in airports. We missed each other. Then we'd get used to the separation and have to adjust again to togetherness. During the first six months of this new lifestyle, I focused my practice on psych testing because it was time-flexible. I ended my relationship with my remaining therapy patients, sad that the kind of psychology work most meaningful to me was exactly what I was walking away from. However, I couldn't in good conscience continue treating those patients who needed to have a therapist consistently present and available to them.

My compensation for that loss turned out to be writing. My deepest thoughts emerged on the page, things I didn't even know I thought until I wrote them. It was an astonishing experience—how writing gave me another way of being me and discovering my philosophy and truth—and I let my imagination take me wherever it wanted. Sometimes, it took me to unusual places like Vietnam or a tropical restaurant with macaws in cages. I studied these things, the most haphazard of education, yet a great intellectual adventure.

My life alone in LA seemed like I'd gone back to being single, except I wasn't. I had no desire to seek attention from other men anymore. I had learned that I wasn't built for affairs or casual sex. Only a committed, long-term relationship gave me the emotional safety to function sexually at my best. And thankfully, Bob was pressuring me less to display myself. He was excited about *Dogfight* being made and busy with meetings and other offers.

140   staying married is the hardest part

One evening, two years into this lifestyle of living in two places, I arrived back from Ashland alone to find an invasion of cockroaches scurrying around in my dark LA kitchen. Horrified, I closed the light and got into bed shivering and hoping they wouldn't crawl all over me.

In the morning, I walked around this one-bedroom apartment with the jumble of leftover furniture from various stages of my life and thought, *no*. The sofa was Rachelle's old flowered one from her office; there was an antique sideboard I'd moved around for years. Polished acrylic wastebaskets from my office sat in the bathroom. My beloved wormwood inlaid table and ladder-back chairs from my old Barry Avenue apartment were in the dining room. Nothing matched. Nothing made sense anymore. Bob was gone to Oregon, and mostly, I was here alone.

In the kitchen, I listlessly opened the cupboards and drawers. The expensive Calphalon cookware we'd received for our wedding was now suspected of causing Alzheimer's or cancer, so I thought it best to throw it away. I'd sent my sterling silver to Ashland with my delicate cobalt and white china. Even when Bob was here, we weren't entertaining in this small apartment with no parking. Old dishes populated the cupboards, glasses from different sets, a sieve, and one measuring cup. In the bedroom, the blankets didn't match. When I was in Ashland for a few weeks, I'd return to find something wrong—the toilet water had turned rusty, or there was a highway of ants, or the bathroom towel rack had become unhinged. Now, the cockroaches.

I was clinging to LA like a hiker who's slipped down the side of a cliff and is hanging on with blanched fingers. Maybe living in Ashland would be okay? Maybe falling through space like that would land me safely somewhere else? After all, I'd be with Bob, and that would make me happy. Maybe one of his movies would hit, and we'd have so much money we'd buy a place here, and he wouldn't be so miserable in it because his career would finally become what he wanted. I could try living in Ashland and writing full-time. If I hated it, I could come back.

I peeled my fingers off that wall and let myself fall.

After I moved to Ashland, it seemed like we drove up and down that I-5 corridor a million times, a trunk full of stuffed carry-ons, books, writing notes, and hiking boots. I could tell where we were by the smells, the garlic fields, the sad fragrance of cow shit from the giant holding area of doomed cattle, sweet alfalfa fields, and the sharp, cool air near Mount Shasta. We were together. That was the best part.

My framed degrees and certificates went into the back of a bedroom closet in Ashland. I let go of my professional life in LA, but I made sure to pass the Oregon State Orals exam and get my Oregon psychology license. I had no sense of the future, nor did I want to set down roots in Ashland, but I needed my insurance policy so that if I ever wanted to practice in Oregon, I could. Meanwhile, I maintained my California psychology license.

I missed my friends terribly. Still, I started living a writer's life, sleeping in till 8:30, reading novels, going out to breakfast, and walking in the woods.

One Ashland friend became very precious to me. When Bob first arrived in Ashland in 1981, he met Steve, a respected entrepreneur in a town known by pretty much everyone. A

142   staying married is the hardest part

Jewish boy who'd escaped from New Jersey to reinvent himself in the Pacific Northwest, Steve was warm, funny, and smart. To me, he felt like home, and we both grew to love him.

Our sex life was better in Ashland. I attributed this to Bob's greater satisfaction with his career, now completely out of TV and exclusively writing movies, and also to this: Ashland is a casual, funky place. The women wore Birkenstock shoes, fleece jackets and pants, little makeup, and no one around us was dressing like Hollywood, including me. My high heels sat dormant. I wore hiking boots and L.L. Bean plaid flannel and would have looked out of place in anything fancy. It was a year of calm between us.

In the fall of 1990, we went up to Seattle to watch the filming of *Dogfight*. River Phoenix had been cast as the lead, supposedly a tough young US Marine, but it was obvious to anyone that it was miscasting. River was a slender, sensitive guy who didn't really fit the part. Bob was upset about it, but he couldn't change it because River was a known actor, and Warner Bros. insisted on that. The female lead chosen was Lili Taylor, a very fine actress but slender and fit, and the role called for an overweight young woman. Lili agreed to put on weight for the role, but after she put on ten pounds, she hated the idea of putting on any more, so the director let her stay at that weight and tried to pad the clothes to make Lili look larger. Bob was incredibly disappointed in this. He wanted to make a statement about how painful it is to be a fat girl and how love goes deeper than the shape of a body, but he lost that casting battle, too.

In Seattle, Bob was invited to watch the "dailies"—the day's footage—and Bob was dismayed to see the changes the

bonnie comfort   143

director was making in his script. He fought her over it to no avail. She had her own vision, and she had the ultimate say.

Warner Bros. released the movie in 1991 to good reviews and modest success. On a quiet LA weekday afternoon, while we were visiting, we went into a Westwood theater where the movie was playing and sat in the audience to watch it.

Bob was inconsolably depressed for about six months after that. His original script was somewhat altered, and he was pained by the new ending and the scenes that had been removed. Because it was his first major filmed motion picture, he had no prior experience to temper his disappointment. He may have known other disappointed writers, but this was new to him personally, and he had to face the fact that unless he reached the status of a hugely successful writer and director like Woody Allen or Quentin Tarantino, he'd never have the kind of complete creative control he'd like as a writer.

Yet, in retrospect, it was probably *Dogfight* that made his career. His name was well-known in the biz after that. He had much bigger directors and producers interested in his work. The film eventually became a cult classic. Still, his disappointment in the finished product was painful and somewhat ruined it for him. I was excited that it had been made at all—a huge milestone in his career—but his tendency to anxiety and depression couldn't be cured by what others would clearly have seen as a big success. It wasn't done *his* way.

One project of Bob's that pulled him out of his *Dogfight* disappointment was his original screenplay, *Friendly Voices*. Lauren Shuler Donner liked the idea well enough to hire Bob to write it as part of her development deal with Warner Bros., and the money it earned made him hopeful again. While I was

144   staying married is the hardest part

writing my novel, Bob banged away at *Friendly Voices*, pacing and reciting dialogue out loud, a half-dozen books on Native American lore lying on the sofa.

Happy in Ashland, and at his best with more career success, everything about Bob was boyishly charming. He cut eyeholes in a camouflage sheet and hung it over the sliding glass door to our balcony where our bird feeder was perched so he could closely watch yellow grosbeaks, blue scrub jays, red-streaked finches, and alongside them, gray squirrels with their almond eyes and lush, fluffy tails. In between long sits at his typewriter, Bob snuck around corners, teasing me, and sang aloud to Nancy Griffith, tears sometimes spilling down his cheeks at her longing voice. He played tennis and went fishing, a tall boy standing on the riverbank for a half hour with a fly rod looking for a bite. He wanted clown shoes and ordered himself a custom pair.

I took over one of the two spare bedrooms as my writing room. My desk was covered with stacks of paper and floppy disks, and the bed was strewn with half-finished novels and how-to writing books. I was teaching myself a new profession.

There was frost on our lawn in the mornings and sometimes snow and ice in the winter months. I hated the cold. Summer was boiling hot in the afternoon: iced tea, air conditioning, hunkering down by 2:00 p.m. My lovely, moist ocean air was gone, and my hair collapsed in the dry atmosphere. But spring and fall were perfect, and I was writing, writing, writing, and loving it.

I joined a small group of other women writers, one of whom became a National Book Award finalist, and I learned a lot from them while sharing our pages, eating their spectacular homegrown strawberries, and drinking their herbal teas.

bonnie comfort   145

One morning, I told Bob I'd written our former basset hound, Frank, into my novel, but I would call him Harry. Bob said, "Why? You think you're going to ruin Frank's reputation?" The absurdity of that made me laugh, and so in my novel, Frank remained utterly himself, right down to his real name.

Although I never felt entirely at home in Ashland, those three years we spent together there were some of our happiest. Bob and Steve went fishing now and then. They went on a few road trips together. It was a period of amazing productivity for Bob, who churned out his own original screenplays as well as adaptations of novels and screenplays requested by producers or directors. I loved my own writing process, how it fully engaged me to the point that sometimes I'd wake up in the middle of the night with an idea, stumble to my computer, and type the whole thing with my eyes closed. In the morning I'd go in and read what I'd written and be amazed by it, almost as if it had been written by someone else.

I rolled around in Bob's love for life, his curiosity, his comfortable flannel shirts, and hilarious one-liners. There was simply no one I'd ever known who was as fun and profound at the same time. We played well sexually too most of the time, me loving him and how appealing I felt in his eyes. His pressure for me to flash myself in public receded as he became more content with his career.

One time at home we playacted an old fantasy of Bob's involving me washing him. Afterward, he came back from the bathroom and accidentally stepped into the bowl of soapy water sitting on the carpet. He hopped around with a wet foot, and we laughed and laughed.

However, he had not lost his biggest turn-on—seeing me in lingerie, heels, and scanty clothing—and often, I was happy

146   staying married is the hardest part

to do it because it was our form of foreplay, but other times, I'd tire of the dress-up, and the pressure to go beyond what I happily saw as sex play.

When we went to LA, there was a lot more anonymity and stress for him, and his pressure on me to flash underwear at strangers would ramp up. We usually stayed at the Hotel del Capri in Westwood. It was a modestly priced old-LA-style hotel, lush with foliage and circled around a central pool, and we both found it cozy and convenient, but on the interstate, he'd still pressure me to flash truck drivers, and I'd get fed up and resentful and refuse, and we'd have to recover.

Bob was hired over and over for various projects, and money poured in. He also wrote another original screenplay of his own, *The Ox and the Eye*, which was set in Oregon. A small production company bought the rights to that movie and committed to making it. They changed the name to *Good Luck* which Bob hated, but they signed Gregory Hines and Vincent D'Onofrio to star in it so Bob was hopeful.

Penny Marshall acquired the US rights to the award-winning Italian film, *Cinema Paradiso*, which we both loved. In 1992, Bob met with her and agreed to do an adaptation of that screenplay for American audiences. It was a perfect film for him to adapt, and the result, titled *The Dreamland*, kept the spirit of the original but had an American twist and sensibility that worked beautifully. It was everything of Bob at his best.

A few months later, Penny asked Bob to write a screenplay for Jack Nicholson based on his teenage experience as a lifeguard at the Jersey shore. Bob met with Penny and pitched his idea of how to do it, and she was happy with it. He poured his heart into the lifeguard movie, studying mythology, Jungian therapy, and New Jersey.

For writing breaks, we often went to the Oregon beaches for a few nights, and Bob collected rocks and shells as if they could anchor him to something more solid than his career and the unpredictability of show business. He'd walked away from a terrible God at the age of thirteen, but it had left a longing in him for the ocean, the vast universe, and his version of something out there.

Once a year in summer, I went to Winnipeg for a week. During one visit, Brenlee and Nate picked me up to drive to a family dinner. I was in the back seat listening as she told him I was writing a novel, and as if I wasn't even in the car, Nate turned to Bren and said, "If she sells that novel, I'll kiss your ass on the corner of Portage and Main."

I said nothing. Brenlee said nothing. Two daughters of Min's, accomplished and respected by others, were unable to talk back to such a demeaning comment. I was instantly eighteen again, sitting at Min's dining table, watching her cater to Nate and laugh at his jokes while I became invisible. Later, I thought about how Min's grooming us to defer to men played into the difficulty I had in being more sharply confrontational with both Nate and Bob.

It was a relief to be back in Ashland after that trip. Bob took me to the Jackson County Fair, where we looked at the pigs and goats and rabbits. We ate cotton candy and hot dogs with mustard dripping on our fingers. We played bingo with ladies who seemed old at fifty with their tired hands and frumpy house dresses. I was an exotic flower in my short skirt and blouse open an extra button. Bob's stream of observations made me laugh so much that my stomach muscles hurt.

Sometimes, Bob licked right in the center of my glasses, so I looked out through saliva and had to take the glasses off and

148   staying married is the hardest part

clean them. It always made me laugh at the outrageousness of it. Sometimes he told me to leave my glasses on while we did it, his librarian fantasy.

His mind was my adventure. Once, he said, "I think birds give me ideas. When one flies close to my head, it might spark a tiny electrical thing in my brain."

"Really?"

"Why not? Our brain's full of electrical activity."

One Saturday evening in Ashland, we had a "tool party" because Bob loved hardware stores and tools. He told everyone to bring the most unusual tool they owned, and weird things showed up: spindles for turning wool, a knob from an old juicer, a strange apple peeler, and a giant metal nut. Our friend Steve brought a long, skinny metal tool with a little claw at the end like fingers. "What the hell is that?" we all asked. "It's a grabber," he said. And we could then see it. To pick up tiny things that have fallen out of reach.

At Halloween, Bob bought a basketful of fake noses on rubber bands and took the whole lot to his weekly poker game, where he had each player pick a nose for a portrait. At 2:00 a.m. Bob crawled into bed, drunk on beer, and said, "It was the most amazing thing how each guy picked a nose that went exactly with his personality!" I giggled and cuddled with him, thinking there was no one else like him. By Christmas, he'd made 12 x 16 prints of these portraits of each guy in a mat frame and gave each one his own portrait.

Bob was terrified of flying, but he took me to places with his ideas I could never have found on my own. It was all of this that kept me wedded to him, this adventure of ideas and stories and humor that spun like sugar from his lips. I'd always had a sweet tooth.

bonnie comfort   149

After I moved to Ashland, I made sure we went to LA during the winter weeks when Min was there. I took her out to fancy lunches, proud I could do it, proud this was still my LA where I knew so many people. Her shoulders and back were painful, so I took her to the best orthopedist. I took her to my dentist and paid for the work. Her disappointment over my dad's late-life mismanagement of their money had distilled into a bitter stew of regret and resentment.

In her late teens, she'd had many suitors, but when she was twenty-two and working as a waitress in a diner, her fiancé had broken off their engagement, and to recover, she'd taken a summer trip to Winnipeg to see where she was born and stay with relatives. There, she met my dad, a man fourteen years her senior with a thriving law practice. He was smitten. She was unsure. After she returned to LA, he wrote long, eloquent letters to her every day while she went back to slinging hash. In 1933, a twenty-three-year-old woman was considered past her marriage prime. With only a high school education, Min's future hung securely on whom she married, and at that point, my father was her best choice.

In August 1934, she married him, left her family, and began her life in Winnipeg, unaware of how cold it would get, unaware of how much she would miss her mother and the avocado and fig trees in their yard. For years, she cajoled and argued and tried to convince my dad to move to LA with her and join her brother Joe's practice, but she lost the arguments.

Now, late in her life, when she had expected to be at least financially comfortable, my dad's judgment had become impaired, and without any of us realizing it, he had trusted a conniving colleague with most of his money and it had been squandered. This was a terrible blow to Min and it was shocking

150   staying married is the hardest part

to hear her talking about buying day-old bread when she had always prided herself on shopping at the best grocery stores.

I loved her. I felt bad for her. When I offered my suggestions for how she might feel better, they were soundly rejected. And I felt invisible to her as a person again. I served her while we were together and was always depleted and tired afterward.

Her misery was oppressive, but I didn't have enough money to ease her disappointment, which seemed to be the only thing that might have helped.

In April 1992, I finished my novel. I sent it to Bob's agent who passed it along to a New York agent. The guy, Tony, sounded warm and knowledgeable, and after reading it suggested I work with a freelance editor to improve it. Three full revisions and nine months later, Tony said, "I think now I can sell it. But I'll have to wait till September. No one reads in the summer."

I waited.

In the third week of October 1993, Bob and I headed down to LA once again. He had turned in *The Dreamland* and *The Boys From Neptune* to Penny Marshall and needed to meet with her.

We checked into the Beverly Ritz Hotel on Wilshire. All was well.

Part II

CHAPTER 12

A Strange Confluence of Events

New cashmere sweaters and velvet skirts were piled on the upholstered chair next to the sofa. Shopping bags from Bloomingdale's and Ann Taylor lay propped against the living room wall of our hotel suite. I'd been giving Bob a fashion show of my morning's purchases. Next, I pulled on a pair of glove-soft Donald Pliner high heels, to which he said, "Perfect for walking from the bed to the bathroom and back!" I laughed at this pleasure of his, then rooted through the bags until I found what I knew he'd love the most—a white angora sweater with a deep V-neck. I put it on over a plaid pencil skirt, then pranced up to him to step between his legs.

His brown eyes were soft, and his eyebrows gave a quick rise up and down. He ran his warm hand up my thigh to the panty line. "Great legs," he said, and that familiar flush spread across his cheeks. I warmed to his pleasure. I loved enticing him.

In spite of our painful conflicts, we still told each other everything. We still slept curled around each other. One Valentine's Day, early in our marriage, he had brought home

154   staying married is the hardest part

a small box for me. Inside I had found two little sculpted mice lying together in a bed of cotton and a small card on which he had written this:

> When you turn over
> I turn over.
> When I turn over
> You turn over.
> If neither of us turns over
> Neither one of us turns over.

The phone rang, and it was Rick. Although Rick had stayed in TV and Bob had immersed himself in writing movies, they were still best friends. I sat down at the dining table, a glass-topped maple with curvy upholstered chairs, and I started reading about earthquake preparedness in the *LA Times*. The fragrance of Asiatic lilies perfumed the air, a lovely touch the hotel provided in cloisonné vases.

Bob and Rick talked for a half hour, and Bob stood and started pacing as he often did while exchanging jokes, holding the phone base in one hand and the receiver in the other. He was in his jeans and socks, a white T-shirt pooled around his hips, a gravy spot in the center at chest height. "That's right!" he said and burst into his staccato laugh. Even while hearing only one side of the jokes, I smiled because his laugh was so infectious.

I returned to my reading. "Do an inventory of your house," the article said. "Identify potential hazards that can fall. Don't hang anything but fabric above your bed." I had lived through the 1971 earthquake when the hospital in which I worked fell, and I could have been killed. Still, I loved LA. I could have written that Randy Newman song.

"I love ya!" Bob said and hung up the phone. Immediately, I looked up from my paper.

"Rick told me about a terrorist who sent out a letter bomb in the mail, but he didn't put enough postage on it, so it came back 'return to sender.' The guy was so happy to get some mail that he opened the letter and blew himself up." Bob shook his head in marvel. "Aaahh, I love a stupid death." He wandered over to the window that faced the inner walkways in this hotel that was once an apartment building. He pulled back the curtain, and the LA light poured in, the tall Queen Anne palms visible beyond the hotel. A loud splash from the courtyard sounded as someone jumped in the pool. Maybe we'd go for a swim later.

The phone rang again. "Hallo," Bob said, his voice going up at the end in his clipped Canadian accent. Then, "Oh hi," in his voice for people he didn't know well.

Then Bob went quiet.

I was at the point in the article where it said, "Create a disaster supply kit—water, food, and basic items for seventy-two hours. Keep it where you spend most of your time."

I looked up in time to see Bob sit down hard on the sofa, still holding the phone to his ear. His shoulders suddenly rounded inward. "What do you mean?" he said. "What?" as if he suddenly couldn't hear. The long phone cord lay lifeless on the cushy carpet. "Okay, okay," he said. "Where?" He covered the receiver and said, "Quick, I need a pen and paper!"

I stood up so fast that my chair almost tipped over. I stepped immediately to the desk, where a hotel pen and writing pad lay in wait. I offered these to him, standing over him, but his body had crumpled forward in the strangest way. His hand shook while he wrote an address.

"Can you tell Bonnie?" he said.

156   staying married is the hardest part

Fear sweat wafted up from his armpit as he held the phone
out to me. His face had gone slack, his eyes rounded. I took
the phone. It was Dr. Agre, our Beverly Hills internist. "Hi,
Bonnie," he said, and I noticed how very familiar his crisp
tone was. "I saw something on Bob's lung X-ray. If I didn't take
X-rays yearly, I'd think it was nothing."

I wrote down tomorrow morning at 10:00 a.m. That
meant we had no time to lose. After I hung up, I sat down so
my thigh was touching Bob's, and I put my arms around his
chest.

"How many times have I joked about getting weird can-
cers?" he said. "Cancer of the elbow. Cancer of the heart. Now,
here it is."

There's before you get a phone call like that, and after. The
light in the room seemed strangely pale now. The Asiatic lilies
too fragrant, like rotting fruit.

"Maybe it's something easy," I said.

Now, he disentangled himself from me, stood, and said,
"Let's go lie down." Of course, I followed him immediately,
wanting to do anything that would be comforting to him,
but when we got to the bedroom entrance, he saw something
from our second-story bedroom window that made him stop.
I stood next to him. Now I saw what he was looking at: a man
in a safety belt, poised in the sycamore tree outside just at the
height of our window. He was sawing away at small branches
and letting them fall.

"Bon!" Bob said. "Take off your bra and go stand in the
window!"

"What?" I said. "Now?" I looked at him sideways. "You've
got to be kidding."

"No!" he said. "It'll help me! Honest! Please do it!"

I couldn't believe that, at this moment, he wanted me to tease and expose myself to another man. It was crazy. I stood rooted to the spot, frozen.

"C'mon. It'll make me feel better, honest."

This was the last thing I wanted to do. I was scared, too. But a helplessness came over me. How could I refuse him at this moment when he'd just learned he might have a terrible diagnosis? Surely, I could do this for him right now if it helped him cope, even though I had to go somewhere else in my head to act out a sexual tease that felt so alien to me.

I stood by the bed, slowly removed the angora sweater, and threw it on the bed. My white lace bra came off next, and my breasts fell against my chest, warm and soft.

"C'mon," he said as I stood there, stricken by the desire to do anything to make him feel better while hating how that particular set of actions made me feel.

I snapped into performance mode. Naked from the waist up, I went to the window in our bedroom and gazed at the man in the tree. The man held his power tool idle while he looked at me and smiled back. I smiled and touched my breasts.

Bob came up behind me, sweaty, his breath quick, and he cupped my breasts from behind while the man in the tree watched.

I was caught in the net like I always was at these moments with my husband—a fish struggling to breathe.

The next morning, we were at Tower Imaging for the CT scan. I held Bob's cold, clammy hand until they took him in. My own stomach was tight, not knowing what they'd find. Later, the doctor called to say there was a tumor the size of a thumbnail wrapped around Bob's aorta. "I'm going to send you to Dr. R, an excellent oncologist," he said.

158   staying married is the hardest part

Dr. R had a solo practice in Beverly Hills. His office was dark, and his receptionist curt. The man was manicured, his graying hair perfectly cut, and his suit had the quiet sheen of money. "You have some kind of lymphoma," he said. "You could either have six months to live or a normal lifespan. We won't know until we biopsy the tumor."

He said this in a casual manner. He might be telling us what movies were playing at the nearby multiplex. The room swirled, and I tried looking at him through the dark air. "Did you say six months to live?" I asked in a small and quiet voice that sounded like a child's.

"Yes. Or a normal lifespan. If you want to speed up the diagnostic process, you can hand-carry the films to Brotman Memorial Hospital. I want you to get the biopsy there."

The endless chauffeuring I did that year began—from hotel to hospital to another hospital to doctors' offices to our apartment. For eight months, Bob was so anxious that he couldn't drive, and I couldn't get to these places fast enough, as if speed cured.

I stayed with Bob in the pre-op area of Brotman Memorial until they wheeled him away for the surgical biopsy to be done by slamming a large bore needle through his chest wall. Sick with worry, I retreated to the empty surgery waiting room. From the waiting room phone, I called our home voicemail, and there was a message from Tony, my New York agent. "Call me," was all he said. I called immediately, and he said, "We have three offers on your book. I think we should take the one from Simon & Schuster, but I'll give you time to think about it."

I shuffled back a step, my mouth open, while he explained the details. After I hung up, I flopped down on the green plastic seat behind me, imagining the possibilities. The room had a

bonnie comfort 159

faint smell of disinfectant and stale coffee from a carafe sitting on a warming plate. The overhead fluorescent light flickered. How could such a confluence of events occur? My husband might die, and my novel was going to sell? I didn't know whether to laugh or cry.

The instant a nurse came to the door and led me to Bob in the recovery room, I tucked away my news and focused on him. He lay on a gurney, dopey from the anesthetic, his hair rumpled and cute. I took his hand and held it, but as he lay there, his hand got sweaty, and he said, "I can't breathe." I assumed it was his panic as usual, but I immediately told the doctor, who assessed Bob and said, "His lung's been punctured. We've got to get a chest tube in him."

So began the endless number of painful procedures Bob had to endure. I stepped away as they pulled the curtain around him. Every minute was long. When they pushed back the curtain, he had a quarter-inch rubber tube protruding from his chest, but he was breathing easier. I stroked his forehead and took his hand. His eyes filled with tears, and he wrinkled his nose, trying to control the tears. "You know I really love life," he said, and I nodded, thinking that for no one was that truer—Bob of the silly antics, the jokes, the games, the parties he threw, the people he regaled with funny one-liners. "I'm not a bad person, am I?"

"Of course not." I squeezed his hand. *But why would you even think that?*

Bob had to stay in the hospital overnight, and I sat next to him in a chair. In the morning, Dr. R came in all bristly and cheerful. Bob lay in bed, feet flat on the mattress, and knees up. "Good news!" the doctor said. "I can cure you!" He pounded his fist on one of Bob's blanketed knees. "You have a good kind

160   staying married is the hardest part

of lymphoma! We'll have to snow you with chemo to get rid of it, but we can do it!"

The relief of an optimistic prognosis was dampened by the word "snow," but for the moment, I didn't mind that doctor's peacock walk and impeccable suit and tie. Bob was only fifty-three, and I was forty-eight, and we both desperately wanted him to survive.

Chemo and radiation would take almost a whole year, so we needed a place to live. While Bob was pacing around our hotel suite in a panic, I found a short-term rental near Cedars—a spacious ground-floor apartment with a patio that looked out on a golf course. It was on Pico Boulevard, just south of the Santa Monica Freeway, and only a ten-minute drive to all the doctors' offices and hospitals we would need. I rented living room furniture but bought a king-size bed, small kitchen appliances, bedding, a TV, and a stereo system. Money was hemorrhaging from our bank account but I didn't care. We essentially had a home again in LA, which I had created in one week to Bob's amazement.

Meanwhile, I had several conversations with my agent about the book offers and decided to go with Simon & Schuster. It was thrilling to sign that deal just for the affirmation of my work. My agent said he'd now turn his attention to looking for a paperback deal and foreign rights. I had to choose a final title for the novel, and when I ran the choices by the Simon & Schuster editor, she liked *Denial* because it had multiple meanings. Denial is the name of a psychological process we all engage in some of the time: not admitting to ourselves the truth, and not realizing it at the time. Denial also had a legal meaning: my character had to defend herself in court. So, *Denial* became my title.

My attention was barely on my novel, though. What felt real was that Bob had a life-threatening illness. We called our closest friends and family to tell them about Bob's cancer. Cards and gifts poured in. My favorite was from Chris and Joyce Cluess, our Thanksgiving family. They sent a gorgeous potted Boston fern which arrived at our door with a card that said, "Bob, you asshole!" We loved this card, which was meant in the best possible way.

While Bob was out, walking around the block, coping with panic about his impending cancer treatment, I called Min. I lay on the couch in our newly rented apartment and burst into tears when I heard her voice.

After she listened to it all, she said, "Honey, he's going to be okay."

My tears slowed to a drip. "You think so?" I asked.

"Yes, I do. He's going to get through his treatment, and things will be all right."

I wrapped her words around me like a warm, comforting blanket. Her voice gave me the old feeling of being held gently, of the whole world being right because she had me safe in her arms. *He was going to be okay. She had said so.*

After that I called our friend Steve in Ashland and asked him if he might be able to drive down to see us and bring me my computer. Of course he dropped everything to drive down. His brief visit was balm for the soul for both of us.

I bought an answering machine and learned quickly to put a daily report on my outgoing message. Friends and family wanted to be kept up to date, but it was enough to have lived through it without having to repeat it ten times a day.

There was no Thanksgiving that year. Just waiting to see how he reacted to the chemo.

162   staying married is the hardest part

The first week went better than expected. His being able to tolerate the chemo made his prognosis good. However, his oncologist and staff were lacking the essential empathy we both needed. After calling around, I switched Bob's care to a wonderful oncology group at Cedars.

Bob's worst problem was panic, which sapped whatever quality time he had and ruined it. He clutched the arms of his chair. He hyperventilated. He couldn't focus on any TV except *Wheel of Fortune*. After all, he'd had panic attacks long before he'd found out he had cancer. Now, the reality of death added to the old anxiety and made it overwhelming.

I arranged for Bob to see John Lundgren, MD, a psychiatrist I knew from the Brentwood VA. John was handsome, careful in his choice of words, and he had one of the most beautiful, deep, comforting voices I'd ever heard. I drove Bob there and picked him up after each session.

Broken as Bob was, with giant holes in his armor of arrogance and defiance, he really did settle into therapy. Dr. Lundgren prescribed an antidepressant and a minor tranquilizer, and within days, Bob was calmer. After his third session, I pulled up on the Beverly Hills corner outside Lundgren's office and saw Bob leaning against the building wall, his shoulders slumped, eyes downcast, looking sadder than I ever remembered, my boy-man broken by fear. He got in the car and said, "I spilled my guts today. I told him the sex stuff."

I glanced over at him, noticing his red-rimmed eyes and his blotchy cheeks. "What exactly did you tell him?"

He wiped his hand across his forehead. "About my lingerie thing. And peeking. And how I've pressured you to expose yourself. I feel so bad about it now—I guess I just didn't wanna let myself know it."

I glanced at him as I turned and headed south on Rodeo Drive. His cheeks were red, his eyes luminous and damp. On this warm, sunny December day, I rolled down the windows and let the wind press my hair against my cheek.

He said, "From now on, I'm going to be a better husband. You've been wonderful. And I don't want you to be unhappy anymore. If I get well, we're going to move back to LA, and I'll never ask you to expose yourself to other men again."

I remember this the way one remembers one's wedding or the birth of a child—clear, bright colors, and time slowing down. His words meant everything. I could feel myself choking up, my skin white hot, my eyes blurring with tears. We passed the glittering store windows of Van Cleef & Arpels, Giorgio's, Gucci's, and a rush of love for this street washed over me.

"That's wonderful," I said. And I let my tears spill down my cheeks while stopped at a traffic light. I grabbed his hand and squeezed hard to stop the swirling in my chest. "But the most important thing is you getting through this treatment and staying alive."

His diagnosis was in early November 1993, and every day after that was some new form of agony—Bob's hair falling out in clumps, his face pasty white, his eyes half closed because the chemo made light unbearable. He lost muscle mass overnight, and his strong thighs suddenly became thin and shaky. There were panicked trips to the ER, him saying he was dying, his blood pressure falling, and his white blood cell count so low he had to be admitted to an isolation room where he couldn't have visitors or flowers. He clung to me like a man drowning in the middle of the ocean, me barely able to keep my own head above water. I had not a minute to myself to the point where I,

164   staying married is the hardest part

too, was drowning, losing strength, immersed in the nightmare of his suffering.

In early December, I called Dr. Lundgren and said, "Is there anything you can suggest to help me? I can't leave his side for a half hour without him panicking."

Dr. L. recommended a private psychiatric service, men who came every day and sat with Bob so I could go to the grocery store or to a doctor for myself. The fees for this private psych care were exorbitant and not covered by medical insurance, but I didn't care. Anything for relief. I had to dip into Bob's retirement account to keep up, money for which we'd later have to pay taxes and premature withdrawal penalties, but at the time, his staying alive and recovering was all that mattered.

I began writing to save my life. I didn't have to think something up. I wrote only for myself, calling it "Cancer Diary." I described the horrors, the weird and funny things, and my agony over witnessing what Bob was going through. There was no one to whom I wanted to tell these awful details. Just my computer, my fingers spilling it onto the page.

Bob wouldn't talk to anyone, Bob the intensely social one, the raconteur. I had to field everything—friends and family calling and sick with worry, running errands every day for something he needed. My back went out, and I ate too much just to soothe myself through each day. I started going to physical therapy. I lived in a big blue heavy cotton sweater that came to midthigh to cover where I'd gained weight.

The light went out of Bob, and he was a fainting, quivering mess of near-death. One night, lying next to him, his arms and legs jerked in his sleep, and he mumbled to himself. In addition, when awake, he started stumbling over his words.

The Wordsmith himself could not pronounce certain words, forgetting and jumbling them. Alarmed by this development, I said to his MD, "The chemo is affecting his brain."

"No," the doctor said with utter confidence. "These drugs don't pass the blood/brain barrier." But no one knew Bob's gift with words better than I did, or that years later it would be called "chemo brain," a known side effect of some chemotherapy drugs.

Meantime, a strange confluence of events: in early December, five weeks after Bob's diagnosis, my new editor at Simon & Schuster wanted a revision, so when Bob was sleeping or not crawling down the hall telling me he was dying, I was rewriting. In between that, I stole moments for myself to keep the cancer diary. I recounted awful trips to the ER, Bob's battle with acute, painful constipation, and his utter physical and psychological devastation. I just had to tell someone the awful details without editing it, and my cancer diary did that for me.

On New Year's Eve, Bob became acutely ill. I managed to get him into the car to drive him to the Cedars ER. He was weak and febrile, and the waiting room was filled with people packed shoulder to shoulder. A cancer nurse named Mel helped us—nice as could be, an angel in the midst of the war zone. He put a yellow mask over Bob's nose and mouth to protect him from all the wheezing and flu coughing and took him back to a bed in a curtained area.

I called Betsy Beers from the ER. She was a dear friend whom we had met through Bob's work. I thought he might be admitted. I thought he might die. Within a half hour, Betsy was there, holding my hand and making me laugh some of the time. It meant so much that she'd dropped everything to be with us, this smart, funny, talented TV and movie producer who was so

166   staying married is the hardest part

loyal to her friends and family. By 11:00 p.m., Bob was stable, doing better, and Mel said I could take him home. The elastic band of the face mask had made deep red indents in Bob's bald head, and by the time we left, he had crisscross marks all over his scalp.

Betsy met us at home with a bottle of champagne. After I put Bob to bed, she and I sipped the champagne and watched an awful Howard Stern New Year's Eve show, but I didn't care. Bob was safe for the moment, and Betsy was with me.

In January 1994, Min arrived for her yearly visit, and I was actually happy to see her. I brought her to our apartment, where we sat outside on the patio while Bob slept. She took off her sweater and let the sun warm her like a cat, closing her eyes to feel it and let it soothe her. She brought me some of Grandma Esther's letters written decades ago in cursive Yiddish, formal and vivid, letters filled with complaints about family members. Like mother, like daughter. But I was fascinated by the history of it. During those brief hours with Min, I felt like I was myself again.

At 4:30 a.m. on January 17, 1994, the Northridge earthquake occurred. It was the largest quake ever recorded in the United States in a dense urban area. The Santa Monica Freeway collapsed just four blocks from our apartment. More than nine thousand people died. We were sleeping when the TV across from the end of our bed flew off its table. We leaped out of bed and stood in the doorway, me yelling, "*Aaayyy!*" When it stopped, we staggered around the apartment, looking to see what else had fallen and broken. Dishes were in shards on the kitchen floor, medicines in the bathroom scattered over the tiles, and magazines and books in crazy piles on the carpet.

Bob was so weak from chemo that he had to sit in his recliner, too afraid to get back in bed. This was one of his worst nightmares. The night after the quake, he sat on the edge of the bed, hairless, folded in on himself, sick beyond anything we could have imagined. His hands shook, and he looked at them, and looked at me standing next to him, and said, "I can't live in LA. I'm sorry. I know what it means to you, but I can't. I just can't."

I sank down on the bed next to him, shivering in the warm room. This was his truth, and I could no longer fight him about it. My chance for us to have a life here if he recovered, was over. It was LA without him or Ashland with him, and by now, I knew I'd never leave him. Cancer had taught me how utterly precious he was to me. "I understand," I said.

A sad heaviness settled inside me as I sat next to him in silence. My shoulders slumped, too, the disappointment writing itself in my body as an irretrievable loss.

CHAPTER 13

Pinky Swear

During cancer, Bob deteriorated into a physically weak and frightened mess, enduring painful procedures and the terror of dying. I had to take over completely in spite of my dread of his possible death and the pain of watching him suffer. I navigated the medical world way better than he ever could have because I was comfortable and experienced in it, and I had a local network of professional friends.

Although I was as patient and loving with him as if he were my baby, I was, at times, emotionally and physically exhausted by the caregiving. While Min was still in LA, I sought some respite by taking her out to brunch. I stopped outside Connie's house, enjoying for a few brief moments the bright orange crests on the bird-of-paradise flowers in her front yard, the moist ocean air, and the perfect temperature, but once Min was in the car, I saw how the shape of her mouth turned down, and every word out of that mouth was a complaint.

We went to Schatzi on Main, Arnold Schwarzenegger's Santa Monica restaurant. She asked the waitress to bring her boiling hot coffee. When it arrived, she put cold cream in it and let it sit for ten minutes, then complained to the waitress that the coffee wasn't hot enough. When the jam came in a little pot, she said to me, "Put your knife in that jam."

I did, and I said, "What?"

"Don't you see? It's not today's jam. It's a little hard on the surface."

I just kept shoveling in food, amazed that in our two hours together, she was only able to focus on me for a few minutes, even though she knew I was overwhelmed with caregiving and that Bob was in terrible distress and might not live. Each time she asked me a question, with what I knew were loving intentions, she interrupted my response and continued with her own unhappiness, which was the exact opposite of what I needed.

When I took her back to Connie's, we sat in the car for a few minutes. Min nodded as if already in conversation and, out of the blue, said, "I admire you, Bon—you—you were the only one who got out."

I could not have been more stunned if she had slapped me. *Now, she admires me for leaving Winnipeg? When she fought me so hard? When she didn't stop lobbying for me to come back until I got married ten years later?* I sat there for a few moments saying nothing, while in my head, I was shouting, *What? Is one of us crazy? I spent twelve years in analysis to cope with getting out because you couldn't let me go, and now you say you admire me for it!?*

"Thanks, Min," I said quietly. But I thought, *Now, you're frail, and your memory is starting to mix past and present, and all I want to do is hold you and tell you how dearly I always loved you, how much I respected your strength and your laughter and your optimism and your philosophy and your cooking and your beauty*

170   staying married is the hardest part

and your talent. But this acknowledgment now is so bittersweet. So filled with irony. The very thing I wanted from you then is only given to me now after I don't need it.

I came inside Connie's house for a few minutes so Min could give me a batch of her freshly baked oatmeal cookies. Before I left, we gave each other a full-body hug. The love between us was still there in the heat between our bodies, in her breath warming my ear.

She walked out with me and stood on the porch in her red cardigan sweater with the different colored buttons she'd sewn on to make the sweater more interesting. The sad yearning for me and missing me was there in the way she waved and didn't take her eyes off me as I slowly pulled away from the curb.

As I drove, I thought maybe we shouldn't expect everything we want from our parents after a certain time. Maybe we continue to love and give back because of what once was there. Maybe we love out of gratitude and the knowledge that one day we, too, will be old and frail and unable to give like we used to.

In March 1994, I finished my rewrite of Denial, and my editor was satisfied with its content. By early June, Bob had endured eight months of cancer treatment, and at the end of it, he was becoming himself again, if you ever become the person you were before such an ordeal. He said repeatedly, "You saved my life. I wouldn't have made it without you," and we both knew it was true.

Cancer had changed the balance of power between us. His respect for me grew enormously, as did my own self-respect. By the time he had recovered, our love for each other was deeper and more palpable than ever. And for the first time I genuinely felt we were equals.

To express his gratitude, Bob bought me a gold ring of hearts entwined, and long gold earrings in the shape of a figure eight. He bought a sleek black Lincoln Mark VIII and drove it back to Ashland while I stayed in the apartment another few weeks to rest and visit with friends.

When I returned to Ashland, Bob was already weaning himself off psychiatric drugs, starting to build up his physical strength, and sitting again at his typewriter. We agreed that in one year, we'd move to Portland, Oregon, because he wanted me to be happier where I lived, and Portland seemed like a decent compromise between LA and Ashland.

That August in 1994, we drove to Northern California for the filming of *Good Luck*. Richard and Shirley Hahn, the owners of East-West Films, were there producing it. We loved them both, but Bob argued with them and the director over changes they'd made, and he lost those battles. Just as had happened with *Dogfight*, the people who had final say did it their way, and it was another instance in which Bob was forced to accept other people's creative decisions. The Hahns had been spirited supporters of Bob, but by the time the movie was released in 1996, they'd run out of funds to pour a lot into promotion. The movie went straight to video.

Once I had the March 1995 release date for *Denial*, I began preparing for a whole other way of being in the world. I hired a publicist and sat in her Beverly Hills office noting how polished she looked—hair dyed black, nails long and red, makeup subtle but carefully done, coordinated dress clothes. She ticked

172   staying married is the hardest part

through her Rolodex, making a tapping noise with the long fingernails of her left hand. With her right hand, she wrote down names and numbers. "You need a makeover," she said.

I went through a whirlwind of specialists—a media expert, a new hairdresser, a wardrobe person who revamped my clothes, and a tutor to teach me how to speak in sound bites and how to sit on camera. It was one thing to have endless hours to compose one sentence at a time at home. It was another to be on live TV or radio and have to come up with something on the spot. My publicist arranged book readings for me in LA bookstores, Palm Springs, Portland, Ashland, and Seattle. She arranged for radio appearances, TV appearances, and speaking engagements.

It was a strange endeavor for me, speaking in front of strangers holding my hardcover novel, but it taught me something important: I had to have something to say to those people that was worth their time.

When Simon & Schuster released *Denial*, *People* magazine chose to do a piece on it.

It was as if I'd boarded a train in one country and disembarked in another—there I was in the March 6, 1995 edition of *People*, a half-page devoted to a positive review of the book and my photo. Sales spiked immediately. Bob bragged to our friends about it, and I asked his LA agent to look into selling the movie rights. I was so grateful to Bob for giving me that kind of access to Hollywood. I would never have had that entrée on my own.

Over the next few months, a steady stream of boxes arrived on our doorstep. First the Simon & Schuster hardcovers, then paperbacks with different cover images from different countries. One Monday in May, I hauled in a heavy box, slid my utility knife through the tape, and opened the flaps to find six big hardcover books from Sweden. I picked up one, felt its heft in my hands, and turned it over and over. It felt so amazing to hold in my hand a physical object that represented all those words I'd chosen and typed, here now in a different language.

Inside the back flap I studied a black-and-white photo of me taken in LA after Simon & Schuster sent their photographer to our hotel room. I examined it as I had backflap photos of other authors, wondering what of their true-life experiences were embedded in this fiction, wishing I could know more about their personal lives and private experiences. This time it was a version of me, a big smile on my face, frozen in a moment of time.

A week later the German paperback arrived, then in rapid succession, paperbacks from Israel, England, and Japan. Opening these boxes was pleasant and strange. My novel had taken on a life of its own.

There was a reception for me at a big bookstore in West LA, and many of our friends came to congratulate me. The same in Ashland. But the one that mattered most to me was the one in Winnipeg, where after a bookstore reading, Brenlee had a reception for me at her house, and Min was so proud. It was deeply satisfying in light of Nate's snarky comment a few years earlier about kissing Bren's ass on Portage and Main. I didn't need to remind either of them about that. My success was enough. There was even a big article about me in the *Winnipeg Free Press,* the kind of article Min had collected so many times about my sisters in past years.

In June 1995, Bob and I moved to Portland, Oregon. We rented a penthouse in a historic 1928 building with thick concrete walls, high ceilings, six-foot French windows, and a

174   staying married is the hardest part

partial second floor. We could barely get Bob's Lincoln into the one-car garage meant for a 1930 Ford, but I gloried in seeing that Portland was definitely much more of a city than Ashland, although I quickly registered how different it was from LA.

Here, the streets were narrow, convoluted, and complicated, nothing like LA's wide, easy grid. People wore mostly rain gear, Nike and Adidas running shoes, Columbia sportswear and L.L. Bean flannels. Families were dedicated to soccer, bicycling, climbing, kayaking, fishing, and skiing. There were many old, funky stores Bob loved.

We bought a new but weathered-looking leather sofa and chair for the living room—not exactly my taste, but hey, the man had just survived cancer, so I let it go. In fact, I'd already let so much go that we'd gutted our retirement account.

Again, we were on a financial high-wire without a net, but I continued believing. Bob's income had started up again. My book was doing well. In the last five years, with the exception of his cancer year, Bob had churned out one screenplay after the next, and we were sure at least one would be made. There were dozens of calls and meetings in LA, and he was writing a new movie of his own, *Jesus on Line Four*, a story loosely based on his early years as a radio talk show celebrity in Edmonton.

Bob listening to Vivaldi or ELO or Garth Brooks soothed my worries. He was himself again. His brain had mostly recovered from chemo, and I had started writing again. I told myself we were going to be okay, but there was an axe hanging over our heads: it was only one year since his treatment had ended, and the first three years were the most critical. Every six months, he needed to have CT scans and labs to monitor for a recurrence of cancer, and now that he was off psychiatric meds,

bonnie comfort   175

it was impossible not to be anxious. For Bob, the only natural treatments for anxiety were gambling and sexual excitement. Now, since he'd agreed to give up his favorite form of sexual distraction with me, gambling was the thing.

Bob loved walking into the big, glitzy Nevada casinos where the bells and music from the slot machines drowned out whatever noise was in his head. Often, we went to Vegas or Reno. I gambled at the slots or roulette tables, but once he settled at a blackjack table after dinner, I'd retreat to our room for a book or movie. Bob never gambled too much money. He wasn't one of those compulsive gamblers who'd drain the family bank account for the chance to win big. He just liked the rhythm of it all, the way it soothed his mind, the feeling of belonging with such a conglomeration of people. Money was for fun, and gambling was fun.

Every year in October, Penny Marshall and Carrie Fisher had a joint birthday party, and this year, Penny invited us. For the first time in our lives together, Bob wanted to go to the quintessential Hollywood party, and he wanted me with him.

We stayed at the Beverly Ritz again. I wore a black tuxedo jacket and skirt from my book tour. Bob looked "spiffy," as he would say, in his navy blazer, white shirt, and his favorite blue jeans. He even went with me to Bloomingdale's and bought himself a pair of soft Italian leather loafers I found so sexy.

The party was at Carrie's house, and what amazed me was the number of people I instantly recognized: Ed Begley, Jr., Sean Penn, Mark Wahlberg, Albert Brooks, Warren Beatty, and Annette Bening, to name a few. Neither Bob nor I wanted to eat. We just drank champagne and stood talking to the one person

176   staying married is the hardest part

we knew—Andrea Asimow, Penny's development director. Later that week, Bob went to Penny's house for a table reading of *The Boys From Neptune*. Richard Dreyfus, Steve Martin, Christopher Walken, Danny De Vito, Ellen Barkin, and more had done Penny the favor of showing up at her table to read Bob's script. Later, she sent Bob the audio tapes of the reading and, oh, how he treasured those.

The movie was not made, but that doesn't mean it never will be. Sometimes a movie is made thirty years after it's written. For now, all I have are those audio tapes converted to CDs—voices from long ago, maybe the only ones that will ever speak those words.

Back in Portland, one morning Bob said, "I'm going out for a drive."

I hugged and kissed him goodbye. "Have fun!" I said, happy for some alone time.

It was early November, and I opened one of the tall French windows in our living room and let the sweet air waft in while I settled down to read yet another book on how to write.

Five hours later Bob came home, his eyes bright, smile big. "I found this great Indian casino!" he said. "Spirit Mountain— it's owned by the confederated tribes of Oregon. Huge and new! You gotta come see it with me!"

"Okay," I said, not thrilled to spend most of a day in a casino with no alcohol, no high rollers, just a country setting with blackjack tables for him and slot machines for me. I did go with him a week later. I didn't love it, but I didn't mind that he started driving out there twice a week, happy to go, happy to come back, exploring rural Oregon on the way and dictating his writing ideas into his handheld. On the way he often stopped at country thrift stores and collectible shops for "treasures," and he'd come home with an inexpensive but odd assortment of items like an ashtray with a cartoon on it, a World War II poster that said, "Save Used Fats for Explosives!" and an old carved wooden chess set.

Although Portland was lovely, it was dull and overcast almost every day in the winter. I so missed the tropical flavor of LA. I felt I had rewound my life halfway to Winnipeg. The specter of Min's homesickness haunted me.

Bob missed his friends and fishing near Ashland. I missed my friends and everything else about LA. Our compromise in some ways served neither of us.

On a warm day in July 1996, the beginning of our second year in the penthouse, Bob sat in his big leather armchair, reading the *Oregonian*. I was sprawled on the sofa, my head resting against the arm farthest from him, my legs splayed out, feet bare, sundress pooled around my calves. The air from the open windows felt soft, and I lay there, content to be watching the top of Bob's baseball cap behind his open newspaper.

Being with him always felt like I was doing something that mattered.

"Another fool," Bob said, grinning. He tossed the paper on the coffee table, took off his cap, scratched his head, and put the cap back on. "This guy went into Chase Bank on east Burnside to rob it, pulled a gun, took a bag full of money, and then walked to the nearest bus to catch a ride home." He shook his head. "Of course, he was arrested ten minutes later."

I shook my head, too. "Too stupid."

178 staying married is the hardest part

Bob kept grinning. "Let me see up your skirt."

I smiled back and inched up the hem of my skirt to midthigh. Then I raised up one knee so he could see my panties. It was fun for me to play in this way, nobody else around.

His hand rested on the antique brass studs of the armchair, and he picked at them with his nails. A scratching sound, restless, irritated. "I wish you'd do that for me in public."

Inside me, a door slammed shut. Here it was again. After he'd promised.

I looked out the window, wishing this wasn't happening. The sky was an unexpected hard blue. A talented song sparrow shouted his territory, and I wished it could have cheered me, but it couldn't crack my disappointment.

I heard his hand slap down flat on the arm of the chair startling me into looking at him. His voice came out angry: "I don't get it. You love to play, you always did! You're beautiful and flirty, and part of you is a little girl who likes hats and scarves and playing dress-up. What's so bad about doing that for me!?"

Late morning coffee rose up in my throat, souring my mouth. "I'm happy to do that *with* you! I just don't want strangers to see."

"But you don't get it." His fingers picked at the brass studs. "Those strangers are *me*. I'm the rejected, lonely guy who can't get a date. And when you show your panties to a guy like that, it feels like you're accepting *me*."

I sprang up from the sofa, my skirt tumbling down to my ankles. "No, *you* don't get it! I feel like your puppet!" I paced, held my elbows, and then sagged against the narrow wall in between the windows. My voice came out pleading, less angry. "I want you to like my naked body without clothes, just you and me, skin to skin . . ."

bonnie comfort   179

Bob stood up and moved to the sofa. He patted the seat next to him and said, "C'mere."

I sat down next to him, my mood ruined, my hopes to be free of this shattered.

He took my hand and stroked the back of it softly. "Bon, I'm fucked up. I'm never gonna be that normal guy. I always had to steal sex. Never felt I had the right to it. I can't change that. When you show yourself to other men, it turns me on so much that it overrides those old church people in my head telling me sex is not okay. And I love you for it."

A slight breeze ruffled the newspaper we'd been laughing about a few minutes ago.

He threaded his fingers through mine. "Remember that doll I bought you? In Eugene?"

Yes. Although it lay in a box in my closet, I treasured it: a two-foot-high little girl with dark brown pigtails and round glasses, wearing a mint and cream striped pinafore and white shoes. We'd seen it in a toy store window while holding hands and wandering a street in Eugene, Oregon. He'd spotted it and pointed, "Look! That's you."

"Really?" I'd said, staring into the display window. And then I could see it: the shy girl who felt self-conscious of her glasses, who didn't play baseball well, who wanted to be pretty and flirty and make guys like her. "I'm gonna buy that for you," he said.

We entered the store and asked the saleslady about it. I held it in my hand and touched the dark eyelashes. "But it's so expensive," I said quietly to Bob. It was $250 in 1991.

"I want you to have it." These were his kind of gifts to me— not the practical, but the magical. And at that moment, I felt seen by him—the shy, insecure me who wanted to be loved just as she was.

180   staying married is the hardest part

The saleslady laid it carefully in its fancy yellow box and handed it to me. It was as if she was handing me a part of myself I'd lost or shoved away. Me, the woman now with stiletto heels in her closet, push-up bras, stockings, and garters, although at that store I was wearing an old Bandon sweatshirt, my Reeboks, and baggy warm-ups.

"I love that little girl," he said now. "I love all your different selves—you in your frumpy sweatshirts wearing your glasses, you in your dress-up writer's suit, you in your trashy sexy outfit. It's all of you at once, and it makes me feel all of me at once."

Something hard in my chest softened and loosened. I could see our young selves, fitting together—me, the ten-year-old playing movie star in the mirror, him the thirteen-year-old peeking in the window to get a glimpse. We *were* all our different selves at once in those moments. Alive.

"You're beautiful," he said. "You have no idea how beautiful you are."

"You're right. I have no idea. Must be why I never tire of hearing you say it."

"And I never tire of looking at you, or taking photos of you, or showing you off in public."

"But you take it too far."

"What if I promise not to?"

"I don't think you can keep that promise."

"I'll do my best." He held out his curved little finger. "Pinky swear."

I threaded my pinky around his.

Later that week, I put on a favorite of his: a white shirtdress and patent leather heels. We went to dinner at The Ringside, an old steakhouse on West Burnside. Dark interiors, quiet carpets, and white tablecloths. My top button was undone. After a cocktail, we ordered their extraordinary steaks, and I slipped out of my chair to go to the bathroom. When I returned, I showed Bob a glimpse of my garter, and his face flushed. "So sexy," he said and raised his glass to me.

I bathed in his love and desire, smiled, ordered a second cocktail, and we laughed our way through that dinner. Later at home, we tumbled into bed, me keeping my dress on, my stockings, even my shoes. What a good time we had that night. The pinky swear was working.

A few months after our Ringside date, Bob was dealing with the usual LA merry-go-round—love, love, love your script, sorry, can't get the green light to make it. The projects the executives pitched to him instead were sometimes infuriating. An executive from Fox Studios wanted him to write an all-animal version of their old classic movie, *All About Eve*.

"An *all-animal* version?" I asked when he told me. "You're kidding!"

"I wish." We were sitting on the brown sofa, me facing him with my knees up near my chin, my bare feet flat on the leather. He was angled away from me, staring at the silenced TV on the wall. "They own the movie. So, it's much less expensive for them to remake it."

"I know, but really—it's a perfect, classic movie. Redoing it with animals? Ridiculous! It trashes the old gem."

"But maybe it would get made?" He shook his head as if to get rid of the aggravation and looked out our tall window to the cloudy sky. "Wanna get dressed up and go for a drink?"

I loved him so much in that moment, how hard he kept trying, how much energy and faith it took to keep banging his

182   staying married is the hardest part

head against that wall for so many years. "Sure!" I said. "Let's go to the Benson. Maybe we'll get dinner there later."

I wore my lacy underwear and a short, pleated periwinkle blue skirt with a filmy overlay. We drove to the Benson because who wants to walk ten blocks in high heels?

The Benson Hotel was the classiest in town at the time— dark wooden walls, heavy chandeliers, a pianist at the baby grand in the lobby. It used to be the hotel where presidents stayed when they visited.

I sank into one of the cushy sofas; my skirt spread out around me. My black stockings showed through the skirt's filmy overlay. Bob sat down across from me, ordered our usual, and gave me a smile with a quick raised eyebrow, as in, "Are you gonna show something?"

I smiled back and inched up my skirt so he could see. It had been two years since his cancer treatment was over, two years since I'd displayed myself to someone else in front of him.

When our drinks came, I leaned forward to clink glasses with him, so glad he was alive and well that when another gentleman sat down near him, I left my skirt where it was, treating Bob to his favorite. The man was overdressed for Portland, a silk tie, a pin-striped three-piece. Probably on a business trip. At first, he looked at my exposed thigh in quick glances, but when he saw me catch his eye and smile, he smiled back, a smarmy smile that said he was available.

Bob's eyebrows gave a quick shove upward again.

Yes, my body seemed to say to the businessman who'd developed a thin sheen of sweat across his forehead. Yes, I'm here for you. But really, it was only for Bob, who was so pleased he was practically squirming in his chair.

Why did I choose to treat Bob to what I knew he loved at that moment? Did some part of me feel I owed him this after how unfaithful I'd been? Did I miss how hot he got for me when he noticed another man watching me?

One thing I know for sure: it was a sudden impulse. I didn't think about it for more than a few seconds. We'd been together now nineteen years, and most of that time, I'd been Bob's sexual playmate. Maybe I missed feeling so desired. Maybe some self-destructive force in me wanted to regress to being his playmate, not the psychologist who'd saved his life and had a novel published in eight countries.

It was like offering a recovering alcoholic a sip of champagne because it tasted so good.

And me, the bartender.

We lapsed back into the old battle. I dressed up, and we played, but it was never enough for Bob. When I was wearing a skirt in any public place, it was "Show him your legs! Bend over so that guy can see your cleavage." Once again, it became tiresome and relentless, and I blamed myself for opening that door again.

Mostly, we were happy together, writing, taking driving trips, and having our friends visit, but once, only once, we had another horrible fight.

Right before my yearly summer trek to Winnipeg, Bob and I went to a bingo game at Spirit Mountain, and while there he saw a three-hundred-pound man across from us, and Bob wanted me to spread my legs for the guy.

I glanced at this sweaty man with thinning hair plastered to his head and blackened fingernails bitten to the quick. "No," I

184 staying married is the hardest part

said, keeping my legs closed, although my skirt was short, and Bob knew I was wearing lacy whites.

"C'mon!" Bob whispered with that kind of urgency I hated.

"*No!*" I stood up. "I'm going to the Ladies.'"

Rage rose up in my throat as I walked quickly toward the bathroom, coughing as I went. I rushed into a toilet stall and hung over the porcelain, dizzy and nauseated but dry-mouthed. And isn't that just like me, I thought. Can't swallow it, can't vomit it up.

When I emerged five minutes later, Bob stood in the hallway outside the restroom with a sour look on his face, his mouth corners down. "Let's go," he said grimly.

Once his mood soured this way, he wouldn't get over it quickly. "Fine," I said.

We drove in silence for an hour; the only sound in the car was a John Prine CD. Here was our power struggle again, an unresolvable difference between us. I felt like an animal in a maze that keeps bumping into the same blind alleys, never finding the way out.

The next morning, he took me to the airport, and our conversation was brief and clipped. A miserable weight lay inside my chest. There was no way out of this other than to leave him.

I had plenty of time to ruminate on the plane.

Why don't I leave him? I asked myself, for the first time since I'd decided after cancer, that I'd never leave him.

At some point after being married for years, whether it's five or thirty, the other person's true habits, coping style, and character become glaringly obvious. Sometimes partners annoy each other. Sometimes they bicker. They may feel unappreciated, discounted, and frustrated with the other's habits. They no longer want to accommodate the other. They have stopped trying to be what the other wants.

Now, they want to be themselves.

As a marital therapist, I see what must be faced: no partner is ever going to give you everything you need, and in some ways, whether major or minor, you're incompatible. I call it The Reckoning.

The Reckoning is a phase when the most difficult work of marriage is required. You see clearly whom you've married, and you must learn to tolerate the "otherness" of the other. It pretty much happens to every longtime married couple. It's as silly and small as, "I hate the way you stack glasses in the dishwasher," and as big as, "If you don't stop drinking, I'll leave you."

Yet a lot of people weather these destructive turns in a marriage and don't separate. Later, many are glad they worked through this phase, although sometimes, circumstances forced them to stay. They may have wanted to wait until their children left home, or their finances were better, or because they were ill. Sometimes, those "temporary" decisions get you through the rough phases, and then things change. By the time your children leave home, you might have created a new business for yourself that's a great source of satisfaction and shifts your attitude at home. Or, you go through breast cancer or a mangled knee, and your spouse is really there for you, and the gratitude you feel repairs the bond between you. Or one of your children gets married and has a baby, and the joy you both feel when with that grandchild makes having stayed together worth it. Each situation is unique, but if that glue keeps you together for a substantial amount of time, a new phase of your life often emerges, where some of the things about your partner that so plagued you in the past fade in importance.

After my casino fight with Bob, after I'd gotten on the plane, I had my reckoning. There was no question Bob and I loved each other. We had a physical passion for each other. He was the single most interesting man I'd ever known. And I remained his dream girl, but each of us was bitter now about our sex fights.

On that plane ride, I made a list of the reasons I had stayed:

- Because every marriage is a trade-off, and I get way more good than bad.
- Because the sex fight only happens sporadically, and the rest of the time, I love my life with him.
- Because he's right: I am that little girl who wants to twirl in the light and have the person who loves me admire me.
- Because he's been through so much, and I feel for him.
- Because of the laughs, his charming quirkiness, and knowing I'm the center of his world.
- Because he cares way more about ideas and fun than whether the house is clean, or the bed is made, or whether I do any of the traditional things women are supposed to do.
- Because he calls me Boss, and I call him Boss.

Now, we had reached rock bottom. I was completely fed up with the sexual fights. *Fed up*. Once again, I had to think deeply and clearly about whether I wanted to stay with him. I didn't know if either of us still wanted to be together.

CHAPTER 14

The Hotel del Capri

When Bob picked me up a week later, we went to Salty's, a waterside fish restaurant on the Columbia River near the airport. We ordered cocktails, and I gulped my Grey Goose. Our talk was sparse and stilted after we'd ordered—petrale sole for me, Crab Louie for him. I knew him so well that I could look at any menu and predict what he'd want. Crab Louis here. Beef stew in a bread bowl at the Tiki bar. Lemon meringue at Shari's. Sometimes, he'd just hand me the menu and tell me to order for him.

This time, though, his face was a map of disappointment, the corners of his mouth drooping. His forearms rested on the table, hands on those forearms, defended, cold, fatalistic.

Seeing me searching his face, he said, "Maybe we should get a divorce."

Those words shocked me. Never before had he said "divorce." I flashed on an old memory of him in the shower in our Glenhaven house, water streaming over his body, and him saying to me, "I'll never leave you, you know. If anybody leaves, it'll be you."

187

188   staying married is the hardest part

That was three years after we married, when I was angry over how he'd shut down sexually, and he knew I was uncertain whether I'd stay. But now? Now I was clear.

"I don't want a divorce," I said.

I knew he didn't really want a divorce, either. He just wanted what he wanted and wasn't willing to stop pressuring me. I suspected the divorce suggestion was another form of pressure. But damn if I was going to give in on this again. After he promised, after I nursed him back to health, and after I'd told him again and again how I felt.

"I just don't understand it," he said. "Such a little thing for you to do. Why won't you do something that's so easy for you when it means so much to me?"

My voice came out intense, hissing. "We're going to have this fight here? Fine! Why the hell do you think it's so little? Or easy? I hate it!"

I looked around to see if this argument had drawn attention, but our table was far enough away from others, and no one was looking. "It embarrasses me! I feel ashamed of myself for giving in to you!" I dropped my fork on the white tablecloth, my appetite completely gone.

The flaw in my position was this: so often, when in a playful mood, I'd done what he wanted, enjoying his turn-on, liking him getting hot for me. I could see how he thought it was "easy for me" because in that mode I was the little doll with the glasses, flirty and fun. It was familiar to me. The problem was, though, that I was unpredictable. I was fine showing myself off sometimes but tired of it at other times. It was confusing for both of us. Complicated.

You think you're in charge of your decisions, but you don't realize that sometimes your early solutions to old problems

bonnie comfort   189

trap you in a repetitive loop. The young Bob had seen how I could revert back to the young Bonnie, who was so practiced at seducing and pleasing, and sometimes he wanted to call that girl up. And sometimes, we both got off on it. On the other hand, young Bonnie never tried to entice unattractive strangers or passing truck drivers. She was flirting with attractive, interesting men. That came easily. Exposing myself to strange men or truck drivers was very different.

We paid the bill and bought a Salty's sweatshirt for him. On the drive home, inside our silence, Bob reached over for my hand, and I gave it to him.

The utter comfort of that gesture was like a warm sun.

When you look back on relationships, you can usually see it was all there from the beginning—the great, the awful, the quirky, the incompatible, the powerful, and the compelling—but you fall in love with the great stuff, you try to ignore what doesn't fit, and you hope the bad stuff won't bite you in the ass. Later, in the worst moments of your relationship, you can't tell yourself you didn't see it or know it might happen. It's the logical progression of who the two of you are and how you do or don't fit together. Bob used to say, "You can't be surprised when a thief takes your money," but of course you can. Love puts a soft-focus lens on everything, and every personality trait has a light and dark side. You hope, or you wouldn't get married.

After three years in the Envoy, we missed grass and trees and having a dog, which was not allowed in the apartment. In June 1998, we found a neighborhood that felt right—Lake Oswego,

190   staying married is the hardest part

with its wide, gracious streets, trees and parks, and nicely kept houses. Our new rental house had a front lawn, a landscaped backyard, and a hot tub.

Within two weeks of moving there, we went to the Oregon Humane Society and rescued a dog. On our way home, the back hatch full of dog crate, leashes, dog bowls, and food, we named him Savvy. He was half border collie, half black Lab, and had a curly tail he held like a flag over his rear section. Bob called him "the dog with the question mark tail."

Playful and inquisitive, we never knew what Savvy would get into next: racing through the living room with a bra of mine, playing hide-and-seek around the sofa, or ripping up the newspaper. Sometimes, when I lay next to him, he'd press one paw into my chest and gaze directly into my eyes in such an intimate way that I felt I'd crossed the species barrier as Jane Goodall had with her chimps in the wild.

After we settled into Lake Oswego, I joined a writing group, and the experience of reading pages aloud was so bonding that twenty years later I am still friends with some of the people who sat at that table. One of them introduced us to a couple who changed our lives.

Andy was a music store salesman by day and a drummer by night, a guy with an irresistible smile, and a quick and funny line for anyone. He soon became Bob's best friend locally. Carol, his wife, was petite and beautiful, with jet black hair and great talent for cooking, art and gardening. We shared food and laughs every weekend.

The Sunday night *Sopranos* TV show was our regular foursome, and it helped keep Bob's mood okay, but his career began taking hit after hit. Just when his next movie production deal seemed secure, something would happen to make it collapse.

Over the years, he'd written seventeen feature film scripts, and for most he had been paid, but only two were filmed. He also wrote six before that with Rick, and one was filmed. Some would say that was a remarkably successful run, but that's not how he felt.

There are only so many times you can have your heart broken as a writer before you begin to give up. Sometimes, he looked like an inflatable doll, gradually losing air. I felt his pain in my own body, the disappointment crunching my lungs.

Within a year of moving to Lake Oswego, Bob was hoarse again from pitch meetings. Two huge movie production deals going bad put him over the edge. The more depressed he got, the more he wanted to use the distraction of sex to restore the feeling that life was worth living. I hated to be used in this way. This wasn't loving sex. It was like a drug that numbed him at my expense. Still, I wanted to cheer him up because seeing him that discouraged and depressed was terrible, an oppressive dark blanket over a bright, funny spirit.

That's how the wife of an alcoholic brings her hubby another drink.

By November 1999, we were still in a rental house, had no retirement savings, were deeply in debt, and dependent on Bob for our income. We arrived in LA for more pitch meetings, and this time, we stayed at our favorite modest hotel, the Hotel del Capri. Our third-floor room near the back looked out on the other wing of the hotel, separated from our wing by a small courtyard. We went out for dinner at I Cugini on Ocean Avenue, which was a favor to me because I loved that restaurant. I wore my black lingerie and

192   staying married is the hardest part

high heels, a return favor to him. To complement my blue V-necked sweater, I wore a delicate gold necklace Bob had bought me years earlier—a thin chain holding a small opal pendant surrounded by antique filigreed gold. It was a fire opal, translucent iridescent turquoise when you held it up to the light, a necklace bought when we were new and constantly wrapped around each other.

I was looking forward to our week here and seeing our friends, although Bob was apprehensive about his meetings. When we walked back into our room that evening at the Del, he turned on the bedside lamp and glanced out our window. He stopped, his voice urgent. "Bon! C'mere!"

I came up behind him and saw a guy across from us in the other wing, naked, pleasuring himself. His light was on, too. He glanced up and saw us, and Bob immediately stepped back and said, "Go up close to the window! Smile and touch yourself!"

Oh fuck. Here it is again . . .

I stood there frozen.

"C'mon! It's such an opportunity!" Bob whispered fiercely. He undid his bulging pants.

In this split second, I had to decide: Should I do what he wants so he'll be happy and we'll have a good week, or should I refuse him and start the whole angry shutdown? Neither choice was good.

But oh, I wanted a happy week.

I went to the window and looked at the guy, who was now looking back at me and handling himself. I was watching live porn. Bob came up behind me, put his hands around my front, and enclosed my breasts through my sweater. "That's great. He's liking it. Now, take off your sweater!" He pulled his arms away, leaving me free.

bonnie comfort   193

I removed my sweater and dropped it on the carpet, but I left on my lacy push-up bra. Bob encircled me from behind, kissed my neck, and said, "Let's give him a show. If we do it on the bottom corner of the bed, he'll be able to see us!"

Do I keep the peace and help him tolerate his misery? Or do I refuse him and start a fight that might ruin his performance in his meetings?

I stepped out of my black panties and climbed on the edge of the bed on all fours. Bob lifted up my skirt—a full black skirt that had a ruffled hem. Now we were doing it doggy-style. No foreplay, no kissing. Just how I imagined making a porn movie must be for the woman.

Bob repositioned me to make sure the guy could see me clearly. I pulled the bottom of my skirt up to my shoulders and hung my head so my hair covered my face. Bob was so excited that his hands dampened where he hung onto me. He was vigorous enough that my necklace swung against my chin over and over as I breathed in the dry-cleaning fluid of the bedspread and the taste of my hair in my mouth. My fancy dinner threatened to return. I swallowed hard, letting some part of me float away from this reality where my elbows burned and I was seasick.

When it was over, Bob closed our curtain, and I sat down on the toilet to pee. I undid my necklace and held the pendant in the palm of my hand. As I held it up to the light, I saw a fine crack in the opal. Yes, there it was—a definite crack running from the upper right of the stone at an angle to the lower left edge.

But it wouldn't break in two. Its antique gold filigree setting would hold it in place.

194   staying married is the hardest part

Consent is usually discussed in the context of dating, not in the context of marriage. Some would say that getting married is a form of lifelong consent. However, spouses often duel over what they will and won't do sexually. Sometimes, one partner shuts down and never comes close again. Sometimes, a partner asks you to do adventurous things, and once in a while, you do, but you don't agree to do it frequently.

With Bob there was often in me a push-pull, wanting to be strong and honor my preferences, yet wanting to please him. Sometimes I said yes, sometimes I said no, sometimes it was fun to excite him in that way, and I didn't care who was seeing me. I was like an old-fashioned slot machine, keeping him pulling the handle because sometimes I paid off.

Did consent have to be like training a dog not to beg at the dining table? Where if you relent and give him a scrap of food from your plate it reinforces him sitting there for weeks salivating while you eat? Or can humans accept that sometimes it's no, and sometimes it's yes, and be fine with that?

When Bob and I were coming of age in the 1960s, asking for consent was not part of the sexual dance. Rape was the only clear-cut situation in which the issue of consent by a woman was examined. Rape was a recognized act of violence. Other than that, men were trained to pressure women for sex, and women were trained to resist. Men who broke down a woman's resistance were often seen as having prowess, being a "bad boy," and kind of sexy. Women were taught to entice, to play hard to get, yet to accommodate themselves to men's preferences, from high-heeled shoes and exceedingly tight corsets to faking orgasm so the man would feel successful.

Over my shared decades with Bob, there were times when I felt shame about not being true to myself. Should I *never* have consented when I didn't want to do what he was asking?

I can't really give a clear yes or no answer. Marriage brings layers of complexity to sexual activity. What about the time Bob had just learned he might die? Even though, at that moment, I didn't want to expose myself to that guy in the tree outside our hotel window, I did it out of love and empathy and concern for Bob. Where does consent fit into that?

Isn't it okay to make a sacrifice sometimes for someone you love?

Bob's meetings went well that time. Buoyed by hope again, he began writing a new movie he'd pitched. He had made the transition to a desktop computer, so I couldn't hear him tapping away anymore, but I was happy to see the new pages accumulating. I spent my days slogging away at a second novel and going out to diners with Bob.

Seven months later, he turned in his screenplay. The studio was uneasy about it. They said they'd work on it. What was the point in continuing to pitch his beloved ideas?

"Nothing's going to come of them," he said.

I looked at him lying on the sofa, listlessly clicking through channels, and the reality could not be ignored. He had just turned sixty, and I was fifty-five. We had nothing but debt, and he could no longer force himself to get up for another pitch meeting.

Worried sick about money, I retreated to my home office. It was late September 2000. Savvy sauntered up to my desk chair, a tennis ball in his mouth, dropped it, and stared at me. I ignored him for three minutes. He picked up the ball again and dropped it closer to me. Off we went to the park, me holding an old tennis racket and ball as we headed for the fenced baseball field. The air was cool, and the fragrance of a wood-burning

196   staying married is the hardest part

fireplace reached my nose, the quintessential sign of autumn in Oregon.

I tossed the ball up in the air as if I were going to serve, then smashed it with the racket as hard as I could. Savvy was already racing to it at top speed, all muscle and focus and heart. I admired that dog. Nothing, I mean nothing, distracted him from his intense speed toward the ball, and he timed himself so he reached it just as it descended toward the grass, and he could snatch it at the end of its arc without letting it touch the ground.

Watching that intensity, that focus, I realized I was going to have to find that in myself. I'd been hanging on, hoping Bob wouldpull another magic act and finalize a new deal, but the time had now passed for waiting, and the stakes were getting too high.

Savvy dropped the ball again in front of me. After another dozen times of this, Savvy threw himself on the grass, panting, and didn't bring the ball back again.

The sky was overcast, and clouds moved and changed shape. There was a heavy, clunking sound I could almost hear inside me: the weight of our present and future dependent on me. For ten years, I'd enjoyed a wonderful freedom from the responsibility of work, and I was grateful to Bob for the opportunity, but now, like an old rusty train grinding back into place on a track, I was going to have to start up my engine, gather my strength, and rescue us.

First, I bought a color printer and a digital camera to take photographs for eBay sales. Then, I taught myself how to use eBay and began pawing through drawers, closets, and garage cupboards for things to sell. Every item had a memory and a meaning, but I shut out sadness like a woman in front of her burning house, caring about only one thing: how to save her family.

I culled everything I could from our possessions and sold them. I also photographed Min's framed oil paintings on my walls and made a series of greeting cards for her with the images, which I packaged and mailed to her. By that time, she had sold her house and moved into a condo not far from my sisters. She was ninety, frail, and too old to travel.

The last thing was a Chevy station wagon Bob had found years before and spent thousands on restoring it. It sat in our garage. He never drove it. Still, the day a man came to buy it, Bob stood in the driveway watching it go in the Portland rain that mingled with his tears.

Now was the time for one more sad sale: the Ashland house, and Bob didn't want to hear anything about it. Everything around him was crumbling.

That September, I visited Min in Winnipeg. We sat at her Formica table in her kitchen, and she made tea with milk and served it in her china teacups. When she sat down, her rheumy eyes looked straight at me through her glasses, eyes soft and sincere, and she said, "Bon, I treasure those greeting cards you made for me. It's one of the nicest things anyone has ever done for me. I'm happy my paintings hang on some people's walls, but these cards—I can send them to anyone, and I'm so proud of them. I marvel that you made them. I can't thank you enough."

There it was: her lifelong ambition recognized, her desire to have her talent out in the world, finally in some form she could

198   staying married is the hardest part

control, and from her daughter, whom she had been unable to control. "I'm so glad!" I replied. I saw her in that moment for herself—a talented woman whose ambitions had been flattened by the culture of her time. Everyone in our family had her paintings on their walls; she had, with my sister's efforts, had a one-woman show in town; she had received praise from some strangers, but those greeting cards were the missives she could drop in the mail to relatives and friends, proud that they could see her work.

By late November 2000, I'd cut our debt in half, but we needed steady, substantial income to meet our monthly expenses. One afternoon, I noticed Bob was half-heartedly trying to write again. I stood in front of his desk, and his typing stopped. He leaned back in his squeaky chair and blew out a long sigh. "I think I should retire from the Writers Guild," he said.

Another crazy idea of his. "But you've just turned sixty!"

"Oh, ye of little faith," he said, pointing his first finger at me. "I can retire any time from fifty-nine-and-a-half on, *and* I can still keep working. If I make more money, it just adds to my pension."

"Really?"

"Yup. That's one good thing about the Writers Guild. Great benefits."

When the pension letter arrived, it explained that we had to choose one of three options: the full monthly pension beginning immediately and terminating upon the writer's death, a reduced monthly pension starting immediately and continuing until both partners died, or a lump sum payment. The kicker: once you made your choice, you could never change it.

In the living room, Bob was in his brown leather chair, his shoulders pressed into the back. He took the letter from me and read it as if it were his funeral arrangements, his hand trembling, his head lowered. The fact that you could never change your choice made the decision enormously important. Bob put the paper in his lap. "I think we should take the full pension now."

That meant the pension would stop upon his death.

He'd already been through non-Hodgkin's lymphoma, two malignant melanomas, and now something new—his hoarse voice, his low energy. Given his history, I'd likely survive him, and we both knew it.

The skin on my arms burned with an instant fury I'd never felt before. My voice came out like a loud howl. "How can you do that!? If you die before me, I'll have no income!"

"But we need as much money as possible now," he said. He looked so defeated, his shoulders slumped, his T-shirt spotted with jam. "Look at the numbers." He held out the Guild pension proposal to me, his hand shaking a little bit with his arm in the air.

I took the document and stood in front of him, studying the numbers again. It was true we'd have about one-third more money monthly now if we took the option he wanted.

"Maybe one of my movies'll get made, or I'll write another few," he said. "I could still turn things around."

I handed back the proposal and left the house without saying another word, my breath coming fast, my face hot and wet as I cried out loud in my car. How could he choose to leave me no income if he died first? It was appalling! Unconscionable after all our years together! After all I'd done for him and continued doing!

200   staying married is the hardest part

There was a wooded park near our house with a trail through trees surrounding a huge, swampy pond. I walked and walked that trail, and then I walked and walked some more— maybe an hour, maybe two.

Gradually, I calmed some as I walked out the rage. I knew his point of view was without malice. He'd always been so generous. No, it was his dread of facing further decline and death that was fueling his choice and a naivety he'd always had about money and hopes for his movies. But I was done pinning my hopes on show business.

By the time I'd circled countless times, I'd made up my mind.

When I returned to the house, Bob was still sitting in that chair, looking blank and stunned. I stood in the middle of the living room and faced him, noticing how listlessly he stared into space.

"I'm going to go back into practice," I said. "That's what I'll do to rescue us. But here's what I want from you: request the reduced monthly pension so that I'll continue to have some guaranteed income after your death. If you don't agree to this, *I'll never forgive you.*" Those words were said with a firmness I rarely used with him. It was a steely delivery.

He saw it all in my face and blinked slowly. "Okay," he said, and that was the end of it. My muscles relaxed, and I breathed a sigh of relief. We applied for the pension, and within a month, we had some money coming in.

Now, in a city where I knew almost no one, I would have to develop a private practice.

A heavy determination settled against my chest like a lead apron for dental X-rays.

I rented a small office in a downtown Portland suite with other psychologists, joined professional organizations, attended boring lectures, drank bad coffee, and introduced myself to other psychologists, chiropractors, dietitians, doctors, and nurses. I took people I'd never met out to lunch to explain my services. If I got one referral from them, I immediately generated a written evaluation report and sent it to them.

Bob's voice got worse, and a Portland ENT doctor recommended a biopsy of Bob's vocal cords. Once again, I was there holding his hand before they wheeled him into surgery. The ENT found no sign of cancer, but Bob's hoarseness didn't abate.

I found a local psychiatrist for him, Dr. Rick Cohen, whom he started seeing twice a week. It gave me some peace of mind to know that at least Bob was talking about his fears, and if necessary, there was someone to prescribe for him whatever might help. However, we both knew we had to see an ENT specialist in LA to assess his hoarseness further.

Leaving the house helped get everything off Bob's mind, so on some weekends, we went to the beach. One time, he found a smooth, oval rock that, from the side, looked like the profile of a man with his mouth open, talking. He called this his "talk rock," and he carried it in his pocket and rubbed it for months: magic to keep away the possibility of no longer being able to speak.

We also drove to Reno some weekends, stopping for a night in Ashland to see Steve and his delightful wife Kelly and then staying in Reno's high-rise hotels. Our focus had certainly

202   staying married is the hardest part

not been on sex these last few years, but his obsession with me showing myself had not gone away. In fact, it seemed to be his most passionate way of treating his depression, and as defeated as he felt, it seemed to be the one thing I could do that would at least temporarily cheer him up. This time, I dressed up in my lingerie and flashed for the poker players in my short skirts. I hugged him in the elevators and kissed him in the hallways, delighted to see a glimpse of the old boyish Bob who could still find some distraction and pleasure in this play. We danced our old dance while the words from Leonard Cohen's song "Dance Me to the End of Love" played in my head.

Then we returned to Portland, and I put on my doctor's suit again.

In April 2001, we sat in a Beverly Hills ENT office, holding the medical records from Portland. This doctor looked at the films and said with animated exasperation, "That guy never biopsied your vocal cord! He biopsied the arytenoids!"

"What are they?" I said, my own voice weak.

"The cartilage the cords attach to."

He threaded a scope up through Bob's nose and down his throat to look closely at the chords. "You have a growth on your vocal cord, and it could be malignant," he said. "I'll try to spare the cord, but it might have to be removed."

How could there be anything worse for a man who had talked his way to a brilliant career? In despair, we drove back to Portland to think things through. My face burned as we drove up I-5, me holding back tears for so many miles. We ate McDonald's french fries and talked about anything but the vocal cord condition. While I went back to work, my dear honey took to the sofa, unable to bear his grief. No faith left. No energy to keep pitching. No voice.

He took anti-anxiety drugs, which didn't help much. His libido went down to zero, and so did mine. We kissed and hugged and cuddled every day, but this wasn't about sex for either of us. We clung together at night like two kids lost in the woods.

Fearing the permanent loss of his voice, Bob began culling through a lifelong collection of his poetry. With Andy, our drummer friend, Bob studio-recorded his best poems onto a CD in his hoarse voice.

I called Dr. Agre, the one who had originally identified Bob's cancer. When I told him about the vocal cord tumor, he arranged a consultation with a talented surgeon at UCLA Hospital. We drove down. Bob went through some tests. "I think I can remove the tumor by laser and spare the vocal cord," the gifted surgeon said. "But I won't know till I get in there." His exam room smelled of antiseptic and fear.

A week later, in May 2001, Bob was admitted to UCLA Medical Center. Once again, I was in a surgery waiting area, the world at a standstill but the light swirling and dizzy. Then the surgeon was there, in green scrubs, his tired eyes. "I was able to spare the cord," he said.

Relief gave me strength, but Bob was nutty—obsessively ruminating, repeating himself, restless and anxious. When we got back home, something was new: he started fighting in his sleep, kicking, punching, and talking out loud. Once or twice, he kicked me while asleep and punched me in the arm. He had no memory of this when he woke, but it startled and frightened me, and for the first time in twenty-two years, I had to sleep in a separate bed. "I'll cuddle you at bedtime till you fall asleep," I told him. "But then I have to slip away so you don't hurt me."

204 staying married is the hardest part

"The last thing I want is to hurt you," he said, and we hugged a long time, both so sad.

In my diagnostic manual, I looked up sleep disorders, and to my shock, I found a description of exactly what was wrong: he had REM sleep behavior disorder. Okay, I thought, we can live with this. I just can't stay in bed with him once he's sleeping.

CHAPTER 15

Transitions

In August 2001, I went to Winnipeg for a quick family visit. Min was ninety-one and had finally vacated the house she'd lived in since I'd left home. Now she was in a high-rise condo, relieved of the need to have her sidewalks shoveled in winter, and her garden tended in summer.

A few days into my visit, Min and I were in Salisbury House, a Canadian chain one cut above Burger King. Waitresses in black uniforms brought plastic menus. I ordered a tossed salad with blue cheese on the side and a cup of pea soup. Min ordered hot tea "with the bag outside," one pancake with syrup, a soft-boiled egg, and syrup, "don't forget the syrup."

After we were served, five minutes went by. Her tea water was cooling, and she hadn't yet dipped the bag. "Your husband should go back to work," she said.

My right trapezius muscle tightened. I had to put my fork down because my hand was shaking. How could she? Judging him at a distance and ripping away the years of pride I felt in how successful he'd been. My cheeks got hot as I said, He's supported me for twenty-three. He's been very sick. So, don't tell him that."

"Oh, I would never dream of saying anything to him."

206   staying married is the hardest part

Right. Always behind someone's back.

Her pancake looked rubbery, but she emptied the syrup jug on it, dumped the poached egg on the soaked pancake, and mashed it. When she picked it up with her hands I thought, *this is how it starts, this is how it ends.*

The back of her hand was a topographic map of her labor, blue veins lumpy against the bones, skin as transparent as the tomatoes on my plate. How those hands had worked, whipping batter, kneading dough, ironing shirts. "Dad was in that condition for eleven years," she said.

It was more like five, but five years with a demented husband could easily feel like eleven, so why argue?

The waitress came. "Is everything all right?"

Min said, "Everything's fine," and before the waitress was three steps away, Min said in her direction, "Except you."

My trapezius clamped down hard enough to hurt my neck. "Min, quiet!" I said.

"Oh, she didn't hear."

And what exactly was wrong with the waitress anyway? Something about not being a perfect servant? As if a servant could make up for those lost years with my dad?

The egg and pancake were gone, and only a shiny pool of syrup lay on her plate. "My friend Mona told me her son is a world-renowned surgeon," Min said.

"Probably published in international magazines. Maybe that's what she means by world-renowned."

She looked at me right in the eyes and said, "That's a big word."

And we started laughing because she was right about Mona and her pretentions.

bonnie comfort   207

As we laughed, the years melted away. It was Min and me laughing in the kitchen at her Aunt Rose imitation; Min and me at the drugstore, on red stools, drinking chocolate milkshakes from metal cans with straws; Min and me laughing so hard at Jackie Mason on *The Ed Sullivan Show* that she had to take off her glasses and wipe away her tears.

Now, we were both taking off our glasses to wipe our eyes. And I could see the hint of veins beginning to show through my own hands. But Min was finally smiling. Her soft cheeks had turned pink like a sweet peach, and she wasn't complaining.

For this one perfect moment, she wasn't complaining.

Gradually, Bob's voice recovered. His agent negotiated a polish-rewrite of one of his scripts for a modest amount of money, and Bob was able to do it. He also called in a favor from his former partner, Rick, who understood showbiz feast or famine well. "Broke, broke, broke," Bob said on the phone.

Rick had an on-air TV show at the time, and he arranged to have Bob paid very well for consulting by phone on an episode script. Showbiz money. Always better than eBay sales or earning it like me, one hour at a time.

By the end of 2001, I had a modest professional income. In the mornings and evenings, I worked for a colleague in Lake Oswego. Tuesdays and Thursdays, I was downtown. My car was crammed full of files, dog toys, maps of Portland, half-used bottles of water, and crumpled takeout bags from Burgerville. As I traveled between offices, I listened to audiotapes reminding me of how to treat depression, how to tackle anxiety disorders, and the best techniques for couples therapy.

208   staying married is the hardest part

Although Bob's voice recovered, some memory problems and word-finding difficulties he'd had during chemotherapy began to return. Sometimes, he mixed up words or couldn't remember the names of objects. "Where's that thing?" I heard often, and yet, with his creativity, he made up charming substitutes for names, like "the run-fast birds" for sandpipers. But the day he drove right by our street on the way home, a fear registered in my chest like a gripping hand.

Something more was wrong.

In February 2002, after a CT scan of his brain, Bob and I sat in a Portland neurologist's office, again preparing for news. The doctor's voice was monotone, and his speech pattern was quick and clinical. "So, Bob," he said, "I suspect you have Lewy body disease. Your scan was essentially normal. You don't have Alzheimer's. But you do have early clinical signs of Lewy body."

I peppered him with questions about this strange diagnosis. He said, "50 percent of the men who have REM sleep behavior disorder—and it's mostly men who develop it—go on to develop Lewy body disease. The other 50 percent do not."

"*50 percent!?*" I replied.

"Yes," he said. "50 percent." To me, he added, "Come around to my side of the desk, and I'll show you."

I leaned over his shoulder to study his computer screen. A fragrance of lime wafted up. His fingernails were clean and very short. He pointed to his screen of scanned images of a brain where there were some darker patches. "These are areas of the brain damaged by Lewy bodies in a man who has died. Lewy bodies are microscopic protein deposits that damage normal tissue. They're also the cause of Parkinson's. You can't see them on CT scan—you only see the damage to the brain they cause over time." He clicked his mouse to another slide. "This is a Parkinson's brain. In Lewy body, the protein deposits first start at random throughout the brain, creating diffuse cognitive problems. In Parkinson's, the Lewy bodies start in the motor areas only. The end stage of both conditions looks clinically the same—dementia and muscle rigidity."

Gray, weak light shone in from his office window. Bob sat facing us, looking dumbfounded. My heart raced, my mouth went dry, and my hands balled up into tight fists. I had just learned that my husband, who could whip out hilarious one-liners nonstop, who came up with complex and touching stories, and who had an encyclopedic memory for history, was going to slide slowly into dementia, and there was not a fucking thing we could do to stop it.

That June, I scrolled through our Quicken accounts. We had no assets and still had some debt, but our friend Andy, whose day job was working at a bank, thought we could qualify for a home loan, and he was right. It took all the cash we had, but in August 2002, we bought a house in another Lake Oswego neighborhood and were able to make payments.

In April 2003, Min was diagnosed with esophageal cancer, and I took time away from Bob and my practice to see her. Slushy, muddy May in Winnipeg, and we were back in Sal's. One egg poached lightly, "I'm a sick woman, you know." One pancake with non-sugar syrup and tea with the bag on the side, thank you. She was nicer to the waitress that day, but she said to me,

210   staying married is the hardest part

"They water down the regular syrup, you know. And I don't want to lose weight."

"Maybe Ensure?" The drink of cancer patients.

"I'm quite frail," she said. I nodded and reached across the table with my open hand. She placed her palm in mine and said, "Speaking of dying, here's my advice: trust people, but always cut the cards, and don't sign anything without reading it." We laughed.

We spent as much time as possible together, reminiscing and talking. On my last day in her apartment, she said, "I have a birthday present for you." She disappeared into her bedroom and returned with a navy-blue jewelry box. I had no idea what was inside until I opened the lid and found my favorite string of pearls of hers, the one with the moonstone clasp. She had always known how much I loved it.

Tears spilled down my cheeks. Forgiveness flooded my blood and bones, filling my whole body. I knew whenever I wore this necklace, I'd feel Min's love wrapped around me. No parent can give everything each unique child needs. Her trying to bend me to her will long ago had paradoxically given me the drive I needed to separate from her and chart my own path. I had succeeded. She had finally seen and respected it. There was only love left between us now.

Back in Portland, I returned to my psychology practice and Bob. Because I was gone every weekday, Bob often took Savvy with him in the Land Cruiser and drove out to the "Gambling Den of Iniquity," Spirit Mountain. On the way home, he'd stop at a little park where a bubbling stream ran through. Savvy would plunk around in the water, then Bob would open the

bonnie comfort 211

back hatch of the Land Cruiser, and the two of them would sit on the open bottom door, sharing a sandwich. Bob would tell me later, "Savvy and I had a picnic."

In September 2003, I went to Winnipeg to help Min go through cancer treatment. She was to have a body cast made for a Plexiglas form to keep her still during radiation. At the hospital, Todd, the cast tech, took us into a private room where she had to strip to the waist and lie on a wooden board. He layered Vaseline all over her torso, then Saran Wrap and strips of fabric soaked in plaster of paris. When the cast had hardened, he pulled it away, and she sat on the edge of the gurney to get her bearings. Before Todd left, he pointed to the sink and handed her a washcloth.

After he was gone, she said, "Will you wash me?" Bits of plaster stuck to her skin.

I ran the warm water, wet the cloth, put soap on it, and then began washing her skin very gently because it was so delicate. I saw the surgery scars on her belly. I put my cloth in her armpits and around her neck and dabbed a spot off her cheek. Very tenderly, I patted her dry. I thought about the countless times when she had bathed me as an infant and as a little girl, of the times she'd rubbed my leg, lotioned my hands, and rubbed my back.

Now, she was my child.

A few days later, we arrived at the radiation treatment area. When it was her turn, she looped her arm through the nurse's on her way in. The room smelled of some bad chemical mixed with putty. Various molds sat on the counter, like the kind you'd see of actors' body parts in a Star Wars film.

212   staying married is the hardest part

Min walked with a smile and a joke up to the radiation machine and used the step stool to climb up to the treatment slab. The tech positioned her inside her Plexiglas mold with her neck supported, her arms above her head. Then the staff and I left, shutting her in alone behind an eight-inch lead door.

In the control room, I watched her on their monitors, and I saw the image of my Min, a red lighted cross through her vertical and horizontal axes at the chest. They were burning her at the intersection of this cross, hoping to shrink the cancer without killing her. "Cooking her from the inside, like a roast," the doctor said, "which keeps cooking after you take it out of the oven."

Afterward, we sat waiting for the doctor outside his office. I held her hand, and my pulse beat with hers till I couldn't tell where my skin stopped and hers began. After all these years, I felt how connected I still was to the one human being that I'd always been connected to no matter where in the world I was, and no matter how distant or angry we were.

My palms got sweaty, I loosened my grip, and we were separate again.

Back in her apartment, Min said, "Look around. I'd like you to have anything you want."

"I want that," I said, pointing to a beautiful black-and-white photo of her taken in the Luxembourg Gardens when she was forty-two. The photo sat on her living room coffee table and had an elaborately embossed silver frame I'd bought for her in Santa Monica a few years before. In the photo her smile was real and warm, a time I knew she was truly happy. "And I want that little glass paperweight," I said—a small round one that held a photo of two-year-old-me in her arms, next to my sisters—Caroline, age nine, and Brenlee, age twelve. The photo shows Min smiling, her deep dimples at their best, and I knew she'd always kept that little treasure on her dressing table.

She found a box, wrapped these things in newspaper for me, and set it by the door. "It's good," she said. "You'll have these things to remind yourself of happier days."

Standing next to her, I started sniffling, and although she was four inches shorter and thirty pounds lighter, she held me tightly and said, "Don't be too sad, honey. Everybody must die. You'll be okay." She rubbed her hands down my back from shoulder to waist a few times. "Always know you were loved dearly. Remember that. I love you more than life itself."

She was so small and so big at the same time.

Later in the elevator she made me laugh. The basement was the parking garage, so we were headed for street level, riding down with five other very old women. Min asked, "Are we going to the main floor?" and another old lady said, "No the basement." And when Min asked, "The basement?" the lady said, "Do you think we have a car?"

No one found that very amusing, and the lady leaned in close to Min and said, "My sense of humor isn't very good."

Min turned around to her and said, "It's okay. I won't report you."

CHAPTER 16

"Bye, Bon"

A year passed, me working every day and taking care of finances while Bob worked out with his trainer, played handball, drove his beloved Land Cruiser, and talked with friends. His charm and humor carried him, and something about knowing he would decline motivated him to keep doing what he'd always done: let his mind take him down any creative path he liked. While driving, he dictated his ideas. At home, he recorded his life stories. We both wanted to preserve that wonderful array of life experiences he told so well.

The sexual conflict between us that had nearly blown us apart was pretty much a thing of the past. He could rarely maintain an erection, and I was preoccupied with work. I continued dressing up for him when we went out, and I enjoyed it for the familiar and lovely thing it was without any pressure to do more. It had taken us twenty-five years to find this peace with each other.

By early 2004, the Quicken accounts were a map of his decline and of my rising. I cast around for something else he could do that he'd feel proud of. A downtown art gallery agreed to have an exhibit of his photography. It was a great day for Bob. People loved his photos. Some were purchased on the spot.

Andy and Carol helped us host: Carol had catering experience and helped set up a reception, and Andy was his charming and warm self. Because people talked about how much they liked the images, we decided to start a line of commercial greeting cards using Bob's photographs.

Andy and Carol agreed to sit at our dining table and help us think up funny captions to go with Bob's photographs. Every Sunday, the four of us gathered and brainstormed. We drank, we ate, we laughed and laughed, and I wrote it all down. Within a few months, we had about sixty images with captions we loved.

Then one Sunday evening in mid-December 2004, my sister Brenlee called.

"Mom's dying," she said.

I left for Winnipeg immediately. I found Min's room in the hospice hospital, and her face lit up as always at the sight of me. "Bon!" she called, reaching out her hand. I bent over to kiss her cheek and pulled up a chair very close to her to hold her hand and chat. I was there for six hours, greeting both my sisters who came for brief stays and left me to talk with Min the rest of the time. Amazingly she was fully conscious and lucid, but she'd stopped drinking water, and she was peeing less. "Are you not drinking on purpose?" I asked.

She nodded.

"Are you thirsty?"

She nodded.

But she was going to call it, and at ninety-four she had decided to call it quits. How I admired her, strong to the end, still making her own choices.

216 staying married is the hardest part

We chatted about the family, always her favorite topic. Then I asked, "Do you think there's anything after death?" She shook her head no.

"Do you believe in God?" Again a no.

I found this strangely reassuring. In a way, it surprised me, since she and my father had attended High Holiday services all the years we were growing up, and we'd had all those Passover seders and Friday night dinners with her saying a prayer over the brass candlesticks she'd inherited from her mother. I could still see her hands circling around the two flames as she quietly said the prayer. But I understood now that her purpose was to give us a sense of community, to solidify our identity as Jews, and share the common religious rituals that bound families together. It was not God she feared, it was Hitler, and the many other persecutors down through the centuries. What mattered to her was family, and personal freedom for Jews unmarred by prejudice against us.

She rubbed the top of my hand in the way she'd always done, gently, with great affection. Amazingly, she was still cogent and lucid. Pronouncing each word for emphasis, she said, "When I look back on my life, you three girls are my proudest achievement."

My voice was foggy. "You gave us so much, Min."

Out of the blue, she looked directly at me and said, "Darling—you know—of the three of you—you're the one most like me."

Shock suddenly stuck me to my chair. This thought had never occurred to me. The light in the room shifted, brighter and more piercing. I was as stubborn as she was, as determined, and at the same time as loving and tender. She too had left a controlling, demanding mother and gone to another country.

She too loved words and poetry and tried to read people. And hadn't she too found a safe haven in her husband, yet deferred to him and lived with her disappointment?

Her words landed in a young part of me that remembered feeling my sisters did everything better, and I could never measure up. I took her hand and stroked it softly as she had mine countless times. "Yes—you and I—yes, so much in common."

She squeezed my fingers.

Her private thought felt like the ultimate recognition: I was more like her than they were.

Whether she might have said that privately to each of my sisters, I'll never know. In her way of cultivating intimacy with each of us, she was capable of that. But often she'd said, "I love all my daughters equally, but differently," and maybe this was the difference? To be the one most like her felt like the ultimate, intimate compliment and I believed in these last moments of her conscious life, she was speaking her truth. It was a great parting gift to me, better than any of her jewelry, better than photographs or her paintings. It explained to me why years ago she had shocked me when she had told me with admiration, "You're the only one who got out."

I stayed for five days, visiting with her for hours each day, happy she was being treated kindly and didn't seem to be in pain. I knew now what I had only dimly realized: I'd had two great loves in my life—Min and Bob—and they were more alike than I'd ever realized. I had partly chosen him because I loved being his darling, the way I'd loved being hers.

On the fifth day, her eyes looked like doll eyes, wide open. I knew it was from dehydration. She said, "They're going to help me along now."

218 staying married is the hardest part

"That's good," I told her. I was grateful the nursing staff could legally do that here.

I kissed her tenderly on her cheek, then stood at the foot of her bed for one last look.

She waved and said, "Bye, Bon," as if she was standing at the railing of an ocean liner that was slowly pulling out to sea.

"Bye Min," I said, and waved back.

During the service for her funeral, I sat in the pew of my childhood synagogue, realizing I'd been searching for her in others my whole life. I had in me a homing device for people like Min, recognizing them almost instantly and being inexorably drawn to them. There had only been four including Bob, and all I had admired and loved most deeply, but each one had an edge. They were the ones I worshipped a bit, the ones to whom I gave up too much power, but with whom I felt most at home. No wonder I'd been drawn to Bob like magnet to metal. No wonder I could never leave him.

Still, time and circumstances had changed me. In my building a full-time practice, managing our business and finances, and navigating Bob's medical care, Bob and I had both begun to see my strength. And in talking to my patients, I had begun listening to what I said, learning my opinions, and acquiring a new level of authority.

Years had been lost between me and Min, but eventually she had given me the respect and admiration I'd wanted, which now came with sadness and loss.

She was buried next to my father in his family's Winnipeg plot—she, still the Californian, put to rest in the Canadian frozen ground.

bonnie comfort   219

Two weeks later, in January 2005, there was a big Portland snowstorm, and the city shut down. I was like a kid when school was canceled—no need to drive to my office and be responsible. Instead, I was home in my warm-ups, eating toast and watching the endless TV coverage of buses and cars slipping and sliding. Bob was writing and rewriting a script that had gone through several versions and had landed in his lap for a rewrite. He typed and typed at his desk.

The downstairs living room was his office, his big black desk facing the windows to the garden, the walls lined with his collection of ball caps. On an adjoining wall were hundreds of his music CDs which fueled his five-disc player to set his writing mood.

On this day I sat near him, reading on the sofa while he worked. After a while he stopped typing, turned his squeaky chair to me and said, "Will you help me?" his voice sadly quiet. He was stuck, he said. He couldn't remember whether a character he'd introduced was in the first act or the second act. He couldn't keep track of the story lines.

I read through the script. There were sections repeated, story lines confused. A small sensation of nausea clenched my stomach as it did more and more when I saw his cognitive abilities slipping. I'd have to track the story for him, type it for him, be his brain.

We worked on that script for five snow-trapped days. There were joyous moments with Savvy outside playing in the snow, his black fur an ink spot on a pristine world. I built a fire in the kitchen wood stove, baked cornbread, and we watched old movies and cuddled and laughed and talked as we always had. But there was the insidious decline, money at stake, the producer calling to ask for the script, frustration on Bob's part

220   staying married is the hardest part

to the point where one evening, sitting next to me on the sofa, he said, "Such a shame . . . a good brain going to waste."

He never wrote another script.

A few weeks later, on a horribly rainy day, I left Bob at home to amuse himself in whatever way he could. I'd been in practice downtown now five years, mostly treating the usual anxiety and depression of adult life, but I'd also started seeing couples for marital therapy.

There were big puddles pooling on the downtown streets, and I was wearing my ugly ankle-length raincoat: military green, shapeless, with a hood that made me look like a Druid. I shook off as much water as I could before sweeping into our inner hallway to hang up my raincoat so I could look calm and dry.

By ten minutes into my first session, I was immersed in someone else's world. It was remarkable how much of an antidote that was to my sadness, a reminder that when it comes to suffering, I was certainly not alone. At the end of my workday I was totally spent. I clomped down the fire escape stairs into a dark, empty parking lot.

The rain had stopped, and the streets were dry. I was looking forward to seeing Bob, but on the drive, I thought about many of the patients I'd seen that day, and how beliefs they'd developed in their young years had shaped their whole lives.

It was true for me as well, particularly Min's teaching which I'd so taken to heart, that marrying the right man was everything. As I drove on autopilot, I thought briefly about the many men I'd tossed aside. I could have been happy with quite a few of those men I'd abandoned.

I didn't regret marrying Bob. I was full of love for him despite our differences, and it was true I needed a husband who had the basics—kindness, generosity, his own achievements—but given that, the formula for happiness was in my own hands, not in finding a perfect partner. I had hurt too many good men in my relentless quest for The Right One, and not given enough energy to being The Right One myself.

At home, I pulled into the driveway and gathered up my things. I felt like a pack animal, the load a bit lighter at the end of the day. Savvy greeted me with the usual excitement. Bob was watching the evening news but happily agreed to go to our local Mexican restaurant.

At dinner I said, "I think we get along better than we used to. We don't fight as much."

To which he replied, "Oh—We've just worn each other smooth like stones in a river . . ."

Later at home he handed me a piece of paper and said, "I wrote this today. How d'ya like it?"

> The Bible tells us if you cast your seed upon the ground
>   it is a sin.
> This is the first warning that there will be a penalty for
>   early withdrawal . . .

I laughed and hugged him. "I love it! So clever!"

I had fought with him for decades over sex and geography, but I saw him in that moment for everything about him I loved—his struggle to overcome those heavy Bible teachings, his humor, his playful gaze, the joy of fun always. He was my person.

222   staying married is the hardest part

Before bedtime, we sat on our leather sofa watching a PBS documentary on Dian Fossey and her research with gorillas in Africa. There was one adult female who had a newborn baby that died. This sad gorilla mom carried around her dead baby for weeks.

Tears filled Bob's eyes. He struggled to speak as his mouth trembled. "I feel like that mother gorilla. My screenplays are my dead babies, and I keep dragging them around."

That March 2005, I officially started our greeting card business, filing it with the state, creating a trademark, and doing research for how to proceed. The best thing was it gave Bob something meaningful to do. During days home alone, he culled through photos, and thought up captions. I'd drag myself home from a long day, and once again it was like walking into the light. Bob would show me his day's efforts—the old comedy genius still intact—and I'd laugh at his world-class humor.

On Sunday evenings, Andy and Carol continued sitting with us at our dining table and brainstorming silly, hilarious one-liners. It was such a familiar format for Bob—a comedy writers' table, eating, drinking, and making each other laugh. No wonder it was so addictive. No wonder after you've had a taste of that you never want to go back to an ordinary desk job.

We launched our cards at the National Stationery Show in New York. A week after the show we had a reputable wholesaler in Seattle.

CHAPTER 17

Humpty Dumpty

Every day, there was a parade through my office, six or seven 50-minute sessions, each patient unique, specific, worried, hurting, angry, or confused. I did my best to be what they needed, this one needing comfort and reassurance, that one needing insight and a new take on circumstances. Each had a specific history that cast a unique shadow on current life.

In between therapy sessions, I often went for a walk to clear my patients' emotions out of my body and return to myself. Doing therapy is like being a tea bag in a cup. You let the patients' stories and feelings flow through you and fill you up, but you remain intact inside your own silky boundaries. Then, when they leave, you withdraw yourself from their cup and get ready to submerge yourself in the next one.

I usually walked briskly past the coffee shops perfumed with baking chocolate and roasted beans. Instead, I tried getting my blood pumping, breezing past the college dorms, library, and restaurants. Back in my office, I opened the door to the next one, ready to let that patient flow through me, but by the end of the day, I was worn out.

224   staying married is the hardest part

At night, my patients' stories sometimes stayed in my head, but only ones in which I worried I hadn't said the right thing. I reminded myself that my presence in their lives was mostly what cures. Rarely did I recall anything specific that was said in my own analyses. What I remembered was the caring attunement of another human being who listened so intently to me. It was the full Presence of the Other that transformed me little by little.

I often feel therapy is like that—that I sit with a person as she thinks out loud, and by my listening and being there, she is able to discover herself and how to navigate her life.

As his dementia progressed, Bob clung more and more to pleasurable activities that soothed him, particularly trolling through junk stores and antique malls. I gritted my teeth every time he came home holding a paper bag because it usually held some odd object I had no desire to own—a Howdy Doody doll, a toy gun, or antique children's puzzles. Gradually, Bob filled up our basement with a diverse collection of objects, most of which I thought were of little monetary value. I was frustrated by these things. I saw he was trying to recapture his childhood, often drawn to things from the 1940s or 1950s, but there were quirky comedy things too—a wind-up toy of a naked couple having sex, a watercolor painting of Jim Bakker and a weeping Tammy Faye, her heavy mascara dripping down her face.

One day, though, Bob brought home the most amazing Humpty Dumpty I'd ever seen. Painted in bright colors, it was wooden, almost two feet high, with articulating arms and legs that allowed it to bend at the knee and sit on a shelf. The top of the head above the eyebrows could be removed to reveal the hollow inside, and we figured it was designed as a toy box. It was an enchanting piece, bigger than life, evocative of the old rhyme, captivating in its colors and cheery paint. "This is wonderful!" I said.

Bob's smile was broad with pleasure.

We left it downstairs with the other collectibles, but a few years later, I hired a decorator to redo the living room and bring in higher, firmer sofas for Bob. Behind those, we secured three tall bookshelves to display some of the things he'd found. There, we put the charming Humpty on top of one of the bookshelves, the legs dangling over the edge. In the dining room, I installed huge, framed posters of our five best greeting cards, so his creative product was on display. It helped him feel his life still mattered.

I realize now that the anguish I felt in seeing him leave for the casino or junk stores was triggered by knowing he was no longer capable of a more productive life. He never lost much money at the casino, so I didn't worry about that, but for as brilliant a chess player as he'd been, now he couldn't even win against me, me who in earlier years could be beaten in three of his moves. Instead, he sat at digital slot machines or searched for dusty relics that reminded him of boyhood days when he and his brother would have a shoot-out with toy guns or keep a large tin can full of their best glass marbles.

By now, it had been two years since we launched our greeting card business, and the enthusiasm of our card reps in Seattle had dwindled. As the months wore on, and the accounting statements looked worse and worse, I closed the business.

226   staying married is the hardest part

One late autumn afternoon in 2007, I looked out the front door of our house and saw Bob pulling into the driveway, back from the casino. The maple trees were turning bright flame, the oaks shedding their yellow leaves over our lawn. Bob was still driving, but he now had a full beard because he'd lost the manual dexterity needed to shave. When he saw me at the screen door, he gave me the full-faced smile that was mine—the one that always said how happy he was to see me, how special our connection was. I felt a start in my chest, a moment of joy like I imagine a male Emperor penguin must feel after keeping his one egg warm for four months until he sees his mate trudging toward him, reuniting the family.

In early December 2007, we went to an ocean resort north of Puerto Vallarta, where we could eat on-site, soak up the hot sun, and watch for whales. One day, we took a taxi into town, browsed jewelry stores, and found a sparkly silver necklace for me. Since we'd married, Bob had only worn his wedding ring, but this time, a heavy silver bracelet caught his eye, and I said, "Yes! Buy it!" He only wore it for a few weeks until I had to have a MedicAlert bracelet made for him instead.

At our resort, I practiced my Spanish with the staff, but as Bob watched me talking with one waiter, his old addiction surfaced, and he said, "He likes you. Come on to him. We could have him in our room, and I could watch."

I gritted my teeth. He hadn't made a request like that in years, and that whole obsession seemed outlandish now but as entrenched as the four blue dots tattooed at the base of his neck for radiation accuracy.

He offered to buy the waiter's hotel jacket and gave him our room number. One evening, the guy knocked on our door and handed it to us in its transparent laundry bag. Bob tipped him heavily, and I politely thanked the guy and said goodnight, disappointing Bob in that way for the last time. When we left, I dutifully packed it and brought it home, where I hung it in the closet.

Eventually, I gave it to Goodwill after Bob stopped noticing it.

Lewy body disease not only impaired Bob's mind; it slowly ate away at his physical abilities, too. I had the toilet elevated and grab bars installed. He was as dear and funny as ever, but his driving was getting dangerous; he needed company and supervision during the day and someone to make meals. He tried to fight losing his driver's license, but when he looked at the written exam he'd have to take, he gave up.

I tried various home care agencies. Finally, we found the perfect caregiver: midfifties, cheerful, and sweet. She reminded Bob of his mother, and he and Dot bonded immediately. She sat with him and discussed his stamps. They took Savvy to the park. When I got home, dinner was ready. As responsible as Dot was, I never worried about Bob as long as she was with him. Evenings and weekends were still me, though, sometimes all night long.

Bob slept in the master bedroom on the main floor; I slept in the guest room right below that. He began wandering at night, coming down to my room, panicky and disoriented. I installed LED runner lights along the steps so he could see where he was going. I put a baby monitor on my night table and could hear him yelling in his REM sleep. I was extraordinarily patient, but one night after he'd woken me for the third time, I snapped, "What do you *want!*"

228   staying married is the hardest part

In a childlike voice, he said, "Everything."

Ugh. The sadness of that fully woke me. "C'mon, get into bed with me," I said. I wrapped my arm around his waist until we both fell asleep.

I attended a weekly support group for caregivers and discovered that many people with dementia were horrible to care for—angry, combative, mean, and without gratitude. How fortunate I felt leaving those meetings to come home to my sweet, muddled husband. He never lost his insight. He accepted that he had dementia. He thanked me every day and was still funny, sometimes unintentionally.

One day, Dot was driving Bob to a store, and he glanced in the car's back seat and asked, "Isn't someone missing?"

"Yes. Savvy. But he's home with Bonnie."

"Bonnie? What Bonnie?"

"Your Bonnie."

"Since when did I become Bonnie?"

I took him to see his psychiatrist, his gerontologist, and his dentist. For his depression and anxiety, he was prescribed a cocktail of medications that helped keep him alert and calm, but at one point, his doctor added valproic acid, a mood stabilizer, and it seemed to help with one unusual addition—it gave him a frequent partial erection, a "chubby" he called it, and it was a very pleasant surprise to him. One day, as he sat on the toilet looking down at his "chubby," he smiled up at me and said, "I like my new friend."

Oh my God, the man was so endearing, as addled as he was by then.

One Tuesday, I attended a conference on meditation. I was impressed when the instructor guided a room full of two hundred people through Mountain Meditation. I experienced the remarkable effect of doing it myself, being the mountain, and watching the seasons change. What a gift to have this perspective. I came home, lightened and feeling good, and Bob greeted me when I walked in the front door. I chattered away about my conference until he looked at me oddly and said, "I have to admit I'm not really sure who you are."

Immediately taken aback, I say, "Are you fuckin' with me!?" Bob smiled his impish smile. "No, but I'd *like* to fuck you."

I laughed, but inside, a dreadful sadness lurked—*he's going to stop knowing who I am.* I took his hand. "Let's sit down on the sofa and watch the news."

We sat, knees touching, and he said, "Well, whoever you are, you're very good company." I threaded my fingers through his and put my head on his shoulder. I was aware of a still, quiet knowledge that Bob and I were both waiting for the inevitable.

After dinner each evening, we'd settle on the sofa with my legs stretched out on his lap, and he would rub me with lotion or Aquaphor. His rubbing relaxed me so deeply I would often doze while we were watching whatever on TV he wanted to see.

And here was the strangest and loveliest thing: after he took his evening pills, we lay down each night in his bed, and he would run his hands slowly over my thighs, torso, and back. "You have such nice skin," he said one time. We spooned, he stroked my back, we turned, I stroked his. It was honey and sustenance, primitive and soothing, like mother and baby, lovers, owner and puppy, and we were all those. How shocking that it had come to this—the most reassuring, loving Presence of the Other, without the struggle for words, the frustrations of the day. Just the simple and deep pleasure of a comfortable bed, soft sheets, and complete communion with one another.

230   staying married is the hardest part

And then I would slip away to go to bed alone, Sudoku, books, recipes.

Every evening around eight, Savvy leaped into action, racing up and down the stairs. Although Bob rarely looked after Savvy, he sang to him, played with him, and made me laugh a thousand times with the things he said about Savvy. That was so typical of our marriage: I lived with a comedian. He paid me in trade.

One day, when I came home from work, I sat next to Bob and said, "I have a patient today who has Marfan's syndrome." Years earlier, Bob had told me about that condition. He looked at me blankly, so I asked, "Do you remember what that is? Abraham Lincoln had it."

"Is it hat disease?" he asked.

My work calendar was crammed full, and I made every decision at home. Sometimes, I wore the same work clothes every day of the week, so I didn't have to take the time or energy to choose something else. Sometimes, if I had a twenty-minute break, I put my head down on my work desk and slept. I barely looked at myself in the mirror.

The last time I took Bob to Ashland, he was sixty-eight, and I was sixty-three, and by then, I saw the value in a small-town life. Ashland offered a gentle pace, the natural beauty of mountains and creeks, and now, twenty-eight years after we'd bought a house there, an interesting array of people, stores, and restaurants. That weekend, I felt sad about taking Bob away from this lovely town. We drove by our old house, visited friends, and strolled the bike path we'd walked so often. After leaving town, we drove through the pear orchards where, so many years ago, I had danced for Bob in my bra and panties in front of the car's headlights, the only light illuminating me under the night sky.

I dreaded Bob deteriorating into some kind of crisis. One morning in 2009, I came into the kitchen and found him holding a large carving knife over an open carton of cottage cheese. He was stabbing the air with the knife and talking under his breath.

"What are you doing?" I asked, loud and alarmed.

He looked up, surprised, shaken out of his reverie. "Oh. I don't know."

"That's very dangerous! Put the knife away!"

He put it down on the counter. "I had to defend myself."

I burst into tears and sank down to the floor, sobbing, my back against our center island.

His tone was quiet and sad; he said, "Why is your heart breaking, little girl?"

I got up, blew my nose, and put my arms around his, those warm, loving arms that still meant the world to me. "You have to be careful with big knives."

Occasionally, Bob would ask to see naughty photos he'd taken of me over the years. I didn't mind. I'd show him the matte 8 x 10s I'd saved—me in French lingerie, stiletto heels, cleavage, tasteful photos like the Playboy girls of the 1960s. I couldn't fit into half of those garter belts now, nor would my feet be happy, but what fun we'd often had over the years and how pretty I'd felt. Sometimes in those earlier days, we'd start fooling around in bed when I was in my favorite nightwear—a

232   staying married is the hardest part

plain white T-shirt—and he'd say, "Why don't you go slip into something uncomfortable?" and I'd laugh and dutifully comply, charmed by his insight.

Now, he would hand back the photos and say, "I wish we could do this again," and although I felt sad for him, I was relieved that it wasn't possible.

Instead, we were having a deep romance. He was in love with my sixty-four-year-old body with its lumps and bumps in the wrong places. He didn't care. He caressed me like he never had before, slowly, tenderly, with complete giving. Was this the same man who wanted to avoid being too intimate with my body? No. It was not the same man. Years of work, disappointment, and illness had changed him. He had lost his arrogance completely. He was naked before me, vulnerable and sad. And I loved him more than ever.

Our last trip anywhere was a drive up to Edmonton to see friends and his family. We stayed in a hotel, because Bob didn't exactly know anymore where in the bathroom to have a bowel movement. Sometimes on the floor, sometimes in the shower. It was awful for both of us.

After spending the afternoon on his brother's farm, Bob's eyes were teary. "Could we move back here?" he asked, the longing making his voice rough. "I'd like to . . ." he said.

But those days of me accommodating his geographic cures were over, and we both knew a move would not hold back the heartbreaking inevitable.

"I have to keep working, honey," is all I said.

A good long-term marriage is earned slowly through forgiveness, acceptance, and devotion. Mutual empathy and admiration give the marriage strength when an argument brings you to the brink of thinking of divorce. Over many years' time, you evolve a genuine acceptance of your mate, this Flawed Other whose quirks and habits don't in some ways fit your own and require strategies for working around your differences.

You can't stay in a long-term marriage without sacrifice. No matter how much you have in common, you're two very different people, and inevitably, there are times when what one wants is mutually exclusive from what the other wants. You either give up something you want because what you have with this person is bigger and matters more to you than that thing, or you leave because losing that thing is intolerable.

Certainly, that was the case with Bob and me. Each of us gave up living in the place we loved best in order to create a viable compromise. I often adapted to Bob's habits, but he, too, made room for my needs, supporting me, encouraging my creative abilities, and, of course, entertaining me in a way no one else ever had. We admired each other. We had compatibility in our attachment styles; both of us were mostly secure with long-term emotional closeness, yet able to tolerate the other's absence, communicate effectively, and turn to the other for support. When we fought, we would both regress to avoidant strategies, withdrawal, distance, and silence, but we were able to repair, sometimes just by holding hands.

Feeling heard, accepted, and appreciated ultimately kept us together.

CHAPTER 18

He's in Room 9

Even when you know someone's going to die in the next few months or years, you don't know exactly when or how. Denial protects you from thinking about it very much. You focus on today, you appreciate everything that's good right now, and you keep the dark presence just out of consciousness, a heavy, oppressive quicksand that could pull you under if you let it. You grasp for every sign that death will be far away and take pleasure in the smallest triumphs.

Near the end of his life, Bob's safety became such an issue that I moved him into an assisted living apartment. The day I moved him there was the worst. He stood in the middle of our bedroom, watching Dot and me pack his meager clothes, the T-shirts and warm-up pants. He'd never been much interested in clothes, but now these were the only ones he'd need. His arms hung helplessly by his sides; his eyes tracked us from closet to suitcase. I was tormented by guilt, but he accepted the situation. When we arrived there, the all-female staff welcomed him, escorted us to his suite, and tried making him feel comfortable.

After we were alone in his apartment, he asked, "Is this a bordello?"

Later that evening, I tidied up his desk at home and found this note: "I love lucid."

A week after I moved Bob out of the house, Savvy came into my bedroom on a Sunday morning, pacing. He couldn't get comfortable sitting or lying down. I drove him to Dove Lewis, the best twenty-four-hour animal hospital in Portland, and they brought a gurney out for him. As I walked toward the front entrance of the building, I saw Savvy lift his head and look at me as these strangers wheeled him away. Our eyes met.

They gave him an opioid. In a few days, they diagnosed him with metastatic prostate cancer, now invading his spine. No cure. Intractable pain. I told them yes, please release him from this misery. Dot brought Bob to the vet hospital so we could say goodbye to him together. They put a nice blanket down for Savvy on the floor, and he lay on it. Bob and I held hands. Then, very quickly, the vet came in and gave Savvy the first injection. Immediately, Savvy's furrowed brow relaxed. A few minutes after that, he received the toxic injection, and in seconds, the life force drained out of him. I had never seen this before. It was shocking to feel that Savvy was no longer there. His body was an empty vessel now.

I took a lock of his tail hair, his paw prints in plaster of paris, his collar, and leash. A week later, I went to the crematorium and picked up Savvy's ashes in a floral black and orange tin container.

One of the last times I saw Bob happy was an afternoon when I arrived a little early at his assisted living apartment. They told

236 staying married is the hardest part

me he'd had a bad day; he'd fallen again, and an assistant had wheeled him up to the third floor to watch a resident couple playing ping-pong. I waited at a distance for a few moments, sad for Bob in that chair, steeling myself for looking after him and watching him suffer. And then, as I got within ten yards of him, he turned and saw me, and the instant infusion of joy practically made him bounce out of his wheelchair. There was that wonderful full-faced grin, that wide mouth suddenly upturned in joy at seeing me, almost as if a strong wind had struck him. His hand hit the arm of the chair, and he said, "There she is!" with such happiness. How could I not feel so loving and sad that now, I was his only joy?

I wheeled him back to his apartment, and we sat side by side on his sofa.

In December 1977, when we went shopping for wedding rings in a Brentwood jewelry store, I had agonized over rings for a good half hour. I loved a pavé diamond ring, but the band was plain. I liked another patterned band, but it had no diamond. The owner offered to make me a new patterned band to go with the pavé diamond, and I agreed. Bob, on the other hand, stood for a few minutes in front of the men's wedding bands, pointed, and said, "That one."

"Don't you want to think about it?" I said. "Take your time?"

"No. That one'll be fine."

Too quick, I thought. Not careful enough. It's a little ornate with those imprinted leaves.

He was happy with it, and how little I understood then his ability to go with his gut and be right. I needed ten months to take the risk of marrying him. He needed only two weeks to know I was the one. And for thirty-two years he never took that ring off except for surgeries.

Now we were sitting on the "genuine fake-leather sofa" we'd purchased long ago in Medford and poked fun at because both ends reclined. I liked that stupid sofa because Bob could stretch out, put his feet on me, and I could rub them while I had my own feet elevated. That was maybe twenty years ago. Twenty years of rubbing his feet, loving his weirdly shaped toes and too-prominent heels. How many thousands of times had I run my hands up his legs, inside his pant legs, sometimes up to the crotch? Too many to count. And now I sat beside him on that same couch in his assisted living apartment. He'd lost nineteen pounds in one month. A few times I'd taken him out for dinner after the thin dinner there—soup, a cheesy bun—and he had eaten all his pot roast at the restaurant. "More food!" I told them. "He needs more food!" They tried, but it wasn't adequate. Guilt-ridden and worried, I wondered if I'd made a horrible mistake in bringing him here.

For a moment, I looked up and away, and when I looked back, I saw that his wedding ring had fallen off his fourth finger and was sitting on his lap. The sight of it struck me like a board across the face: that he'd lost so much weight his ring had fallen off his hand, that the symbol of our marriage, which he'd rarely taken off, had simply fallen off by itself. That he could lose it. That I could lose him. That I was already losing him. Every day. Every pound.

Early the following Sunday, I took Savvy's ashes to the wooded park where we'd walked together so many times for twelve years. There was fog all around, heavy and humid, and no one on the walking path, just me and my floral can holding

238   staying married is the hardest part

the boy I'd loved and cared for. I scattered his ashes in his favorite spots, returning him to his playground, saying a little prayer to the universe for his dear soul.

On Christmas Day, Andy and Carol came to the house for a quick lunch before we all went to spend the rest of the day with Bob at his assisted living apartment, but during lunch, I got an emergency call from the facility. He was deteriorating. They couldn't get him to eat or drink anything.

We raced there and found him in bed, a bit incoherent and severely dehydrated. I called for an ambulance, and they rushed him to the ER. Andy and Carol drove their car and met us there. They waited nearby after Bob and I were settled in one of the few private ER rooms. Mewling, moaning, and bustle wafted in, along with the smell of antiseptic and disinfectant. Doctors and nurses and aides milled around the command desk.

As we kept waiting, my stomach clenched into a knot. I was desperate for Bob to get help. Suddenly, I recognized the senior doctor in the ER and went to her for help. To my relief, she immediately barked orders to a nurse who came into Bob's room minutes later and hooked up an IV. They took blood samples while I watched the life-giving liquid drip into his vein. The doc came back an hour later and said she thought he should be admitted. I thanked Andy and Carol and told them to go home. By midnight, the end of Christmas Day, they'd settled Bob in a room on the fourth floor and brought in a cot for me.

All night, they checked on him, pumped fluid, and took his temperature. In the morning, the change in him was remarkable—back to his usual loquacious self, back to joking.

He wanted to talk to Claire in LA. I dialed the number. "I'm having a close call," he said, and we all laughed.

The doctor ordered soft food for him—applesauce and pudding. He couldn't eat any of it. He choked on a spoonful of water. The dietitian said she would give him thickened water to see if he could swallow that.

In the late afternoon, the dietitian brought thickened water. Bob choked and coughed and spit it out. Outside, a heavy snow was falling, and in the wedge of light from the streetlamp, I could make out the flakes rushing to the ground, sharply white in the waning light. The room smelled of hospital food and bleach. The footsteps of visitors and staff in the hallway gradually faded. I slept again on the cot, still in my velour outfit. Christmas music played quietly over the loudspeakers, interspersed with the usual paging announcements. On TV, *It's a Wonderful Life* played continuously hour after hour.

Ten o'clock the next morning, Dr. Hodges arrived, a smart gerontologist who had guided us through Bob's decline over the last several years. She took me into an empty, darkened windowless chapel where she left the light very dim in the quiet.

"Well, Bonnie, Bob's been very clear he doesn't want to go on living by artificial means. Now he's unable to swallow, so the only way to keep him alive would be to give him a feeding tube, and I know he doesn't want that."

It was one of those moments when the surreal carves itself into your memory for good. Her soft strawberry blond hair, her small, clean hands, the faint sound of announcements on the incessant hallway loudspeaker. "So, if you disconnect the IV, how long will it take him to die?"

"A week or two."

240   staying married is the hardest part

Seven to fourteen days before he would take his last breath.

We went to his room and stood next to him. Dr. Hodges said, "Bob, I'm sorry to say you won't be able to survive without a feeding tube. So now is the time to unhook the IV and let you slip away."

He looked at both of us, acceptance calming his cheeks, his voice steady. "Okay, that's fine. I'm okay with it." He was fully conscious and clearheaded and didn't need to ask any more questions. Dr. Hodges explained she'd try to get a bed for him at a good hospice facility.

After she walked out, I stood next to the bed, holding his hand.

Still so himself, he said, "On further consideration, I would like to have lived longer."

I chuckled. I kept holding his hand, profoundly grateful that he was cogent, that he was gracious in accepting death, and that I didn't have to be the one making that final decision.

That afternoon, I watched the nurse remove his IV—the final life-sustaining fluid withdrawn. The ambulance drivers wheeled Bob down the hall on a rolling stretcher while I put on my heavy blue rain jacket that had been hung on the wall the last three days. I found my car in the parking lot. It was December 28, 2009, and remnants of snow were piled on the side streets. By the time I arrived at Hopewell House, a Providence hospice facility that at one time was a private mansion, it was midafternoon, and the sky was a heavy gray.

I called all my patients and told them I'd be out of the office for several weeks. At the moment, it was only Bob and me.

"He's in Room 9," the nurse said, pointing to a room with a glass window directly opposite the nursing desk. I stepped into the room and saw Bob lying there with his eyes closed, a hideous red patchwork quilt covering him. Funny how your mind latches onto the smallest thing you can control at a moment like that. I immediately went back to the nursing desk and asked if they could replace the patchwork quilt with a simple one in a neutral color. "Sure," they said and brought him a plain beige. I felt oddly better. I didn't want him going out under a clown blanket.

I dialed a few last calls for him on my cell. His speech was thick, the words not articulated too clearly. The last call was to Dr. Cohen, his longtime psychiatrist. I explained before I put Bob on the phone. They talked briefly, and then Bob said, "Well, I love you." After he gave me back the phone he told me Dr. Cohen replied, "I love you too."

We held hands. The staff checked on us very often and began giving him morphine tucked inside his cheek and moisture swabs for his mouth. They changed his diaper regularly and offered me food, but I couldn't swallow much myself. I alternated between Sudoku puzzles and knitting. I was making a complicated scarf from alpaca yarn we'd bought on one of our last outings, that time to Hood River, where we'd stopped at a small winery and an alpaca farm.

I went home long enough to shower and change my clothes and bring back a portable CD player and my laptop computer. Bob wanted to listen to a favorite relaxation CD of ours, one we often fell asleep to. When I got back, he was still conscious, and I put the music on and settled into the chair. The smells of antiseptic, bleach, and hand soap peculiar to hospitals infused the air. Each time the nurse entered the room, he rubbed hand sanitizer between his fingers.

I composed a long email to our friends and relatives, saying Bob was dying and that if they wished to say some last words to him, I would read their emails to him. I explained his illness, Lewy body dementia, adding that he had called it the "Louis the Fourteenth disease."

242   staying married is the hardest part

A flood of emails came in, but I couldn't read them aloud without crying. A close friend from my writing group, Diane Ponti, kindly read them to him, a great act of generosity on her part. Barbara and Rick flew up from LA to see him before he died. His brother, Doug, flew down from Edmonton. Steve drove up from Ashland to be with him and burst into tears as he sat at the foot of Bob's bed. I left them alone to commune with each other.

Other friends visited, and for a few days, Bob could still respond. On New Year's Eve, Andy and Carol brought champagne and food in a wicker basket, and Barb, Rick, and I joined them in the Hopewell dining room. Their kindness and generosity meant so much.

The hospice home had a huge living room right outside Bob's room, and each day, one nurse brought her golden retriever, who lounged on a doggy bed and radiated calm. Having just lost Savvy, I found this homey presence comforting, and each day, I paused to pat the dog.

Friends continued to visit and call—Bob's squash coach came, as did his exercise trainer, a squash buddy, my girlfriends, and his hairdresser. Bob slept longer periods of time, and he gradually became less responsive. Emails were read to him by our close friends while they were visiting. Andy and Carol spent a great deal of time there.

By January 6, Bob was no longer responsive, but the nursing staff continued looking after him superbly. They asked if I'd like them to increase his morphine dose, and I said yes. There was no point in prolonging anything now.

As he lay there, his eyes closed, his body sunken into the mattress, I sat snugged up to his bed, and I held his still warm hand, and I said over and over, "I'll love you forever, Boss." The nursing staff told me hearing is the last sense to go when someone is dying. I wanted that to be the last thing he heard.

It was so clear to me he was on his own path now, letting go of life, reaching into the universe, into eternity, toward the blue light he described seeing when he was doing a guided imagery exercise during cancer. There was peace in his body, and the nurse who was so kind to him said, "He's having a good death," and I saw the truth of it, the peace in his face, his acceptance without a fight. Fortunately, he had not been in pain. He had suffered indignities, loneliness, loss of his home and his dog, and his mental faculties, but the wisdom in his core remained, and his spiritual acceptance of death allowed him this peaceful end.

In Bob's room, I opened my laptop and composed my email letter telling everyone he had died. I left it there ready to send because I knew I wouldn't be able to compose it later. In the morning, I smelled toast coming from the little kitchen area where relatives can fix themselves something simple. I drank coffee.

On the last day, I saw Bob stop breathing sometimes for a few moments, and it frightened me. They told me they expected he would die within a few hours.

I took pictures of his face on my phone. I sat out in the living room some of the time near the retriever. I went into Bob's room countless times and watched him breathe. I cried. I told him over and over I would always love him. He stopped breathing for a few seconds and then started again. I panicked. Then I told the head nurse, "I can't bear to see and hear him actually stop breathing. I'll stay just outside his room. And when you know he's gone, please take the ring off his finger, bring it out to me, and put it in my hand, and that's how I'll know he's died."

244   staying married is the hardest part

If you have witnessed the death of one you love, human or animal, you've seen how one moment it's your dearly beloved, and then it isn't. The life force leaves, and immediately, that body no longer holds the Presence of the Other. I had just witnessed that moment with Savvy. I didn't want to remember Bob like that. He was a man always so full of life.

Andy and Carol were there on the sofa with me. The nurse came out at 5:30 p.m. and placed the ring in the center of my palm, the gold ring with the overlapping leaf pattern. I put it on the third finger of my left hand, right next to my own wedding ring.

I walked behind the funeral home duo who came to take him to their cremation building. They gave me paperwork, I signed things, and I was to go there tomorrow to wrap up the legal work.

It was a Friday, 9:10 p.m. A light rain was falling, and I walked out of Hopewell House for the last time. I said goodbye to Andy and Carol in the parking lot and assured them I'd be okay to drive home. On automatic, I drove over the shiny, wet streets, the smell of damp air activating a faint lingering scent of Savvy in my car.

The house was quiet and dark. I went downstairs to my bed. The kiddy gate sat against the wall where I'd left it since Bob had moved out five weeks ago. One of Savvy's beds lay in the middle of the downstairs living room, his toys scattered around the room where he'd dropped them for the last time.

The carpet felt cushy and comforting on my bare feet. Exhausted beyond what I can ever remember, I fell into a dark sleep in this dark room. There was no reason I had to get up in the morning. My caretaking duties had ended. I was utterly alone in a 3900-square-foot house.

CHAPTER 19

Owls

Bob died on January 8, 2010. A week later, I drove to the memorial center to pick up his ashes. A short, thin woman in a black silk dress greeted me and told me to wait. I wandered around the showroom looking at mementos until the woman in black reappeared, walked toward me, and handed me a white cardboard box, eight inches square, weighing about ten pounds. "This is it?" I said, hearing my voice from a long way off.

"Yes." Her face was blank as she gave me an envelope to go with the box.

I nodded my thank you and walked like a robot to the door. The heft of the box surprised me, and how ordinary it looked. I put it on the passenger seat, and for one crazy moment, I wondered whether I should secure it with the seat belt. No. Just drive carefully. No sudden stops or sharp curves. I took the back roads to my house, concentrating on getting home safely as hot tears blurred my vision.

Bob. In that white box.

Bob. Nothing left of him but the contents of that box.

My husband of nearly thirty-three years, the love of my life, in that box.

246   staying married is the hardest part

I stumbled into the house and put the box in our bedroom closet. The hanging poles were full of his old jackets and shirts as if he might still need them. I wrapped my arms around those clothes and sagged against them, sobbing.

The sudden expanse of time made me aware of how alone I was. Rick, Bob's former partner, called me three evenings a week, and hearing his voice made me cry, but after an hour of talking and him regaling me with Bob stories, I always felt better. It was almost as if Bob was alive, and just not home.

The house was comforting, the rooms filled with our joint possessions as if we were still there living together. I discovered that grief made me impatient in an odd way: if I was home alone for too long, I had to get outside, and no matter the weather, I walked and walked. If I visited with friends, I felt better for a while, and then I had to get back home. Everywhere I went felt okay for a while, and then I had to leave. After so many years of shared laughs, after that smile of his that lit me up, after the force field between us, here was me remembering, holding it all, and putting one foot in front of the other. It was as if I was walking through a dark forest with a penlight that could only illuminate what was right in front of me.

I saw meaning in things I wouldn't have otherwise—a hummingbird hovering near me, the clicking and clacking sound prompting me to feel Bob's spirit had come to reassure me he was okay. Me who still doesn't believe in an afterlife, me who thinks once you're dead, nothing of you outlives you. And yet I felt his spirit. Sometime later, when my sister Brenlee and I took a tour of the Grand Canyon, our guide told us the legend of a Native American chief whose spirit was immortalized in a massive rock that connected both sides of the canyon, the rock in the shape of an eagle in flight. Enormous. The rest of that trip I couldn't stop thinking of that eagle rock formation as Bob's spirit, his love of birds, and his larger-than-life being. Later, Bren sent me a coffee table book of photos from our trip, including images of that massive bird.

A few weeks after that, I started watching a live feed on a nest of baby owls. They were always touching and leaning on each other and sleeping snuggled up. The older baby had hatched two days before the other and was already 25 percent bigger. I named them Huey and Lois, and I watched them every minute I could. On a windy or rainy day, or even on a soft warm day, they leaned against each other. They slept touching, sometimes tail to head, but mostly vertical, propped up against each other, safe in their togetherness. When the mother came back with her freshly caught prey, they snuggled up to her so she could shove meat strips into their eager mouths. Every other day she brought back an egret, most likely its brilliant white feathers like a neon sign for her at the marsh edge, the egret sleeping on one long spindly leg, unaware of the silent wings of the owl beating toward it, about to steal its life.

One morning Huey began practicing to leave, standing straight up in the nest and flapping his wings. On the day he made the first foray out of the nest, Lois watched her brother flap his wings hard and hop up onto a branch. I felt bad for her, suddenly alone in the nest.

And then it hit me, why I couldn't wait to get to my desktop and turn the feed on again:

I was Lois.

I had no idea how the mere stability of our daily lives supported me—the predictability to having Bob there on the

248 staying married is the hardest part

other end of the phone, to him lighting up when I walked in the door, to the sound of his laugh, staccato and joyful. I could see his face when he was playful and teasing, the way the eyebrows would go up, the way laughter spilled out of him almost as if he was in church and wasn't supposed to laugh like that. He was daring to defy his father, daring to defy the pastors; he was irrepressible in his playfulness and joy. I relied on that, I was buoyed by his joy, although there was also the darkness in him, the depression, the days when he felt so angry and disillusioned by people that he took to the couch and watched baseball and boxing and stupid pet tricks just to get out of his head.

I was now surrounded by the artifacts of our lives together the way Lois sat on feathers and discarded remnants—a comforter with tiny pastel flowers that no matter which house and room always has exactly the right amount of warmth and coolness, the toy rubber chicken Bob gave me "because everybody should have a rubber chicken," his other quirky collectibles, our books carted around for decades, his screenplays, my novel in six different languages, his photography closet, my stained-glass windows, hard drives from old computers as if anyone but me cares what is on them.

I had to fly on my own now.

In these first few months after his death, I did everything I could to memorialize Bob. I felt lucky to have TV footage of him, recordings of his radio shows, his poems, and movie scripts. I collected all the videotapes and CDs I had—professional TV footage of him in his shows, and some home videotapes of our lives—and put them together in two large grocery bags.

bonnie comfort   249

I hadn't looked at any of them for many years, but I wanted to make a thirty-minute DVD to show at the memorials in LA and Edmonton.

I found a private editor on the east side of Portland who said we could play all the tapes together, and I could choose what footage I wanted on the DVD and in what order.

On my first visit, I met the guy in his one-person studio, ready to work with me at his bank of computer screens. He was tall, scruffy, with a tattoo of a camera on his forearm, and had a sweet smile, and a soft voice. We started with Bob's old children's show, *Wacko*, the one he'd been producing when I met him. Our first editing session was three hours. We got through all of the professional videos, and I picked out the most entertaining bits for the DVD.

For our next appointment, we went through home videos almost all taken by me—us on car trips, Bob on our couch in Ashland reading a newspaper blurb to me, footage of snowy mountains on the way up to Edmonton. We were partway through another travel video when the image suddenly switched to me in the Benson hotel, and as the editor and I viewed it together, I realized this guy was looking at a bare beaver shot of me because Bob had zoomed in on that when my robe was open.

Oh my God. I had no memory of that being filmed—Bob almost never held the camera, and this was a video taken fifteen years earlier, when I was wearing an outfit I would never have bought for myself, a red lacy bra, matching garter belt, black stockings with a filmy knee-length robe over it. I had a sudden rush of the experience, how annoyed I was, how the room service guy had just knocked on the door, how Bob was signaling for me to stay just like that.

250   staying married is the hardest part

"Whoops!" I said to the video guy. "Better speed through this!" But my cheeks went hot, and all the old anger I'd suppressed over the countless times I'd acted out Bob's fantasy came bubbling up. Goddammit! He got his way again! Even after his death!

The editor fast-forwarded until there was a travel shot of the San Joaquin Valley. I brushed my hair away from my face and said, "I have to use the restroom," before abruptly getting up and disappearing into the little bathroom behind him.

I sat down on the toilet, my face on fire. How many times had I choked down embarrassment over those scenarios? Pretended to some stranger that it didn't matter if he saw me, glad it would only last a few minutes? I ran the cold water tap in the sink, cooled my hands and patted my cheeks. This is the last time a stranger will see me like that!

When I resumed my seat next to the guy he asked, "Ready?" as if he hadn't seen what he'd seen, as if he wanted to move on as much as I did. We searched through the rest of the home movies, some funny, some endearing, and I let go of that awful moment. When we were done, I was really happy with the final DVD. We'd been at the editing bay from 9:00 a.m. to 1:30 p.m., but I wouldn't have to come back. I paid the guy. I had what I wanted.

"Hey, are you hungry?" he asked.

"I am, actually."

"I've got another client at 2:30 p.m., but we could run across the street and get a burger if you want."

"Sure, okay." I didn't think he meant anything other than lunch in between appointments. But I did have that old sixth sense that if I'd wanted more, he'd have said yes. After all, he'd already seen me.

bonnie comfort   251

We walked across the street to an old bar Bob would have loved—funky advertising signs mounted on the walls, the yeasty smell of beer, and the jukebox playing a Rod Stewart song. I ordered something I don't usually eat, a juicy hamburger that dripped down my hand as I bit into it. If Bob were alive, he would have loved this moment: he'd be turned on knowing the guy got a look at me. He'd be encouraging me to go home with him.

As I dipped crispy French fries into ketchup, the guy was telling me a story about something, but instead I was listening to my own thoughts: *How embarrassing I'm having lunch with a guy who's accidentally seen me naked. But I'm in control now. Even though this guy saw me, it doesn't matter if he's now interested. I don't want to see him again, or bang him in the back room, or go home with him and lie in his bed with the probably rumpled sheets and the smell of old carpet rising up to meet us. I will walk out of this bar and never see him again.*

When I focused my attention again on the present, the guy was paying the bill. Outside the bar, I thanked him for lunch. I kept enough physical distance that there was no opportunity for a hug or a handshake. There was just a moment when he searched my face.

He could not have known the pain that video moment had caused me with its sudden rush of bad memories. And I was not about to tell him. Bob's urgent desires for that had faded in our later years together. We had finally gotten past that, and I was not about to revive it.

My chest felt light and full of air. I even chuckled on the drive home, thinking of that guy's shock at seeing me.

So, one more man got an unexpected peek at me. So what! It would be the last time.

252 staying married is the hardest part

In LA, my friend Betsy Beers and her husband, Bruce, helped me with food and beverages for a huge party to celebrate Bob's life. The party was hosted at the home of Richard and Shirley Hahn, the producers of *Good Luck*, who generously arranged audiovisual equipment, chairs and tables, and someone to run all of it. When we ran the compilation DVD of Bob on camera over the years, everyone laughed. There were door prizes for getting the quiz answers right to forty-eight questions about him. The number one prize was a one-foot-high ceramic statue of the See no Evil, Hear no Evil, Say no Evil monkeys, but due to a manufacturing error, two of the monkeys had hands over their eyes. Claire gave it to me. Barbara and Cort won it. Nobody else could have been better.

That June 2010, I flew up to Alberta with the white box holding Bob's ashes. We had another memorial party for Bob, this time at the lovely home of Abe and Toby Silverman, Bob's closest friends there. The next day, Bob's brother Doug and his wife, Darlene, took Abe and me to the best hill overlooking Drumheller, Bob's boyhood town with the Red Deer River running through it. The bluff overlooked the places the brothers had run and played and hiked and learned about birds and magic.

We walked to the edge of the lookout. It was the perfect spot. I opened the white box, took out the heavy plastic bag, and began scattering the ashes. There seemed to be a lot, and only some took off into the air down the hill. The rest landed too close together on a cactus, looking like someone had dumped cement powder into the grass.

"Look!" Doug said, laughing, "You put him right on that cactus!"

For some reason that felt terrible, as if Bob could feel it, as if it was disrespectful. I bent down and plunged my hand into the pile of white remains and lifted them into the air and scattered them some more. My hand was now covered in Bob's ashes, which made me cry. I sorted through what was left on the ground and discovered there were small pieces of bone. I picked up nine of these tiny bone fragments and kept them in my hands. I didn't want the powder, but these tiny pieces of his strong and hardy bones reminded me of his strength. I wrapped the little pieces of bone in a Kleenex and shoved them deep into my pocket.

Back home I put the little pieces of bone in a silk bag and began searching for something permanent to hold them. My close friend and officemate, Lynn Moore, looked through stores with me, but nothing was right. I kept gravitating to decorative owls because they reminded me of Bob—a strong creature of wisdom and presence—yet I wanted something of me there, too. I finally found the right thing online: a small Limoges keepsake with a hollow bottom to hold something. It depicted the classic British poem, "The Owl and The Pussycat," and fittingly it was being sold by Geary's, the Beverly Hills store where I'd purchased our wedding china.

When the little hand-painted porcelain figurine arrived, I was delighted until I discovered it wasn't perfect. Over the owl's right eye there was an accidental ink mark. I set the piece on my nightstand, but every time I glanced at it, my eye went right to the flaw.

I brought it to work the next day to show Lynn. "Look," I said. "There's a black brush mark over the right eye."

"But that's so right," Lynn said. "We're all flawed, and our relationships are flawed. It perfectly represents that, too."

"True," I said. But it didn't satisfy me.

I called Geary's, and they said they'd replace it with a new one. "Please send me the new one now," I said. "I'll pay for it.

254   staying married is the hardest part

And when I get it, I'll send back the flawed one, and you can give me a refund then."

I took the flawed keepsake home, thinking I'd use it till the perfect one arrived. I carefully installed the little pieces of Bob's bones in it and put it on my nightstand. I looked at it every night before I went to sleep. Weeks later, the second one arrived, and it was indeed perfect, but to my surprise, I'd grown attached to the flawed one. I remembered what Lynn had said: Bob wasn't perfect, nor was our marriage—the little piece was flawed just as we were. So, I kept it. And every night, I looked at it and said good night to him, flaws and all.

The summer of that first year I had a garage sale and sold some of Bob's things—crabbing nets, audio music cassettes from his car, a radar detector—and things I didn't want to see anymore, like two packs of plastic bibs I had to tie around his neck that last year to keep him clean while he was eating. Later, I made a list of all the things I sold, and the one thing I regretted seeing go was his pair of clown shoes.

When we were living in Ashland, Bob had ordered those custom-made clown shoes. And of course, Bob and I both imagined them to be like the usual circus clown's shoes—huge, black with big red toes sticking out. When they arrived, we discovered they were brown leather, with the toe section big, bulbous and closed, and one shoe had a fake toe sewn on it at an odd angle.

Bob was very disappointed. He perched on the edge of the bed, put them on, and sat quietly looking at them. Then he said, "I'm probably the only man in America right now who's sitting on his bed, unhappy with his new clown shoes . . ."

I lay on the other side of the bed and smiled.

That was the way to put disappointment in perspective. I missed the reminder.

bonnie comfort   255

It's surprising how long grief lasts in its various forms. In that first year, I was awash in tears and felt like an electrical cord that had been ripped in half with the wires dangling. As long as I was living in our house, I felt Bob's presence everywhere in it, and that helped anchor me. I relied on those things that we shared to give me a sense that I hadn't lost everything. My psychology practice also secured me because I was doing something that mattered, and my life in that realm was unchanged.

What I didn't anticipate was how grief came at me a year or two or eight later when I unexpectedly encountered something that triggered it. I opened a rarely used drawer and saw a seashell that Bob had brought home from the beach. A flood of memories rushed back of mornings on the sand with him, the salt making his hair thick and wild, the peace on his face soothing to see. Other things still trigger grief years after, like the date of his birthday, our anniversary, the date he died, or a photograph of him I encounter.

Sometimes, I wished I could have one more conversation with him in which I could ask him a few things, like, "Honey, when you told me to fool around, did you really want me to?"

I can guess what his answer would have been. He told me years later that suggesting I fool around was his way of preventing me from leaving him. Did he really want me to fool around? I don't think so. He wanted me to accept the dry spells, and to stop asking him to go with me to couples therapy.

One thing I have learned: death is not the end of a marriage. It's a fabric permanently torn asunder, and I see in my patients and in myself, that although you repair yourself, there are threads left hanging, questions unanswered—a song he loved, a restaurant you enjoyed together, a greeting card you never threw out—and when you encounter these reminders,

256   staying married is the hardest part

grief wells up for how much you loved him or her, how much you still love this irreplaceable and unique person and the many years you shared that are now gone and can never come back.

There is, though, the continuing gift of memories—for me it was the sound of his laugh, the way he opened his arms to hug me, the feel of his body against mine as we fell asleep.

CHAPTER 20

Epiphany

Who am I without you? This was the question that greeted me in the dim light of morning as that first year wore on. I was your adored wife, sexual playmate, number one fan, admiring audience, best laugher at your jokes, and your travel companion in your Land Cruiser. I was your cook, your typist, and your first editor. Safe in the crook of your arm when we lay together in bed, I loved the sound of your heartbeat, that slow steady thud. The loyalty of you, your honesty, your affectionate teasing. So rarely a harsh word. So much play, so much laughter. And still, after you'd taken your last breath, I knew who I was: your grieving widow, the keeper of your vast body of creative work, your memorial maker who gathered people in different cities to celebrate you, the man I adored, who adored me right back and was memorable to so many people.

But now? Who am I now?

I had given away more things of Bob's: fishing gear, rifles never fired, baseball caps, and books on the battles of World War II. And now almost a year had crept by. I had preserved his words, his photographs, his jokes. I had reminisced with old friends about his antics. And that quiet question began to get

258   staying married is the hardest part

louder: who am I without him? Of course, I'd never be without him in my mind and heart, but like a slim slip of the new moon I saw there was a core of me that had always been there, basking in his sun, but different from him. I liked Fleetwood Mac and the blues. I was an early riser. I liked to draw and paint. I missed LA. I didn't really want to wear high heels again. Or a push-up bra. Unlike him, I wanted to fly to Spain and Japan and Iceland. I liked doing psychotherapy. I was not an entertainer. I loved to laugh, but I also liked being heard.

On the first anniversary of Bob's death, I lit a tower candle that could burn all day. I put it in the greenhouse window behind my kitchen sink. It's a Jewish tradition, lighting a candle on the yearly anniversary of a loved one's passing. Yahrzeit, it is called. All the sadness came welling up, and I looked out the window through smeary tears. "Let's go out and buy me a present from you," I said aloud.

That afternoon I went to an antique jewelry store in an upscale section of Portland and looked quickly at everything. I remembered how fast he'd chosen his wedding ring, and now I didn't anguish over what to choose. One thing immediately caught my eye as the right thing: a thick rose-gold rope from which hung a small square locket embedded with semiprecious stones. I walked out of the store wearing it, and strolled along NW 23rd Avenue, looking in store fronts, and feeling close to him. The Fireside restaurant was two corners down, and I went in and took a window seat. A friendly fire burned in the fireplace. I ordered hot chocolate with whipped cream and savored it. I was comforted by this day, this ritual, and I decided to make it a yearly event, a present from him to me on the anniversary of his death.

Now that Bob was gone, all my choices were available. Twenty years after I'd left LA, I could move back, walk away from my practice in Portland, throw away the dozen raincoats and jackets, the waterproof boots, the winter hats, and gloves. I could run screaming back to my dearest long time LA friends—Rachelle, Barbara, Claire, and Betsy. I could live without accommodating someone else's tastes and habits, walk every day on my beloved Santa Monica bluff and gaze at the curve of the bay down to Palos Verdes and up to Malibu.

But I didn't do it. When Betsy came for a visit, I said, "I don't know whether to go back. . . ." We were half naked in the locker room of my sports club. My hair dripped cold water on my bare shoulders.

"Well if you're gonna go back, you better do it soon or you won't," she said. Was she right? I ran through that scenario in my head. There were still professional people there who knew me and would refer to me. I was still licensed there. But I'd be leaving my sure income in Portland, and it was so expensive in LA.

I wandered the rooms of my house, took in the mess of Bob's screenplays, his collectibles, his photos, and his baseball caps. I couldn't bear to leave this feeling that he surrounded me, that here in the house he was still with me. I put the option aside for a while. Here's what I knew: I had to keep working. When I was with my patients, the pain of his absence was held at bay for those hours. Other people were hurting. I could say something meaningful. That work and my house were my anchors, the only things keeping me from floating away like an astronaut unhooked from her spaceship. I decided that maybe in the distant future I would move back to LA, but not now, not until it felt right, if it ever felt right again.

260　staying married is the hardest part

At the end of that first year without him, I took a hard look at my finances, and my lack of retirement money became a disturbing reality. I decided now to earn money as full force as I could. I filled up my work schedule completely, supplementing my therapy practice with psychological evaluations and reports for attorneys who needed my work to bolster their cases. On weekdays, I saw therapy patients and these legal clients. Evenings and weekends, I wrote the reports. While my professional office remained a peaceful sanctuary, my home office began to look like a hoarder special. Reams of paper sat on shelves, alongside file folders, staplers, and psychological testing forms. Bills, canceled checks, deposit books, and tax forms were stacked next to those. When I walked into that home office each evening I had to ignore the crowded mess and just focus on writing reports and patient chart notes.

Who am I without Bob? played in my head often. Who am I without any man?

One evening when I came home from work early, the many editions of my novel in the hall bookcase caught my eye—paperbacks and hardbacks from seven countries. Even though they'd been published from 1995–1997, I'd always kept them in that prominent spot where I passed by them every day. My favorite cover was on the hardback from Germany: the title *Verleugnung Psychothriller* in hot pink against a deep black background, the image a woman's naked back from the shoulder blades up, her thick blonde hair in a French twist with a long, sharpened pencil stuck through it. The Japanese edition had sold 100,000 copies.

The dramatic American hardback cover showed a large scissors cutting through a long stem rose. I pulled it out of the line of books and felt the heft of it in my hand—302 pages on which I'd agonized over every word. Why had my book taken up so little space in my mind? It felt like a footnote to my life. I settled in the living room and leafed through my author's copy, stopping to look at notes in the margins, my underlined paragraphs—cues for my publicity talks.

I laid the book on the cushion next to me. By my definition it was not a hit—not a big enough seller, and no movie adaptation. It did make a lot more money than most first novels. It did go out to thirty Hollywood producers for possible option, and one actress wanted to make it at the Lifetime network, but that never happened. How did all that seem like not much to me? And what was wrong with commercial fiction anyway?

My body felt strange, as if I was looking at it from the outside. I watched myself go downstairs to the stacks and stacks of Bob's screenplays that I'd so carefully organized. These were the things I'd guarded so carefully. Why was my novel a "so what"?

I turned away from the scripts and stepped outside onto my back patio, wandering first among the flowerbeds, and then down the cement steps to the broad swath of lawn under my towering fir trees. I inhaled that fragrance of oily fir sap, remembering Savvy running full force toward the Frisbee. The internal voice I'd lived with for years hacked away at me: "Your novel only happened because Bob's agent sent it to a NY agent, who sent you to a private editor you had to hire. None of it would have happened without Bob. So, Bonnie, how much of an accomplishment of yours is it really?"

The night deepened, and I shivered in my thin sweater. The distant hills sparkled, etched against the purple sky, and I wished Bob was with me on this grassy spot, holding my hand.

262   staying married is the hardest part

I softly said out loud to him, "You were the talented storyteller, the one who had things to say to the world, not me." It wasn't a bad equation—the therapist married to the storyteller. When asked about my book, I had never said I was a writer. I always said, "I wrote a novel, and it was published."

Cold enough that my fingers had turned white, I walked back and forth across the lawn. Clearly, whatever faith I'd had in myself as an "author" dribbled away—not only in a ten-year slog through my second novel, but also in the comparisons I made between myself and Bob, the person I saw as the real creative talent in the family.

In my internal court of judgment, I argued for myself: "Even though you had an opportunity not available to some, it wouldn't have necessarily resulted in a book sale. Simon & Schuster had to believe *Denial* was worth publishing, or they wouldn't have chosen it no matter who introduced you. So Bonnie, didn't your novel ultimately stand on its own?"

Maybe, just maybe, I was a storyteller, too.

Sometimes I think there's music at the core of everyone, a small tune that is yours and yours alone, and in the quiet of sadness or loss, you can hear it in a new way, a way that inspires you and regenerates hope and allows you to redefine yourself.

Three years after Bob died, I was ready to tackle the closet where I'd put his photography gear and photographs. This closet was large and deep, in the downstairs living room near Bob's desk, and overwhelmed with all the things I'd stuffed in there—his cameras, tripods, and slide viewers, large binders, and thousands of photos in packets. The photo packets were stacked and labeled in Bob's printing, among them: Silly

bonnie comfort   263

Pictures, Middle East, TV shows, Canada, Pretty Bonnie, Naughty Bonnie.

I dislodged all the Bonnie packets, laid them on our old drop-leaf table, and began sifting through them. There were funny and sweet photos: me posing in front of a lattice-topped apple pie in Ashland; me laughing in our Palisades pool, my snorkel mask on my head; me hugging a giant dinosaur at Prehistoric Gardens near the Oregon coast. Then dozens and dozens of me posing in sexy outfits, looking at the man who loved to capture me like that, the time and place of each photo still vivid in my memory.

How pretty I had felt in many of those photos, but often how compromised. I leafed through them quickly, another and another, years of these: me in a white lacy bodysuit, gazing over the railing of a Santa Monica hotel balcony; me in a pale silk dress displayed against a window that made the dress transparent; me in backless high heels and a miniskirt, laughing. I studied my face in these photos, a gaze that usually held the warmth of love toward Bob, but sometimes I looked like I didn't want to be there, my eyes downcast or looking off in the distance.

Then, I came across a shot of me in a black bikini by the pool at the Hotel del Capri in LA, my face hidden by sunglasses and a floppy hat, the corners of my mouth turned down. The memory of the night before that photo came surging up—the guy across the way from our window watching us having sex as my opal necklace banged against my chin.

I stood up and began pacing, past the stack of Bob's screenplays, past his desk with his old computer sitting dark, and past his shelf of baseball caps. I stopped in front of another shelf with screenplays. A barrage of questions flooded my mind as I scanned those titles, feeling how alive he was for me in that room.

264   staying married is the hardest part

Bob had always said hearing about my affairs had turned him on. But what if there was another explanation for the obsession he developed after that? What if he'd been stunned and angry, but had held it in because he'd promised he wouldn't be angry?

Nausea built in my stomach.

I went back to the table and plopped down on the chair, letting my hands rest on top of the scattered pictures as these questions sank in. There was one of me in my red pencil skirt on the day I'd confessed all. I remembered watching the eucalyptus leaves waving outside the window on that long-ago afternoon, and Bob's body snugged up to mine a while later on the bed, as he shook his head from side to side and said, "Bonnie, Bonnie, Bonnie," smiling, while he stroked my arm. "I thought you might have fooled around, but I had *no idea.* And you hid it so well!"

I started moving the photos around the tabletop like pieces of a jigsaw puzzle. I never thought Bob was lying to me about his feelings. But could he have been lying to himself?

My hands came to a stop.

Oh my God. Any man hearing the kind of stories from his wife that I told Bob would feel hurt and humiliated.

Why had I not seen this until now?

I shuffled through those photos quickly, looking at the evidence of his obsession.

I pictured him lying next to me that afternoon, saying "I won't be angry" but his face was flushed, and his body restless, as he insisted, "This turns me on! I wanna see you with that lawyer! Let's call him right now!"

He had just heard devastating news and then turned it into a triumph by saying he *loved* the idea of seeing me with someone else. Not only did he love it, but he also wanted to be in charge of it.

Of course! Any first-year psychology student watching Bob at that moment would have recognized his response as reaction formation—behaving and feeling the opposite of one's true feelings—and understood that this defense mechanism would not necessarily be conscious. Bob himself might not have realized what his mind was doing.

So many things suddenly took on new meaning—our awful fight at Salty's when he said, "Why won't you do something that's so easy for you when it means so much to me?"

"Why the hell do you think it's so little? Or easy?" I had said, but why would he believe me when I'd been so promiscuous?

Another time, when he was sitting on the edge of our bed, his jeaned legs frogged open, his white tube socks planted on the carpet, he said, "You had a good time, now why won't you do this for me?"

How could I have been so blind?

My legs shook as I stood up. The answer now seemed so obvious: I had not wanted to know how hurt and angry he must have been.

All these years I'd been in a state of denial.

Denial. The title of my novel.

I didn't want to have to face my own wrongdoing. I didn't know where it would lead. Instead, I had preferred his reaction of excited fun, so I didn't have to face his righteous indignation. My behavior had been shameful, and I feared the possible consequences.

I left a huge mess of photos on the table, and climbed the stairs to my home office where my favorite photo of Bob was

266   staying married is the hardest part

framed on the wall. It was a black-and-white image taken after cancer, his hair not fully grown back, his big eyes curious and open, his character and heart so present in those searching eyes.

I paced in a circle, digging my nails into my elbows. Then I shouted to those eyes that seemed so alive, "Why didn't you tell me!? Why did you stifle it and pressure me like a lunatic!?"

My breath was loud and shallow as my part in all this registered.

I had been outraged that he'd said, "go and get it somewhere else," and I had acted out of defiance. It was *revenge fucking*.

And I had relished the lie of a secret life, just like I had as a teenager when I slithered out of my bedroom window to run to my boyfriend's house at midnight. My telling Bob about all my infidelities was a triumph, an antidote for feeling powerless.

My body felt suddenly limp, and I sank down to the carpet, no longer wanting to look at those eyes I loved so much. Tears spilled onto my sweater. If only I'd thought of all this before. If only I'd considered that Bob had been saving face when in fact he was crushed.

No matter what a psychologist may know about others, it doesn't mean she'll be able to see what she doesn't want to know about herself.

I wrapped my arms around my waist and rocked until my tears abated. My legs were still shaky as I stood up. "Breathe slowly," I said out loud. "In for three, out for four." In the guest bathroom, I blew my nose and splashed cool water on my face, continuing to calm.

Back downstairs I sat at the drop-leaf table in front of the evidence of our mutual craziness. Slowly, I picked up each photograph of me, considered it, remembering where and when it was taken, and then I made two piles: the discard and the keep. Doing this soothed me. Here was me at a truck stop on I-5, in a pink V-necked sweater, cleavage showing, pink high heels, bare legs up to there, a loving smile on my face after a sweet afternoon at the aviation museum in McMinnville. I put that one on the "keep" pile. Here was another, on the road to Reno, posing in front of a sign that said PUTA CREEK, me in my red pencil skirt, holding it up to show my black stockings and garters, me laughing and happy. Another one for the keep pile. And here was one taken in our Ashland house, a filmy black shawl over my lingerie, my eyes downcast and my face sad. I remembered not wanting to pose that day. That went on the "discard" pile, along with another one: me taken through the front windshield of the car, in the passenger seat at a Chevron station, my legs spread, my panties showing, but no smile.

As I went through these photos, I tried processing my new knowledge.

Other people might look at how Bob had behaved and say he was sexually abusive, but I never felt so. And some people might say how I violated my marriage was unforgiveable, but I don't think he felt that way.

We had hurt each other badly, each in our own way, yet marriage is a complex agreement between two people to give each other what they can and learn to accept what cannot be given. We had accepted, had forgiven, had made allowances, each of us knowing our unique histories, and we had remained passionately in love.

Discard, discard, keep, keep. I sorted and tossed, kept, and rejected. When I was done, I had one pile of keepers which was about twice as high as the pile of discards. Those keepers went into a large envelope to be kept in the bottom of my bedside

268   staying married is the hardest part

table, a private item only for me. The smaller envelope of discards went into the trash.

For now, I was ready to close that closet. I knew next time I opened it I would go through another round of grief as I touched those possessions that had meant so much to Bob, but I wouldn't spend more time on the photographs of me.

I had made my peace with them.

There was something else I learned from that evening: it's always easier to see how you'd be happier if the other person changes, but such a focus interferes with thinking about the only thing you can control: your own behavior. So now when my patients describe their relationship problems, my exploration usually includes two questions:

What do you think your own role might be in the conflict? And how might things improve if you changed your part?

CHAPTER 21

The Great, the Awful

Eventually, I had a new dating life, and during sex with a few men, the old insecurities I thought were gone forever came roaring back—self-consciousness about my body, worry over whether I'd orgasm, and how the man would feel if I didn't. Seamlessly, as if it was an old piano tune I could still play perfectly, I fell back into faking it. After all that psychoanalysis, after thirty-three years with Bob when I never faked it, here I was regressing to my younger self. What a blow.

Books on sexuality took up one five-foot long shelf in my hallway, as if the printed word could save me from years of embarrassment, shame, and self-criticism. From my early twenties, I had believed there was something sexually wrong with me, and although plenty of men were reassuring, my belief persisted.

Long after I met Bob and had agreed on our vibrator compromise, I continued seeking solace and understanding from my books, not only for myself, but for the hundreds of women I'd seen over the years with their own sexual troubles. Yet for all my reading, here I was, in my seventies, discovering I was still not free of my old tendencies, and in my psychotherapy practice, women decades younger than I still grappled with

270   staying married is the hardest part

issues that the women's movement and current empowerment messages had failed to heal.

Struggling with the resurgence of my impulse to fake orgasm, I once again sought more information. A patient of mine had told me with enthusiasm that her all-woman book club was reading *Come As You Are*, a book written by a professor of sexuality at Smith College, Emily Nagoski, PhD.

Why not? I thought. I ordered it.

At the same time, I read a glowing reference to an older book on the women's movement in America, *The World Split Open*, by Ruth Rosen. I ordered that one, too.

Both books arrived on my doorstep at the same time, and I put them on my night table. Nagoski's had a bold pink cover, with the photo in the center of an unzipped little makeup bag with a red interior, an image that looked just like a vulva. Hard to ignore on a bookshelf.

One Friday evening, settled in bed, the antique Chinese lamp throwing a soft pool of light around me, I opened Nagoski's book on the science of sexuality. The style of her writing was conversational, accessible, and authoritative because she backed up her information with extensive source material references. Here was documentation of the wide variation between individual women in their expression of sexuality, all affirmed as normal.

When I got to the section on vaginal orgasm, I was stunned.

Research has shown that only about 30 percent of women can orgasm reliably from intercourse alone, while the majority 70 percent occasionally or never orgasm with intercourse. That is considered normal, and those 70 percent of women who don't orgasm during intercourse do so from other types of stimulation, all considered normal. The explanation I read astonished me: ". . . the distance between the clitoris and the urethra predicts how reliably orgasmic a woman is during intercourse . . ."

"Oh my God!" I said aloud. "That's all!? Not some dark psychological problem!?"

Three to six millimeters! Maybe an eighth or quarter of an inch made the difference and was just a normal variation in anatomy. How I had blamed myself for not living up to the movie standard of being quickly orgasmic during intercourse! How it had left me feeling inadequate, apologetic, self-conscious, and demoralized, because not only had I believed I had to be that way to be normal, I had also believed that in not being like that I was disappointing to my partners.

This fact was followed up with something else equally important: context is everything in what turns you on or turns you off. If a woman is worried about her sexual performance, she may be inhibited. If she's afraid she might get pregnant, she may be inhibited. If her baby is crying, or she's embarrassed by her body, or self-conscious, or being sexually forced, her arousal capacity is likely to be inhibited. On the other hand, if she feels loved, accepted, and is freely participating in sex without distractions, she may be less inhibited. The same potential for arousal inhibition applies to men as well. If circumstances are unsettling, a man may have difficulty getting or maintaining an erection or may have difficulty reaching orgasm.

The next morning, I opened the full-length curtains to let the sun in, but I went right back to bed to read the second book. I settled in again, my head comfy against my white pillow, my reading glasses on. This book was a cultural history of the women's movement. As the morning wore on—fragrant coffee, sourdough toast in bed—I read about the years

272   staying married is the hardest part

when I had come of age during the sexual revolution. Rosen also meticulously researched her book, with many references cited at the end. She reported that when casual sex began in the 1960s, women felt tremendous pressure to be "good in bed," and they were terrified of being seen as "frigid," a term of the 1950s. Yes, oh how I remembered that. She went on to report that in the "consciousness-raising" groups of the 1960s, when women began sharing their sexual experiences, one such instance was a woman confessing she was faking orgasms with her husband and she thought she was "the only woman on the planet who had ever been sick enough to do this," until every woman in the room said, "Oh you too . . ."

So, I wasn't a secret liar different from others! I'd been one of millions of women caught between the old and the new—no sex before marriage versus the sudden rush of birth control pills and casual sex. Why, with all my research, had I not known how frequent this was?

I read it in black-and-white on the page, backed up by research and printed confessions: millions of women had faked orgasm and *never told anyone*. I was a product of that moment in women's history—still needing too much to please men, even if we had to fake it.

I had known these patterns in myself for a long time, but until I read this history of the faked orgasm, I thought it was my own private struggle, my personal defect. I had chastised myself for deceiving the men I was with and not having the courage to disappoint them with the truth. I did not fully realize that I was massively affected by the social climate of the time.

By the time I put down those books, I was a changed person. My heart raced, and my skin felt prickly and strange:

Maybe there has been nothing wrong with me all along, except that I believed there was something wrong with me?

The history of the faked orgasm combined with Nagoski's careful explanations of what is normal broke through to me like never before. Hadn't I had men tell me I was fine? Hadn't I read about sexuality for years? Yet this time, reading this recent sex book and the women's history book together was it for me.

I began to cry, thinking of all the pain I'd put myself through, and the men from whom I'd hidden my embarrassment, with whom I thought I should be very sexually responsive despite the context or how I felt about them. "Oh my God," I said aloud, over and over. I put my hands over my face and sobbed, shaking my head from side to side like a swimmer throwing off water.

When I was cried out, my fist full of wet Kleenex, I relaxed my head back into my pillow. I stared at the smooth white ceiling and said, "All these years—there's been nothing sexually wrong with me."

I wish at least one of my analysts had said, "You don't have to fake it. The way you reach orgasm is perfectly fine." I particularly wish that one of them hadn't implied that my sexual fantasy during sex meant I wasn't fully present with my partner. All my analysts were men raised in the 1930s and1940s, and in my thousands of hours in their consulting rooms I had never taken that into account. I needed women to cure me, women who straight talked me out of the old mythology and did actual research on the history and physiology of women.

I got out of bed, wrapped my bathrobe around me, and stood in front of the full-length mirror. "There is nothing wrong with you," I said aloud, as if I were saying it to someone new.

274   staying married is the hardest part

I wandered to my living room and then my kitchen, trying to absorb this newness. Nagoski's explanation of context explained so much in my own history: I'd been tutored by my mother to be pleasing to men. Her consistent message was that finding and securing the right man was the key to long-term happiness. Layer on top of that the women's movement of the 1960s and 1970s, when casual sex became the norm. Then I was expected to be blatant about wanting sex even on a first date, and highly orgasmic, and if I wasn't, I would be disappointing to men. Then there was that boyfriend when I was twenty who said with great authority, "There's something sexually wrong with you, and it's psychological." Layer on top of that my years of psychology study, resulting in my deep values of being authentic, assertive, and strong, yet still thoughtful and accommodating to my partner.

This was my core sexual dilemma: how to please a partner yet be authentic and assertive enough to stand up for what I needed. This dilemma was at its worst with a man who impressed me, because I cared too much what he thought of me which resulted in my inhibition. Yet of course I still wanted to choose a long-term partner who impressed me.

With Bob, I'd found a hybrid that worked for me: someone who impressed me and whose opinion of me really mattered, but who was also sexually flawed.

No wonder I had agreed to our compromise.

After a fresh cup of coffee, I sprayed and polished the counters, while processing my newfound insight which led to this: too much need to please doesn't only apply in the bedroom, and it doesn't only apply to me. My friends and women patients struggle to advocate for themselves. At work, the stakes relate to job advancement and money. At home, women must sometimes find the courage to disappoint, and learn to tolerate the other's disappointment. Silencing our needs damages our self-esteem and autonomy and shortchanges our relationships.

After I loaded the dishwasher, I returned to the bedroom, dropped my robe, and stood naked in front of the mirror. Yes, there was saggy skin, and imperfections, but it was my unique body, with its little scars and specific shapes, and I sent love to that image. "There is nothing wrong with you!" I said again to solidify this new self-acceptance. Looking at myself with kindness was a small miracle.

My favorite black L.L. Bean warm-up pants felt light and soft as I pulled them on. I laced up my running shoes, and walked out my front door with the lightest, most expansive feeling in my chest I could remember. My front lawn looked greener; the huge rhododendrons were still full of blossoms the size of grapefruit. Crunchy autumn leaves were coloring the walking paths, with the promise of pumpkins and fragrant fireplaces and kids in blue and yellow raincoats.

Psychotherapy is in the business of offering empathy and compassion, but it's harder to give that to yourself. I feel compassion now for the young woman I was then. Like many women of my era, I believed I was sexually defective, and it influenced my choices. I feel compassion for Bob, too. He had developed sexual kinks—women's lingerie, the desire to watch—but he felt shame about those desires despite how blatantly he talked about them to normalize them. The prohibitions of his family's religion left an imprint on him of self-hate and self-judgment,

276 staying married is the hardest part

and he suffered with it his whole life, as I had suffered with my private, secret shame from believing I was sexually defective.

I loved the fun and attention Bob gave me. I felt special, and a part of his grand and hilarious life. Much later, I had to reckon with what I gave up: the place where I wanted to live, and a satisfying sex life with my husband. I could have gotten up the courage to disappoint him, and say a firm no to our sexual compromise, or to leaving LA. Perhaps I would have felt more self-respect. Perhaps I would have been happier, but only in some ways. I still feel that what he gave me was irreplaceable.

Sometimes in our later years, knowing the history of our struggle, Bob would ask, "If you could to it all over would you still marry me?"

I always said yes, and most of the time I meant it. There is no marriage without compromise, and there is no compromise without loss.

In my bedside nightstand is the envelope of Bob's photos I saved—photos of me in lingerie, brimmed hats, high-heeled shoes, me seated on chairs, lying on sofas, posing in open car doors or out in the woods, my garters showing, my low-cut bras lacy against my young skin, my camera smile on my face, and my red lipstick. I rarely look at those photos, but I know they're there. They stand for all that was wonderful and terrible about our sexual connection—my need to be admired colluding with his need to watch and control, the pocket of wrong inside a love so right.

I forgive all of it now, and I know the best and deepest part of our love was not in that sexual dance between us, but in the laughs and fun together, the shared insights, the frequent and heartfelt physical affection of cuddling, lying in bed talking, and sleeping together, and the mutual respect we had for each other.

After witnessing my own marriage and so many others, I believe long-term love always has its difficult parts, even the truest and most robust of loves. We humans are complex and strange creatures, even the ones who have framed degrees on our office walls and listen very carefully to others.

One afternoon, five years after Bob died, I brought thirty-two years of lingerie into my living room and dumped it on the broad ottoman in front of my sofa. I had left these things in my lowest drawers, only opening them in passing, drawers full of memories that always triggered a fleeting sadness, so I shut them quickly.

Such a mixture of loss and regret welled up in my chest as I now riffled through the lingerie. I had loved them and hated them, delighting in exciting Bob, yet hating how compliant I'd been, and how I'd sacrificed my authentic sexual self for some idea of how to please men. I still had a way to go to forgive myself, but I tried at these moments to wrap my arms around that young woman who was too dependent to be brave.

I spread the lingerie out on my big dining table, grouping together the black panties, the white panties, the matching garter belts, and bras, and I photographed the whole surface of my table. I gazed at them, how feminine and artful they were, how expensive. I touched those laces and satins and silks for the last time as I packed them carefully in white plastic bags to take to Goodwill.

It was a hard moment, giving those twelve-gallon bags to men who didn't know and didn't care what was inside as

278   staying married is the hardest part

they dumped them in their bin, but I felt lighter when I drove away.

In this latest house purge, I walked into the guest bathroom and glanced at the framed photo I'd chosen to display on a wall that any guest might see: the photo of Bob taking a photo of me. In it, I'm dressed in a gray business suit, jacket open to reveal a lace body suit, a five-strand pearl necklace of Min's around my neck, and I have on my red lipstick and sunglasses. There's a closet mirror behind Bob facing the bathroom mirror in front of me, and you can see multiples of me in the closet mirror behind him. And there he is, camera to his face. I look pretty in the photo, but you cannot really see Bob's face because his features are obscured by the camera, and you cannot really see me either because I have sunglasses on, indoors.

I lifted the framed image off the hook on the wall and held it in my hands, gazing at the woman and man we were in our younger years, caught in a play of our own making. I didn't want to lay that photo on the discard heap. It memorialized too much of my marriage, too much of both of us for me to toss it away. Instead, I put it where I put all the things I still value but no longer want to make part of my daily life: in the back of the downstairs closet.

To be clear, mine is not a story of trauma recovery. My story is about how even the ordinary task of growing up in a loving home includes some kind of distress that defines one's life and is influenced by social issues of the day. When we're little we're like warm candle wax, and the way we're shaped by early and adolescent experience cools and hardens into adult patterns that are difficult to change.

Through hard work, luck and grace, many people secure a good long-term love. There is a kind of music in your life that flows from being with a dedicated Other who is there at the crisis moments of life, whose steady presence is like a good experience of childhood—a parent you hear humming from another room while you read or play with your toys. It's the sense of always being connected, something that helps the lonely condition of us all.

When Bob was doing stand-up comedy for the Canadian Forces, his entertainment group did a gig at Alert, an island near the North Pole dedicated to monitoring weather, global atmosphere, and threats from Russia. In addition to the monitoring stations, there were buildings for housing and feeding the troops working there.

Upon their arrival midwinter, when it's dark so many hours of the day, Bob and his crew were told that between the buildings a rope had been installed that bounded the path from one building to another, so when there's no visibility, people can hang onto it. In the dark, subzero air, when the wind is blowing the snow every which way, the only protection against getting lost is keeping your hand on that rope.

In some ways, this is like a long-term loving marriage: inside its bounds, we can each learn to be ourselves as we go forward in the darkness, knowing the other is a rope we can hold at those moments when we feel we might otherwise be lost.

Author's Note

This memoir draws from my personal experiences as both a psychologist and a wife navigating a complex, decades-long marriage. While I occasionally mention my work as a therapist in general terms, I have included only a few statements attributed to clients, and those have been kept anonymous to protect confidentiality. No identifying details have been shared.

Additionally, I respectfully acknowledge that my late husband's history and memories are presented here through my own lens, with deep love and care. Aside from my direct experience of his behavior, the stories I have shared of his upbringing and family are based on his memories and opinions as told to me, and may not be factual. They are things he believed, and as such they have served to deepen my understanding of who he was and how that affected our marriage. I continue to have the utmost empathy and respect for him and his family, and I hope that comes across in what I have written.

Acknowledgments

I am a person who often discovers her own truth in dialogue with others. I am, therefore, deeply indebted to the members of my writing critique groups. My first was in Ashland, Oregon, with Sandra Scofield, a finalist for the National Book Award, and a generous and brilliant reader. Thank you to Liz Scott, a psychologist and writer soulmate who invited me to join Carolyn Altman's critique group in Portland, Oregon in the early 2000s. I learned an enormous amount and made lifelong friends. Exceptional thanks to my current critique group, Diane Ponti, Tamara Greenleaf, and Connie McDowell, for the last four years of laughs, inspiration, and the privilege of going on three other writing journeys not my own.

I am grateful to Lynn Moore, a superb psychologist, officemate, and dear friend, whose wisdom and encouragement have meant the world. I am indebted also to Frank Wuliger at the Gersh Agency, whose commitment to Bob's work has buoyed my spirits when I think of his unproduced screenplays, and again to Frank for having enough faith in my work to represent me.

Profound gratitude to Henry Ferris, whose incisive developmental editing of my manuscript has been like a beacon in the dark, and whose humor has made me laugh when I needed

284   staying married is the hardest part

it most. Incredible appreciation to Brooke Warner and her publishing team at She Writes Press for all they've done to help me bring this work into the world.

Love and gratitude to Andy and Carol Gauthier, who kept Bob and me laughing until the end, and who still miss him, and to Steve and Kelly Sacks, Joyce and Chris Cluess, and Sheila and Bob Goodwin for their enduring love, laughs, and support. Thank you to my dearest LA friends of so many years---Scott Adler and my dear god-daughter Alycia Adler, your generosity and humor have buoyed me, Debby Cannon for her talent and inspirational courage, and those whose deep conversations have anchored me in this transient world: Rachelle Adler for her wisdom and endless support, Barbara Casady for the insight, joy and love she brings, Cort Casady for his encouragement and great contribution to the title of this book, Claire Covington and her children Scott and Julie who all loved Bob so much, and Rick Kellard whose optimism, humor and loving presence have gotten me through many a grief-filled evening.

I am grateful to Peter Newman, the producer of *Dogfight*, who always answers my emails immediately, to Richard and Shirley Hahn, the producers of *Good Luck*, who offered their home to me for Bob's LA memorial, and to Betsy Beers, Bruce Cormicle, and Ruth Vitale for their generosity to me when I was at my worst.

Thank you also to my dear Canadian friends—Abe Silverman for his love and generosity to Bob and me for so many years, and to Randy and Faye Broadhead, Linda Cullen, Betty Chadwick and Larry Musser for our continuing love and connection. Thank you to Bob's family---to Dave and Dorothy Comfort, and Darlene Comfort and their children. I have appreciated your memories.

Gratitude to my sister Brenlee (now deceased) and my sister Caroline, who has always been encouraging, and my nieces Shelley Werner, Janet Werner, and Elaine Cramer for their careful reading of my manuscript and incisive comments. Thanks also to Paige Berdan Burrows for reading it and offering enthusiasm and support.

Profound gratitude to Laure Redmond whose dance classes helped bring me out of acute grief, and who has remained an exceptional and wise friend and my 911 at midnight when I'm overwhelmed with angst and confusion. You are my heart.

I reserve my deepest gratitude for my writing partner of thirteen years, Diane Ponti: Diane, who read to Bob the emails sent to him as he lay dying; Diane, who for more than thirteen years has been my Saturday afternoon writing partner, offering excellent critiques along with hot tea and Trader Joe's chocolate-covered almonds; Diane, who has encouraged and helped me in every phase of writing this book. I couldn't have done it without you.

Finally, eternal love and gratitude to Doug Covey, who witnesses my life and gives me his loyal and loving presence when I need it most. Thank you for putting up with the thousands of hours I've been sequestered in my home office searching for the exact right words while you have waited patiently for our evenings together. I hope the banana muffins have helped. You are the guardrail that keeps me from being lost.

Book Club Topics and Questions for Discussion

1) The author observes that it didn't occur to her at the time how she was shaping herself to fit the man she was with: "It happened so seamlessly, so subtly, that I barely noticed." As partners bond and choose a life together, each usually adapts to the other's tastes and preferences to some extent. What criteria can help a person know when adapting becomes too much?

2) The author says, "This is how your family of origin shapes you: in ways you admire them, you emulate them; in ways you hate them, you try to be different. In ways you don't realize, you live out what they taught you." Which of your life choices were prompted by the desire for a life different from your family's? Can you think of a way you might have lived out what they taught you without realizing it at the time?

3) The author observes: "I was most drawn to men I saw as brilliant, charismatic, and powerful, the precise men least likely to offer the patience and kindness I needed in bed." As you consider your relationships, what contradictory qualities in your partners have created problems for you?

4) The author reports that sexual fantasy is a kind of magic that appears in your head unbidden in late childhood or

early puberty, and although the particulars may sound strange or perverted, those fantasies remain what sexually excites you most throughout your life. Many people feel shame or self-consciousness about those private fantasies. What might happen if you share them with someone close to you?

5) As the memoir progresses, we see power struggles between the author and her husband. The author notes that every marriage includes some power struggles. What have you found to be the most effective ways of resolving power struggles between yourself and your primary partner?

6) In describing the view from her home in Pacific Palisades, the author thought, *I've made it. LA is my home for life. I could die right now.* Eventually she chose to leave this place she loved so she could stay with her husband. Is there a place you feel is your heart's home? And if it is not where you live, how have you coped with that?

7) As the author's husband begins directing her to satisfy his fetishes, she says: ". . . this sex play with my husband fed my childhood longing for the power of beauty . . ." This is a clash between the desire for beauty and the cost of seeking it. Has that played out in your own life, and if so, how?

8) The author writes, "The Reckoning is a phase when the most difficult work of marriage is required. You see clearly whom you've married, and you must learn to tolerate the 'otherness' of the 'other.'" In what ways have you learned to accept the differences between you and a partner? Do you still struggle with this?

288   staying married is the hardest part

9) The author writes, "You know something but you don't want to know it. You ignore, suppress, and distract yourself. You tell yourself it will get better. You live around it, not in it. You don't shake yourself by the shoulders like someone who cares deeply about you." We have all used these strategies from time to time to avoid what we know to be true. Is there anything that makes it easier for you to face the truth?

10) The author's husband repeatedly suggested she have an outside sexual relationship as a way of her getting what she needed and taking the pressure off him. This was not the so-called open marriage in which both spouses agree to be with others. Do you think it's possible that sex outside a marriage can sometimes save it? If so, why?

11) The author's central dilemma was whether to leave the marriage or stay in it. What made the decision so difficult for her? If it were you, would you have stayed or left? Why?

12) In the author's search for forgiveness for herself and her husband, she realizes some of her choices contributed to the difficulties between them. Usually, each of us plays a role in a relationship problem. How might this apply to you?

13) Some years after her husband's death, the author had certain realizations about her sexuality after reading books about female sexual response and the women's movement. What are your thoughts about that?

A Note on Sources

Personal psychotherapy is a mandatory requirement for the training of psychotherapists. In 1968 when I began my career as a clinical social worker in Los Angeles, traditional psychoanalysis was considered the most transformative and in-depth therapy for professionals learning to offer therapy to others.

I started this journey with my first analyst, two days a week for a year and a half. I lay on the couch in his Beverly Hills office, while he sat in a chair behind me like a New Yorker cartoon. My second analysis was four days a week and lasted seven years, also on the couch. By that time, I was in my doctoral program to become a psychologist. My last analysis was three days a week for five years, again on the couch. In those years, I studied psychoanalytic theory, in particular the works of Freud, Jung, Winnicott, Guntrip, Masterson, Kernberg, Klein, and other thinkers in object relations theory. Once I became a psychologist and went into private practice, I focused on techniques of therapy for individuals, couples, and groups.

To cope with my own issues, I read extensively about human sexuality and the complexities of love and marriage. My bookshelves are lined with works by Louise Kaplan, Robert Stoller, Nancy Friday, John Gottman, Terrence Real,

290   staying married is the hardest part

and Esther Perel, to name a few who have published research and theories on sex in general, and marriage in specific.

I have come to believe that the field of psychology is like the old parable of the blind men and the elephant: six different blind men feel different parts of the elephant and are asked to describe the whole animal—an impossible task, since each man has a vastly different experience. Similarly, human experience is such a complex interaction between biology, genetics, attachment experience, joy, and trauma, that it is always a challenge to develop a comprehensive picture of any one person in front of you.

At some point in my thirty-year practice, I began trusting that my theoretical knowledge was deeply embedded in my own psyche and had to serve as background for my being fully present with my clients, listening to help them find insights, new ways of thinking, and better coping skills. Because my ideas have evolved into a belief system and philosophy of my own, I have chosen not to cite specific authors whose ideas have informed my work (other than Nagoski and Rosen, about whom I wrote in my last chapter.)

My greatest learning has come during the journeys I have shared with my clients, from whom I experienced what cannot be taught in a book. Psychotherapy is a living, breathing space between therapist and client, where something intangible but powerful occurs, much like the dynamic between infant and parent, or life partners, or deep friends—a connection beyond words, an enduring presence in each other's lives.

About the Author

Bonnie Comfort has been a practicing psychologist for thirty years. She has an MSW from the University of Manitoba and a PhD in psychology from the the Chicago School of Professional Psychology Los Angeles. Her novel *Denial*, a psychological thriller from Simon & Schuster, was published in eight countries and translated into five languages. As an expert on marital therapy, she has been a frequent guest on podcasts about marriage. She currently lives in Portland, Oregon, with her long-time partner, Douglas Covey, MD.

Looking for your next great read?

We can help!

Visit www.shewritespress.com/next-read
or scan the QR code below for a list
of our recommended titles.

She Writes Press is an award-winning
independent publishing company founded to
serve women writers everywhere.